THE ILLUSTRATED HISTORY OF FOOTBALL HALL OF FAME

THE
ILLUSTRATED
HISTORY
OF FOOTBALL
HALL OF FAME

DAVID SQUIRES

CENTURY

1 3 5 7 9 10 8 6 4 2

Century
20 Vauxhall Bridge Road
London SW1V 2SA

Century is part of the Penguin Random House group of companies
whose addresses can be found at global.penguinrandomhouse.com.

Copyright © David Squires 2017

David Squires has asserted his right to be identified as the author of this work
in accordance with the Copyright, Designs and Patents Act 1988.

First published by Century in 2017

www.penguin.co.uk

A CIP catalogue record for this book is available from the British Library.

ISBN 9781780895598

Printed and bound in Great Britain by Clays Ltd, St Ives Plc

Penguin Random House is committed to a sustainable future for our business,
our readers and our planet. This book is made from Forest Stewardship Council®
certified paper.

FOR FREDA AND DAVE

CONTENTS

THE GODS (part one)
1

GOALKEEPERS
ARE DIFFERENT
37

CULT HEROES
(part one)
51

ANTI-HEROES
65

THE BOSSES
83

THE GODS
(part two)
101

MIDDLE MEN
141

PIONEERS
155

FORWARD
THINKERS
169

CULT HEROES
(part two)
183

OH YEAH,
DEFENDERS
197

INTRODUCTION

The chances are, you aren't a professional footballer. That's fine, few of us are. You probably don't have a boot deal, or a seven-figure Instagram following. On balance, it's unlikely that you chew on a packet of protein gel as you enter your workplace, or have choreographed a special handshake with your colleagues for when you accomplish a basic task. However, if you still harbour dreams of making it as a soccer superstar, or plan to live vicariously through the footballing abilities of your children, history has taught us some valuable lessons on how to accomplish your fantasy of owning a big, stupid car and retiring before the age of fifty.

In researching this collection of some of the sport's greatest players, a number of commonalities became clear that provide a helpful blueprint for football immortality. Ideally, your youth would have been spent in a South American *favela*. There, you will have honed your football skills by doing keepie-uppies with citrus fruits. If you live in Britain, don't worry; child poverty rates are soaring, so there's every chance your little cherubs will still be able to shake their brittle bones on the world stage.

An alarming number of the game's legends also struggled with destructive addictions: booze, drugs, gambling, sex, and the modern curse of marathon PlayStation sessions. Many of them were also heavy smokers. Johan Cruyff, Bobby Charlton and Sócrates all indulged in the habit that has largely fallen out of fashion for all but a handful of cool cultural icons like Jack Wilshere. Again, the lesson is clear: if you want to make it at the top, get hooked on something that limits your life expectancy. Who wants to live for ever anyway? Have you bloody *seen* it out there?

Fate cruelly trampled upon my own ambitions of becoming a footballer, having been raised in the relative comfort of a well-sanitised suburban housing estate and being too scared to try drugs. Damn you, random accident of birth. However, the real unsurmountable obstacle was a complete absence of talent.

One may argue that there are many players who have enjoyed long and successful playing careers, despite apparently possessing the poise, technique and game-management skills of a newborn camel. However, it's a sad fact that even the most awkward-looking of footballers is still more talented than me, you and everyone we know. Phil Jones may look like he's just mastered how to stand on four legs, but he's an international footballer and has played over a hundred games for one of the world's biggest clubs. By contrast, the closest I ever got to being a player (in all senses of the word), was when I fibbed to a girl I liked at university that I'd once had trials for Luton Town. Not Manchester United, not Liverpool, not even Aston Villa; *Luton*. It's impossible to say for sure whether this was the most pathetic lie ever uttered by one human to another, but it's probably in the top three.

Then there is the issue of physicality. The modern footballer is a fluorescent-shoed, base-layer-wearing, Drake-listening, instrument of athleticism. I, on the other hand, have got a bad arm from the exertions of drawing a book of cartoons and a big fat arse. Establishing yourself at the elite level of the game also requires an absolute commitment and seems to involve a *lot* of going to the barber. Frankly I'm just not equipped with that much dedication for small talk and lack the confidence to have a shooting star shaved into the side of my hair.

Over the years, I've learned to downscale my expectation. As I approach my mid-forties, I begrudgingly recognise that it's unlikely that I'll ever play in a World Cup final. To stand any chance, I'd need the world's population to be massively reduced by an unhinged man-baby beating his fist against a nuclear launch button because of something he read on Twitter when he got out of bed at 3 a.m. to force out a piss, and *that's* not going to happen.

The gradual process of acceptance is familiar. As a young player, you hope that a club scout sees something in you that your PE teachers have missed. A rough diamond, whose natural ability is masked behind thick-lensed spectacles and a disinclination towards hard work. When that doesn't happen, you sign up for a Sunday league team, recalling the many players spotted at amateur level who later shone in the top flight. Are you the next Ian Wright? No. Maybe five-a-side is the place where your skills will reveal themselves: a zippier, more technical form of the game. Smaller pitches, shorter games, like how they do it in Brazil. Are you the new Neymar? Again, no, you are not. Eventually, you reach the stage where you'd settle for an approving nod from one of the other dog walkers when you toe punt a soggy tennis ball in your local park. That's *real* football.

When I was writing *The Illustrated History of Football* (still available in all good charity shops), I realised that there were so many footballers with spectacular careers and interesting lives that I just didn't have the time or space to explore further. I've tried to redress that here, with this collection of cartoons about the individuals who have become part of football folklore, and also a few who slipped between the cracks.

As with all collections of this nature, selecting the subjects was a challenge. Where possible, I've tried to provide a balance of individuals from different clubs and nationalities. There are some people who simply demand inclusion: Maradona, Pelé, Best, Tomas Brolin; others have been incorporated due to their character or the merits of their story. Most are in there because I saw something that was interesting and hopefully amusing enough to build a cartoon around. Inevitably, there are some who didn't quite make the cut. If your favourite player isn't included, console yourself with the fact that they will definitely be included in the next book and that you're probably too old to have posters of footballers on your wall anyway; treat it as a self-development experience. No, *you're* welcome.

THE
ILLUSTRATED
HISTORY
of FOOTBALL
HALL OF FAME

THE GODS (PART ONE)

DIEGO MARADONA

Let's start with the greatest.

Whether tearing through a defence, hollering at his teammates about his massive balls, or ripping his shirt open and peppering journalists with air-rifle pellets, the world has never seen anything like Diego Maradona. As a footballer, he was a whirlwind; a tiny, spiralling Tasmanian devil in short shorts who could dribble, pass and shoot like no one before or since. A chest-thumping street fighter who was capable of both scattering an entire unit of startled Belgian defenders *and* making your uncle swear at the television ('Handball! Hand-*bloody*-ball!'). Unlike the controlled professionalism of Pelé, or the refined grace of Cruyff, Maradona was a wild-eyed, emotional live wire; so highly strung that you could be forgiven for thinking he had a long-term addiction to an ego-enhancing narcotic. However, his first obsession was with football.

Maradona followed the traditional route to football stardom of being born into abject poverty. He was raised in a shanty town in the outer suburbs of Buenos Aires, living in a shack with none of the comforts most people take for granted: electricity, running water, Wi-Fi. It was his cousin who gave him his first football, for his third birthday; by the time he was eight, he'd been signed by Argentinos Juniors. Even at this young age, Diego was plied with pills and stuck with injections to help accelerate his growth.

1

By the age of ten, Maradona was entertaining the Argentinos Juniors crowds with ball-juggling displays during the half-time intervals; a small boy flicking the football casually off his knees, shoulders and substantial head. He then repeated the tricks with an orange, after that a bottle. Just five years later, on 20 October 1976, the same kid would be coming on as a substitute to make his professional debut. His coach, Juan Carlos Montes, had sent him on with a simple brief: to play as he knew he could and to try and nutmeg an opponent, both of which he accomplished. His marker that day, Juan Cabrera, is proud of his part in the Maradona tale, despite suffering the kind of humiliation at the hands of a teenager that is usually preserved for online gaming or supply teaching.

Diego scored his first international goal in a 3–1 win against Scotland at Hampden Park in 1979; a performance that featured a dribble through the heart of the Scottish defence, almost identical to the one he would produce against England at the Azteca Stadium seven years later. The run even began with the same pirouette in midfield to evade a clutch of pink-faced opponents. This was Scotland. *Nobody* did this to Scotland!

By now, his stock was rising, to such an extent that there was talk of him signing for Sheffield United. However, the military regime at home was determined that such a superior example of Argentinian athletic prowess should not be allowed to leave, so it was agreed that he would sign for Boca Juniors, in 1981. This was no great hardship for Diego, as he'd always been a Boca fan, but the club was in dire financial straits and could barely afford his wages. He stayed for one year and, once the junta had crumbled, joined Barcelona for a record transfer fee after the 1982 World Cup. The tournament had given Barça a glimpse of what they could expect from his time at the Nou Camp: astonishing individual skill and occasional acts of petulant violence (his World Cup had ended in disgrace after a knob-high foul on Brazil's João Batista, just as his Barcelona career would end in a flurry of flying karate kicks in the aftermath of a bitter Copa Del Rey final against Athletic Bilbao).

It was four years later, at the Mexico World Cup, that it became clear that Maradona might actually be from another planet; one populated by a race of fleet-footed maniacs with hair like Detroit rockers from the 1970s. The performance for which he is most remembered didn't come in the final against West Germany (although his perfect through-ball set up Jorge Burruchaga for the late winner), nor was it the semi-final win against Belgium, where he scored two goals, one of which involved a surge past three defenders and an off-balance finish. No, it of course came in the uncle-infuriating quarter-final defeat of England, with a pair of goals that perfectly demonstrated Maradona's status as both the player of the century, and as a sneaky bastard.

When he stretched out his arm to punch the ball over Peter Shilton's head for the famous 'Hand of God' goal, Maradona may as well have been extending one long middle finger across the Atlantic Ocean to merry old England. For the Argentinians, it was an occasion packed with meaning. As a nation they were still coming to terms with the events of the Falklands War four years earlier. They needed no motivation when it came to taking on an England team that represented all the hardships faced by their countrymen, even if it's unlikely that Steve Hodge was directly responsible.

However, Maradona was also generous towards his defeated opponents, saying that his incredible second goal wouldn't have been possible against any other team, as he would have been hacked down before he had the chance to run from the halfway line to score. 'The English,' he said, 'are noble people.' This largely overlooked the fact that Terry Fenwick had been attempting to separate him from his legs all afternoon and that Terry Butcher tried to kill him as the ball rolled into the net.

Maradona had dragged an average team to accomplish a feat way beyond their wildest dreams. This would prove to be no fluke, as he became the driving force that enabled Napoli to win two Serie A titles in the most successful period of his career. By now, Maradona's status was only matched in size by that of his courtege.

The substance abuse would eventually end his time in Italy and would later cause serious health concerns, but he mercifully recovered and continues to be a boisterous, opinionated presence, always willing to share a controversial opinion or to have a sly dig at Pelé.

BEFORE THE ARRIVAL OF MARADONA, THERE WAS A TENDENCY FOR NORTHERN ITALIANS TO HAVE A SNEERING ATTITUDE TOWARDS THE SOUTH, ITS PEOPLE AND ITS UNDERACHIEVING FOOTBALL CLUBS.

Oh God, did you see their attempts at winning a Scudetto? It was embarrassing. I couldn't look.

I know. And they will insist on wearing those tacky duck-egg shirts. It's not 1971 any more, chaps! Well, not north of San Marino anyway.

Oh, Stefano; you are awful. The poor things. Tee hee.

EL DIEGO WOULD CHANGE SOME OF THAT FOR A BRIEF PERIOD OF TIME. ON A SUNNY DAY IN JULY 1984, BETWEEN 70,000-90,000 EXCITED FANS PAID 1,000 LIRE EACH TO SEE THEIR NEW HERO AND HIS ENTOURAGE ARRIVE AT THE PACKED SAN PAOLO STADIUM BY HELICOPTER.

This is lovely and all, but did you really need to bring your cousin's proctologist?

Hey! You got a problem with Doctor Steve, we can go straight back to Barcelona, 'Mr President'.

HE'D ALSO USED A SERIES OF BACK ROUTES AND DECOYS TO AVOID BEING MOBBED BY ADORING SUPPORTERS.

There he is! Let's get him, to show him our love!

Dieg-huh?!

AAAAH!

You idiot!

Don't preach, Papa.

THERE WERE 253 JOURNALISTS PRESENT, ALONG WITH 78 PHOTOGRAPHERS. ONLY ONE JOURNALIST WAS BOLD ENOUGH TO ASK THE CLUB OWNER, CORRADO FERLAINO, ABOUT RUMOURS THAT THE CAMORRA HAD CONTRIBUTED TO DIEGO'S £4 MILLION TRANSFER FEE.

That is a ludicrous and insulting suggestion. Paulie Thumbs, Vinny Two Shoes, get this mook outta here.

THE PRESENCE OF THE MAFIA WOULD LOOM LARGE OVER MARADONA'S TIME IN NAPLES. WHEN HIS BUSINESS MANAGER, JORGE CYTERSZPILER, TRIED TO RESTRICT THE ROARING TRADE IN UNLICENSED DIEGO MERCHANDISE, HE WAS WARNED OFF BY THE CAMORRA.

We got a problem here?

No, no...

MARADONA'S FIRST OUTING FOR NAPOLI ENDED IN A 3-0 DEFEAT TO VERONA AND THEY STRUGGLED UP UNTIL THE WINTER BREAK. THEIR FORM PICKED UP ONCE OTTAVIO BIANCHI WAS HIRED AS HEAD COACH. DIEGO DISMISSED HIM AS BEING 'TOO GERMAN', BUT THE NEW BOSS HAD THE GOOD SENSE TO LET HIS CAPTAIN DO WHATEVER HE WANTED ON THE PITCH.

AT THE END OF THE SEASON, MARADONA APPROACHED FERLAINO WITH A LIST OF SUGGESTIONS FOR TRANSFER TARGETS. HE ALSO OFFERED AN IDEA FOR HOW TO DECIDE WHICH PLAYERS SHOULD BE SOLD.

Just sell anyone who gets whistled by the crowd when I pass to them.

You're going to start passing to people?

BRUNO GIORDANO JOINED FROM LAZIO AND LINKED UP WELL WITH DIEGO AND ANDREA CARNEVALE. WITH THE TIRELESS MIDFIELD RUNNING OF FERNANDO DI NAPOLI AND SALVATORE BAGNI, AND THE DEFENSIVE SOLIDITY OF CIRO FERRARA, NAPOLI BEGAN TO LOOK LIKE A TEAM.

Stefano!

NAPOLI GRADUALLY IMPROVED AND EARNED MORE IN GATE RECEIPTS IN MARADONA'S FIRST TWO SEASONS THAN IN THE PREVIOUS 24 SEASONS COMBINED. NOT SURPRISINGLY, THE CLUB INDULGED HIS EVERY DEMAND, TURNING A BLIND EYE TO HIS LAVISH LIFESTYLE AND WILD PARTIES.

I think Diego might have an addiction for buying chandeliers

He could have a long-term dependence on cocaine for all I care; look at all this cash!

THEIR SCUDETTO-WINNING SEASON DIDN'T HAVE THE SMOOTHEST OF STARTS. IN SEPTEMBER 1986, A LOCAL, UNEMPLOYED ACCOUNTANT - CRISTIANA SINAGRA - CLAIMED IN A TV INTERVIEW THAT DIEGO WAS THE FATHER OF HER NEWBORN SON; AN ACCUSATION HE DENIED.

It wasn't me. It was the glans of God.

HIS PHILANDERING WAYS WERE FAMED. ACCORDING TO HIS FORMER DRIVER, PIETRO PUGLIESE, MARADONA SLEPT WITH 8,000 WOMEN DURING HIS TIME AT NAPOLI. HOWEVER, THIS WOULD HAVE REQUIRED HIM TO SLEEP WITH AN AVERAGE OF 3.2 WOMEN PER DAY SO IT SEEMS UNLIKELY.

You were away on international duty for five days, so you have to have sex with sixteen women today to make up, Mr Maradona.

I'm gonna need another cortisone injection. Sheesh, you know when you start a project and grow to regret it...?

THE NAPLES POLICE ALSO RELEASED PHOTOS OF HIM AT A PARTY WITH SENIOR MEMBERS OF THE GIULIANO CRIME FAMILY. WHEN QUESTIONED ABOUT IT BY A MAGISTRATE, MARADONA CLAIMED TO HAVE NO MEMORY OF EVER MEETING THEM, NOR EVEN KNOW WHO THEY WERE.

Parlour games.

Well this all seems perfectly normal.

BUT EVERYTHING CLICKED ON THE PITCH AND NAPOLI SECURED THE TITLE WITH A 1-1 DRAW WITH FIORENTINA IN THE PENULTIMATE GAME OF THE SEASON. THE RESULT SPARKED WILD CELEBRATIONS. PEOPLE FLOODED INTO THE STREETS, MURALS WERE PAINTED AND NEW-BORN BABIES WERE NAMED IN HONOUR OF THE CITY'S SAVIOUR: DIEGO.

Ok, that one definitely isn't mine.

A HUGE SPONTANEOUS PARTY ERUPTED. SOMEONE WROTE ON THE WALLS OF THE CITY GRAVEYARD: 'YOU DON'T KNOW WHAT YOU'RE MISSING'. VHS RECORDINGS OF THE CELEBRATIONS WERE ALREADY BEING SOLD ON THE BLACK MARKET WHILE THE PARTY WAS STILL GOING.

I don't remember this bit.

MIRANDINHA

DESPITE WINNING THE UEFA CUP IN 1989 AND A SECOND LEAGUE TITLE IN 1990, HIS RELATIONSHIP WITH NAPOLI WAS BECOMING INCREASINGLY STRAINED. THE CLUB EVEN HIRED A PRIVATE INVESTIGATOR TO KEEP AN EYE ON HIM.

He's working on something with his driver. I can't work out what it is, but he disappears into a room for hours and emerges looking drained and a bit sad.

He's probably just watching the video I lent him of the 1987 scudetto celebrations.

THEY WERE HAPPY TO INDULGE HIM WHILE HE WAS STILL TURNING UP FOR MATCHES, BUT IN NOVEMBER 1990 HE REFUSED TO TRAVEL TO RUSSIA FOR A EUROPEAN CUP TIE AGAINST SPARTAK MOSCOW, AS HE WAS FEELING THE EFFECTS OF A LATE-NIGHT PARTY.

⇒Thin Cough⇐
Yeah, I think it's just one of those 24-hour things. Through the eye of a needle, mate.
⇒Exaggerated groan⇐

HE THEN MADE THE SCHOOLBOY ERROR OF **GOING IN TO WORK AFTER YOU'VE CALLED IN SICK!** HE HIRED A PRIVATE JET AND MET UP WITH THE TEAM, BUT HE WAS BENCHED AND THEY LOST ON PENALTIES.

THE END CAME WHEN HE TESTED POSITIVE FOR COCAINE AFTER A GAME AGAINST BARI ON 17 MARCH 1991. PREVIOUSLY, HE'D BEEN ABLE TO HIDE HIS COKE HABIT BY USING A FAKE PENIS, FILLED WITH SOMEONE ELSE'S URINE, TO PROVIDE A CLEAN SAMPLE. HOWEVER, ON THIS DAY HE WAS UNPREPARED.

He's been cheating!

AS JONATHAN WILSON EXPLAINS IN HIS SUPERB HISTORY OF ARGENTINIAN FOOTBALL – 'ANGELS WITH DIRTY FACES' – THE FAKE PENIS WAS DISPLAYED IN A MUSEUM IN BUENOS AIRES, BUT WENT MISSING DURING A NATIONWIDE TOUR IN 2003 AND WAS SADLY NEVER RECOVERED.

Nonno, look: an exotic shell from across the seas!

HAND-CRAFTED SCULPTURE OF THE FAMOUS LEANING TOWER OF PISA! 'AUTHENTIC'!

€200·00

MARADONA DIDN'T STICK AROUND FOR THE PUNISHMENT. INSTEAD, HE BOARDED A MIDNIGHT FLIGHT FROM ROME ON 1 APRIL. IN HIS ABSENCE, THE ITALIAN FA HIT HIM WITH A 15-MONTH BAN.

Diego, are we not waiting for Doctor Steve?

What, you don't think I've already got enough people up my –

Sit down and fasten your seat-belt please, sir.

THE ROMANCE WAS OVER. ONCE HIS SUSPENSION WAS SERVED, HE AGREED TO JOIN SEVILLA, WHO HAD JUST APPOINTED CARLOS BILARDO AS HEAD COACH. HOWEVER, DIEGO STILL HAD A YEAR TO RUN ON HIS NAPOLI CONTRACT, SO SOMEONE WAS BROUGHT IN TO ARBITRATE ON TRANSFER-FEE NEGOTIATIONS. SOMEONE TRUSTWORTHY. SOMEONE RESPECTED. SOMEONE LIKE...

Here's Blatty!

Seriously?

Sorry, Vinny Two Shoes wasn't available.

ROBERTO BAGGIO

Despite the number of penalties Roberto Baggio scored, people mostly talk about the one he missed. Throughout his career, he converted 108 spot-kicks, the most in Italian football history. The one he skied over the bar in the 1994 World Cup final penalty shoot-out stands out as an anomaly, but serves to highlight his exceptional record. It's reassuring in a way, if even Roberto Baggio can screw up at work sometimes, then maybe it's ok that the rest of us do. Accidentally sent an email to a supplier calling him Captain Bellend? Hey, Bobby Badge leant back too far that one time. Flashed a gland at the Christmas party? Mate, The Divine Ponytail ripped out the heart of a nation. It's *fine*.

That Baggio should suffer that fate was even crueller, given the fact that he had been largely responsible for getting Italy to the final. He scored five goals during the tournament and lit up an otherwise uninspiring team – all this whilst carrying a hamstring injury. Yet, he was still regarded with suspicion by their coach, Arrigo Sacchi. When goalkeeper Gianluca Pagliuca was sent off in a group game against Norway, it was Baggio who was substituted. 'We needed our fittest and strongest players', reasoned Sacchi. Ouch.

It was an attitude that Baggio would be confronted with throughout his playing days, but he was adored by the supporters of Vicenza, Fiorentina, Juventus (where he inherited the number 10 shirt from Platini), Milan, Bologna, Inter and Brescia. Serie A was the best league on the planet in the nineties, and the sight of Baggio whipping a free kick into the top corner, or skipping around a sea of legs contributed hugely to its popularity. It was only boring when he lined up to take a penalty, because you always knew he was going to tuck it away.

IF YOU LIVED IN A WEALTHY WESTERN DEMOCRACY, THE 1990s WERE A GENTLER, STRANGER PLACE. IT WAS A TIME OF BUM BAGS AND POGS AND 'FANTASISTAS' LIKE THE GREAT ROBERTO BAGGIO.

Any of you lads got a spare scrunchie for this nostalgic cultural reference?

BAGGIO WOWED A GENERATION OF FANS WITH HIS INCISIVE PASSING, GLIDING DRIBBLES AND DEADLY FREE-KICKS. HE PLAYED AT THREE WORLD CUPS, DRAGGING ITALY TO THE FINAL IN 1994. HE WAS A MASTER FROM THE PENALTY SPOT. EXCEPT THAT ONE TIME...

This is the perfect occasion to unveil my Julian Dicks Special. Stand back, everyone...

HE ANNOUNCED HIMSELF TO THE WORLD WITH A STUNNING SOLO GOAL AGAINST CZECHOSLOVAKIA AT ITALIA '90. FOR BRITISH TV VIEWERS IT WAS A GOAL AS MEMORABLE FOR ALAN PARRY'S ORGASMIC COMMENTARY.

Oh yes! Oh yes! OH YES!

I'll have what he's having!

Actually, no; I've completely lost my appetite.

'ROBI' WAS ALREADY ADORED IN ITALY BY THAT STAGE. WHEN NEWS BROKE THAT HE HAD LEFT FIORENTINA FOR JUVENTUS, FANS RIOTED IN FLORENCE FOR TWO DAYS.

Too far?

No! A man has changed employer! Let's burn this whole city down!

INJURIES WOULD BLIGHT BAGGIO'S CAREER. IT WAS WHILE RECOVERING FROM A CRUCIATE LIGAMENT INJURY THAT HE DISCOVERED BUDDHISM; CHOOSING A DIFFERENT RELIGION FROM ONE'S PARENTS BEING THE ULTIMATE ACT OF MIDDLE-CLASS REBELLION.

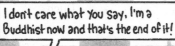

I don't care what you say, I'm a Buddhist now and that's the end of it!

How exotic! We'll have to get you some of that incense.

Cuh! I'm growing a ponytail too. You can't stop me, it's my body, yeah.

Ooh, that'll look cool. You should put some little beads in it too, that'd be snazzy.

GAH!

HIS HUMANITARIAN WORK AND GOOD CHARACTER MEAN THAT IF, AS HE BELIEVES, REINCARNATION IS REAL, THEN HE MIGHT NOT COME BACK AS A SPECIES OF ANIMAL THAT HE LIKES TO HUNT IN HIS SPARE TIME.

This is actually preferable to working for Lippi.

BAGGIO SCORED 205 SERIE A GOALS AND IS THE AZZURRI'S FOURTH-HIGHEST SCORER OF ALL TIME. BUT AS THE SPORT BECAME INCREASINGLY ATHLETIC, SOME COACHES CAME TO SEE HIM AS AN EXPENSIVE LUXURY. SOON THE FANTASISTAS WOULD BE ALL BUT EXTINCT.

Be very, very quiet.

GEORGE BEST

George Best's most famous goals are burned into the collective consciousness of most British football fans. Only the lucky few would have been present to see his drifting run against Sheffield United, his delicate lob against Spurs, or his composed finish in the 1968 European Cup final, yet the footage survives in the memory alongside other culturally significant images like the moon landing, the falling of the Berlin Wall or that kid phoning *Going Live* to swear at the pop group Five Star.

Those recollections of Best trotting back to the muddy halfway line, one arm raised, a trail of humiliated defenders and exasperated teammates in his wake, sit alongside memories of his off-field activities: the handsome, side-burned charmer delighting a throng of beauty pageant contestants by pouring bubbly into a pyramid of champagne flutes. Not for George the short-back-and-sides, brown-ale-and-plain-crisps lifestyle of his more mature colleagues.

Within two days of signing for Manchester United in 1961, Best had done a runner. The homesick teenager had taken a boat back to Belfast, along with fellow trainee, Eric McMordie. Manchester was wet and frightening, unlike Northern Ireland. It was a disappearing act that would become a regular feature of his later years at the club, as alcoholism effectively ended his playing career by his late-twenties. But in the meantime, he was convinced to return by United manager, Matt Busby, and within two years of his professional debut he'd won his first league title; by 1968 he was the best player in Europe.

Best didn't really adhere to tactical instruction. His approach was based mostly on improvisation. It's no coincidence that Bobby Charlton had a full head of hair before Georgie signed. But as United struggled to recapture the feats of 1968, Best became increasingly frustrated. His influence diminished, his drinking worsened, eventually fatally. But before the fame, before the fortune, before the fall, came a famous performance in Lisbon in 1966. Life would never be the same again.

SL BENFICA v MANCHESTER UNITED EUROPEAN CUP QUARTER-FINAL, SECOND LEG, 9 MARCH 1966

EVER SINCE HE WAS A CHILD, WATCHING WOLVES' FRIENDLIES WITH SPARTAK MOSCOW AND HONVÉD ON HIS NEIGHBOUR'S TV, GEORGE BEST HAD WANTED TO PLAY IN EUROPE.

Just imagine playing football in Wolver**hampton**, the birthplace of the automatic traffic light!

Settle down, George or you can go home.

BY THE TIME UNITED ARRIVED IN LISBON TO FACE BENFICA, THE 19-YEAR-OLD BEST WAS A FIRST-TEAM REGULAR, A FAR CRY FROM THE HOMESICK BELFAST BOY WHO JUST A FEW YEARS EARLIER HAD BEEN PUT UNDER THE CARE OF LANDLADY MRS MARY FULLAWAY.

I'm probably only about 35, you know.

BEST WASN'T YET THE ROCK STAR HE WOULD LATER BECOME, BUT MANAGER MATT BUSBY HAD ALREADY WARNED HIM ABOUT THE EFFECTS LATE NIGHTS WOULD HAVE ON HIS GAME.

I've heard about you. Gallivanting around town, with your tie-dyed T-shirts and your Mike Summerbee. You're out of control, son; out of control.

Another half of Shandy, George?

Not for me, Mrs Fullaway, it's only six days before a match.

The relentless march of time...

...Twenty-nine...

TWO SEASONS EARLIER, UNITED HAD LOST 5-0 IN LISBON TO SPORTING. THE HOME FANS WHO BEAT ON THE SIDE OF THE VISITORS' BUS REMINDED THE PLAYERS OF THAT SCORE AND GESTURED TO BEST TO GET HIS HAIR CUT.

Ha ha, no thank you, friend; I like my hair the way it is.

BENFICA WERE GIANTS OF THE GAME, HAVING WON THE EUROPEAN CUP IN 1961 AND 1962 AND FINISHING AS RUNNERS-UP IN 1963 AND 1965. THEIR STAR PLAYER, EUSÉBIO, WAS PRESENTED WITH THE EUROPEAN FOOTBALLER OF THE YEAR AWARD BEFORE THE MATCH, BUT BUSBY HAD A PLAN TO KEEP HIM IN CHECK.

Heh, you're not going to follow me around for my whole career are you, Nobby?

Maybe.

IN THE UNITED DRESSING ROOM, PADDY CRERAND BOOTED A BALL AGAINST A MIRROR, SMASHING IT. SOME OF THE TEAM FREAKED OUT, CONVINCED THAT BAD LUCK WOULD BEFALL THE CLUB. A SILLY SUPERSTITION MAYBE, BUT JUST 33 YEARS LATER, THIS HAPPENED:

Do you think the motorway hard shoulder is there for your personal use, sir?

I've got a funny tummy! I need to get to a toi—

Never mind.

BUSBY'S SIDE HELD A SLENDER 3-2 LEAD FROM THE FIRST LEG AND THE PLAN WAS TO KEEP THINGS TIGHT AND SILENCE THE 80,000-STRONG CROWD.

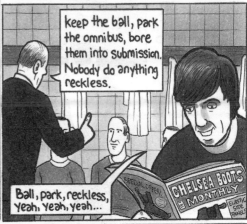

keep the ball, park the omnibus, bore them into submission. Nobody do anything reckless.

Ball, park, reckless, yeah, yeah, yeah...

CHELSEA BOOTS MONTHLY

AFTER JUST SIX MINUTES, BEST ROSE BETWEEN TWO BENFICA DEFENDERS TO HEAD IN TONY DUNNE'S FREE-KICK; HIS MARKER LOSING HIM LIKE SO MANY OF HIS FUTURE MANAGERS LATER WOULD.

I'm glad you see things my way, George. I think this is the start of a fresh chapter for you. I'll see you at training on Wednesday then...

George...?

Where'd he go?

Um, you'd better look at this, gaffer.

But...

The Scum
GEORGE ZEST!
BESTIE ON 12-HOUR LGBT RAMPAGE WITH ENTIRE MISS WORLD PAGEANT

He was literally just here!

FIVE MINUTES LATER, A LONG PUNT FROM GOALKEEPER HARRY GREGG IS HEADED DOWN BY DAVID HERD. BEST RACES ON TO IT, SPLITS TWO DEFENDERS, SKIPS PAST A THIRD AND LIFTS THE BALL BEYOND THE KEEPER FOR 2-0.

Oh I blame Mike Summerbee entirely for this.

BEST THEN STARTED THE MOVE FOR THE THIRD GOAL, FINISHED BY JOHN CONNELLY AFTER ONLY 16 MINUTES. BY NOW BENFICA WERE A SORRY SIGHT, STUMBLING AROUND WITH AS MUCH COMPOSURE AS A DRUNKEN CELEBRITY ON AN EARLY EVENING CHAT SHOW.

And now... the irascible, the irreverent, the irrepressible, Benfica defence

Ehhhh.. Wod ju say?....you big fuc

BENFICA PULLED ONE BACK VIA A SHAY BRENNAN OWN GOAL, BUT CRERAND AND CHARLTON ADDED TWO MORE TO COMPLETE THE ROUT. ALL THE TALK WAS ABOUT GEORGE BEST, THOUGH. UPON RETURN TO ENGLAND, HE FAMOUSLY DONNED A SOMBRERO AND SUNGLASSES FOR THE WAITING PRESS.

Blow me down. First the Kennedy assassination and now a man is wearing a hat!

They'll be putting a chap on the moon next.

THIS MAY SEEM TAME BY MODERN STANDARDS...

Alright?

...BUT IT WAS A HUGE DEAL IN THE MID-SIXTIES, WHEN MOST FOOTBALLERS RESOLUTELY REFUSED TO 'SWING'.

A DIVIDE WAS EMERGING BETWEEN THE OLD FOOTBALL OF BRYLCREEM AND DUBBIN, AND THE NEW FOOTBALL OF SIDEBURNS AND FASHION BOUTIQUES. BEST EPITOMISED THE NEW ERA AND WAS ADMONISHED BY THE OLD-SCHOOL HARRY GREGG, WHO DISAPPROVED OF THE SOMBRERO STUNT.

You're making a bloody fool of yourself, son. The sombrero is more commonly associated with Spain and its former colonies; principally, Mexico. Sure, wide-brimmed hats are part of traditional Portuguese dress, but not **sombreros**! You've gone too far this time; too far.

EVERYONE ELSE LOVED HIM THOUGH AND AFTER HIS PERFORMANCE IN LISBON, HE WAS NICKNAMED 'EL BEATLE' BY THE PORTUGUESE PRESS. THE FAB FOUR WERE ALSO SAID TO BE BIG FANS.

STEPOVER

CLEAR PARALLELS EXIST IN THE STORIES OF GEORGE BEST AND THE BEATLES. THEY WOULD BOTH LEAVE ENORMOUS CULTURAL FOOT-PRINTS, BEFORE BURNING OUT IN THE EARLY SEVENTIES AND GOING OFF TO WORK ON OFTEN-SKETCHY SOLO PROJECTS.

A one-off appearance for an amateur team in Australia? Sure, but I've got to run out to 'We All Stand Together' by Paul McCartney and The Frog Chorus.

UNITED WERE EVENTUALLY KNOCKED OUT BY PARTIZAN BELGRADE IN 1966 (BEST WAS OUT, INJURED), BUT THEY FACED BENFICA AGAIN TWO YEARS LATER IN THE FINAL AT WEMBLEY. BEST SCORED AGAIN IN A 4-1 WIN, HIS CHILDHOOD DREAM OF BEATING EUROPE'S ELITE REALISED.

Did you see that?!

He went round him like the ring road that will relieve congestion around the great city of Wolverhampton!

That's it. Home.

GIUSEPPE MEAZZA

'To have him in your team meant to start 1–0 up,' said Vittorio Pozzo, the coach of Italy's World Cup winning teams of 1934 and 1938. Having Benito Mussolini intimidating opponents and officials probably helped too, but there's no denying Giuseppe Meazza's status as the most formidable striker of the pre-war era.

Equally adept with both feet, and an early exponent of the bicycle kick, Meazza was a forward who seemingly never failed. He scored 216 goals in 367 Serie A games, and would have bagged more if it weren't for the outbreak of war and the serious foot injury he suffered at the age of 29, which sidelined him for a year. Along with his two World Cup winners' medals, he also claimed Olympic gold in 1936 and for a while his tally of 33 goals for Italy stood as a record. When the record was broken by Gigi Riva in the 1970s, Meazza was refreshingly grumpy: 'He scored a lot against Cyprus and Turkey. My goals were more important.'

Meazza scored twice on his Inter debut, at the age of 17. In his second season, he notched up 33 goals, setting a precedent for the rest of his career. He still had to overcome some hostility from his older colleagues. Leopoldo Conti was particularly vexed by the arrival of this young upstart and gave him the nickname 'Balilla'; the name of the military youth groups organised by Mussolini. Meazza seemed about as fussed by this as he did by opposition defences and training schedules.

Blessed with talent and charisma, Meazza became Italy's first football superstar and his image was used to advertise a range of products. Football made him tremendously wealthy, and he even played himself in the 1951 film 'Milan Billionaire'. Meazza enjoyed the fast life and could often be seen driving around the streets of Milan in a flash car, possibly with wheel rims that lit up after dark, bass pumping, Pozzo nodding in the passenger side. Bounce, bounce. Damned cobbled streets.

LIKE MANY OF FOOTBALL'S GREATEST PLAYERS, GIUSEPPE MEAZZA ENDURED A TOUGH START TO LIFE. AS A CHILD, HE SUFFERED SUCH A SEVERE CHEST INFECTION THAT HE WAS SENT TO AN 'OPEN AIR SCHOOL', WITH ITS OWN POOL AND ZOO.

I'm not sure this constitutes a zoo.

When you're paying five liras a month it's a zoo, Lung Boy.

HIS MOTHER TRIED TO DISCOURAGE HIM FROM PLAYING FOOTBALL BY CONFISCATING HIS SHOES, SO HE LEARNED TO PLAY BAREFOOT. HE DIDN'T OWN A PAIR OF FOOTBALL BOOTS UNTIL HE WAS 16, BUT WAS BANGING IN GOALS FOR INTER BY THE AGE OF 17.

Sorry, son; I hope this makes up for it. The man in the shop said they were the best ones.

Quasar. Yeah.

Thanks, mum.

MEAZZA'S TRADEMARK MOVE WAS TO DRAW THE KEEPER OUT BEFORE EITHER SKIPPING AROUND HIM OR SLIPPING THE BALL IN TO THE NET. ALTHOUGH OPPONENTS KNEW THIS, THEY WERE OFTEN POWERLESS TO STOP HIM.

Don't let him do that thing.

Don't let him do that thing.

Don't let him do—

BAST!

HIS INTERNATIONAL CAREER SAW HIM WIN TWO WORLD CUPS AND ONE OLYMPIC GOLD. NOTHING COULD PREVENT HIM FROM SCORING, NOT EVEN WHEN THE ELASTIC IN HIS SHORTS BROKE DURING THE RUN-UP TO TAKE A PENALTY AGAINST BRAZIL DURING THE 1938 WORLD CUP SEMI-FINAL.

Wow.

Quasar boots.

MEAZZA'S TALENTS AFFORDED HIM CERTAIN FREEDOMS. HE RARELY TRAINED AND LIVED CLOSE TO INTER'S STADIUM, SO WOULD SOMETIMES ROCK UP FIVE MINUTES BEFORE THE START OF MATCHES

Sorry, sorry. Bloody trains!

Your house is literally over there and the trains are notoriously efficient now.

Giuseppe! Great to see you! Get changed, lad. Giuseppe, guys!

STORIES ABOUNDED ABOUT HIS PLAYBOY EXPLOITS AND THERE WERE EVEN RUMOURS THAT HE LIVED IN A BROTHEL. HOWEVER, IT SEEMS LIKELY THAT THESE TALES WERE EMBELLISHED BY MUSSOLINI'S PROPAGANDA MACHINE.

Say he's a mighty alpha male who dominates Milan like a big silverback gorilla.

I hate my life.

THE REGIME LOVED STORIES THAT PROMOTED THE IMAGE OF ITALIAN MASCULINITY AND MUSSOLINI ONCE TOLD MEAZZA THAT HE HAD DONE MORE FOR ITALY THAN ANY OF HIS AMBASSADORS.

All these stupid dummies. I should feed them to my dogs. I should.

THE SAN SIRO STADIUM WAS RE-NAMED IN MEAZZA'S HONOUR IN 1980, MEANING HIS LEGEND WILL LIVE ON THROUGH THE AGES.

I can't believe we're going to the San Siro!

Sorry, The Giuseppe Meazza Stadium.

Oh!

The where?

Why didn't you just say that then?

MICHEL PLATINI

If you grew up in England in the 1980s, you didn't get to see much Continental football. Action from Europe was often limited to a brief round-up of the goals on the BBC's *Football Focus* on a Saturday lunchtime. When none of the Home Nations qualified for the 1984 European Championships, broadcasters decided against screening the tournament, with coverage being limited to a highlights package of the final, tucked away deep in the schedules, where no one could stumble across it and write a letter of complaint. And yet, despite this uncharacteristically insular approach, there was still one player that all the kids in my school wanted to be during the lunchtime kickabout: Ian Rush. But we couldn't all be him, so some of us chose Michel Platini instead.

I wouldn't say that I became obsessed with *Le Roi*, but for a short time I did try to convince myself and my peers that I was French. This mostly manifested itself by me wearing my shirt untucked and demanding that others pronounce my surname 'Squi-rez'. Naturally, my parents tried to suppress my Gallic style, telling me that the most exotic branch of my family tree was an uncle from Neath. Their denial of my imagined cultural heritage extended to a flat refusal to buy me cigarettes, even though I'd learned that Platini smoked about a million a day and could still run faster than anyone I knew. Reluctantly, I accepted that I wasn't French.

Just like me, Platini had to navigate some early setbacks in life, with a succession of serious skeletal injuries that suggested he may have possessed a level of physical durability similar to that of Samuel L. Jackson's character in the film *Unbreakable*, or Daniel Sturridge. Yet he persisted, thanks in part to the encouragement of his father, Aldo, who probably wasn't a total baby about buying his boy smokes.

Aldo was also a director at AS Nancy, and when young Michel was rejected by Metz, the old man put a word in for him. Platini impressed in the reserve team and progressed through to make his full professional debut in 1973. Within three years, he was turning out for the national team and was selected for the 1978 World Cup, where France were eliminated in the group stage, after defeats to Italy and Argentina. Back home, some held him responsible for the early exit and he was heckled in French stadiums the following season, yet he was named captain after the tournament.

If there was any justice in the world, Platini would have led the France team out for the 1982 World Cup final, against Italy; but a penalty-shoot-out defeat to the dastardly West Germany proved once again that football almost never delivers a gratifying ending. France had led 3–1 in extra-time, having overcome the shock of seeing Patrick Battiston wiped out by one of the most brutal challenges in World Cup history, delivered via the airborne hip of German goalkeeper, Harald Schumacher. Having apparently never heard the stories of the 1954 or 1974 World Cup finals, nor seen any horror films ever, they then set about underestimating the Germans, which went about as well for them as can be expected. Naturally, it was Schumacher who saved the decisive penalty.

However, France enjoyed better fortune two years later, with Platini lifting the European Championship on home soil. In the first half of the decade, France were a joy to behold, if you lived in a country that televised any of their games.

At club level, Platini was now bossing the midfields of Italy, having joined Juventus from Saint-Étienne, showing trademark balance to narrowly avoid signing for Terry Neill's Arsenal. In Turin, he linked up with several members of Italy's World Cup winning side and formed a midfield partnership with Zbigniew Boniek that saw them win Serie A in 1984 and 1985, the European Cup Winners' Cup in 1984 and the European Cup in 1985.

That last accolade was, however, tarnished by the stain of the Heysel disaster. Platini scored the winning goal, from a penalty that should never have been awarded, in a game that should never have been played. He faced criticism for the enthusiasm with which he celebrated the goal, but claimed to be unaware of the death toll in the stadium. However, Juventus's lap of honour at full time was, at best, spectacularly misjudged.

In Platini's view, his best performance came in the Intercontinental Cup final against Argentinos Juniors later that year. He scored one and set one up for Michael Laudrup in a 2–2 draw, and then scored the decisive penalty in the resultant shoot-out. By this time, I had forgotten about being French, having consumed too much American television and adopted a mid-Atlantic drawl that infuriated my parents. The moral of this story: buy children cigarettes.

IF YOU'RE A PERSON OF A CERTAIN AGE, REMINISCING FONDLY ABOUT YOUR CHILDHOOD HEROES HAS BECOME PROBLEMATIC IN RECENT YEARS.

Telly in the eighties was ace. Jim'll Fix It, Rolf's Cartoon Club, It's A Knockout, The Cosby Show. They don't make them like that any more.

I'M THE LEADER OF THE GANG

CLEARLY, THERE'S NO SUGGESTION THAT MICHEL PLATINI HAS COMMITTED ANY CRIMES OF THAT NATURE, BUT HIS CONDUCT AS AN ADMINISTRATOR HAS CRAPPED ALL OVER THE REPUTATION HE EARNED AS A PLAYER, FROM ROUGHLY THE HEIGHT OF THE EIFFEL TOWER.

Monsieur, what are you doing?

This is me throwing my weight behind Qatar's World Cup bid. There's a video of all my best goals down there. We're in Paris. It's art. Keep up.

THE TEMPTATION IS TO THINK OF PLATINI AS A PRODIGIOUS TALENT, SEDUCED BY THE DARK SIDE OF TOP-LEVEL FOOTBALL BUREAUCRACY...

Join me and together we'll rule planet football like an old man and a slightly less old man.

BUT HE WAS ALREADY IN HIS FIFTIES BY THE TIME HE DEPOSED LENNART JOHANSSON TO BECOME UEFA BOSS, SO WAS HARDLY A DOE-EYED APPRENTICE.

PLATINI OVERCAME MANY OBSTACLES TO MAKE IT AS A FOOTBALLER. HE SUFFERED SERIOUS BREAKS TO HIS RIGHT LEG AND ANKLE IN SEPARATE INCIDENTS WHILST PLAYING FOR NANCY. EARLIER, A DOCTOR AT FC METZ TOLD THE YOUNG MICHEL THAT HE HAD THE SYMPTOMS OF A WEAK HEART AND SHOULD PURSUE A CAREER OUTSIDE OF FOOTBALL.

So, should I quit smoking too, Doc?

Christ, it's not that serious.

IT WAS AT JUVENTUS WHERE HE CEMENTED HIS STATUS AS A GIANT OF THE GAME. HE WON THE BALLON D'OR THREE YEARS IN A ROW, BETWEEN 1983 AND 1985, AND ACHIEVED NOTORIETY AS A DEAD-BALL SPECIALIST. THE WORLD'S MOST NIMBLE GOALKEEPERS WERE POWERLESS TO STOP HIS SIGNATURE RANGE OF FREE-KICKS.

THE TREBUCHÉT

THE CROISSANT

THE SOUTH PACIFIC NUCLEAR TEST

IT WAS HIS FREE-KICK – ONE OF NINE GOALS HE'D SCORED OVER THE COURSE OF FIVE GAMES – THAT OPENED THE SCORING AGAINST SPAIN IN THE EURO '84 FINAL. THE SLOWER DELIVERY SQUIRMED UNDER THE BODY OF LUIS ARCONADA AND SET FRANCE ON THEIR WAY TO THEIR FIRST MAJOR TROPHY.

Just about got away with that one, Luis.

ALONGSIDE MIDFIELDERS ALAIN GIRESSE, JEAN TIGANA AND LUIS FERNÁNDEZ, PLATINI FORMED PART OF THE 'CARRÉ MAGIQUE' (MAGIC SQUARE) OF THE FRENCH TEAM OF THE 1980S. ACCORDING TO NATIONAL COACH MICHEL HIDALGO, 'EVEN HIS FEET ARE INTELLIGENT'.

One ticket for 'Police Academy 4: Citizens on Patrol' and two tickets for the Wim Wenders retrospective, please.

HIS LAST GAME FOR FRANCE WAS A EUROPEAN CHAMPIONSHIP QUALIFIER AGAINST ICELAND, IN 1987. HOWEVER, HE CAME OUT OF RETIREMENT TO PLAY A FRIENDLY FOR KUWAIT IN 1988, AT THE REQUEST OF THE KUWAITI EMIR. THIS WOULD NOT BE THE LAST TIME PLATINI WOULD HELP OUT AN OIL-RICH, MIDDLE-EASTERN STATE.

A World Cup hosted by a country with zero football heritage? Stadiums built by a migrant workforce, in conditions likened to slave labour? A climate so scorching that it renders any activity more strenuous than sweating impossible? Yeah, go on then.

Look out below!

AFTER A SPELL AS FRANCE'S NATIONAL TEAM MANAGER, HE TURNED DOWN THE OFFER TO COACH REAL MADRID IN ORDER TO HELP ORGANISE THE 1998 WORLD CUP. IT WAS A HUGE SUCCESS AND A CELEBRATION OF FRENCH MULTI-CULTURALISM.

Racism is crushed. The politics of hate and division defeated forever. The name Le Pen consigned to an historical footnote. Vive la France!

HE ROSE THROUGH THE RANKS OF UEFA TO BECOME PRESIDENT IN 2007 AND SEEMED CERTAIN TO ASCEND TO FIFA OVERLORD, BUT IN 2015 HE BECAME MIRED IN INVESTIGATIONS INTO CORRUPTION, WITH SWISS PROSECUTORS DISCOVERING THAT HE'D ACCEPTED A £1.3 MILLION PAYMENT FOR UNSPECIFIED SERVICES TO SEPP BLATTER.

FIFA'S ETHICS COMMITTEE BARRED HIM FROM FOOTBALL FOR EIGHT YEARS; A BAN THAT WAS LATER REDUCED TO FOUR YEARS BY THE COURT OF ARBITRATION FOR SPORT. THE GOOD NEWS WAS THAT PLATINI NOW HAD LOADS OF SPARE TIME TO WATCH EURO 2016.

Come on, I earned that money.

Bit to the left. Oh yeah, that's the sweet spot.

My God, this is dull. Who's idea was it to expand this tournament to 24 teams?

GARRINCHA

It was his sister who came up with the nickname 'Garrincha', the local description for a wren, or simply a 'little bird'. It was a poetically apt description for a fragile, beautiful footballer. She coined the term when he brought an injured bird home one day. It was like him, she said, because it had a busted leg and was no use to anyone. No wonder he drank.

His other nicknames were 'The Joy of the People' and 'The Angel with Bent Legs'. Polio had meant he was born with an S-shaped spine and legs that curved to one side, making his feats as a player all the more remarkable. In fact, Garrincha seemed to use it to his advantage; defenders were apparently mesmerised by his misshapen legs and the speed with which he was able to flick the ball this way and that. By the time they'd worked out what he was going to do, he'd already fluttered away from them.

Not that Garrincha probably gave much thought to this; he just enjoyed playing for the sake of it. He had about as much interest in tactics as he did in staying home on a Friday night and often had no idea who was marking him or even who his opponents were; he only wanted to play in his own way, dribbling and crossing, drifting and shooting. The other players were simply props for his improvisation.

As well as his legendary ball skills, Garrincha also had a shot like a cannonball and was capable of bending the ball with great accuracy. On four occasions he scored directly from corner kicks, which almost certainly isn't an indictment on the quality of post-war goalkeeping.

Garrincha had no ambitions to be a professional footballer, but his performances for his local works team led to others convincing him to attend a trial at Botafogo, who signed him up in an instant. It was there where he enjoyed his best years, playing 579 games and scoring 249 goals, including a hat-trick on his debut.

Sadly, Garrincha's career needs to be seen through the prism of his turbulent personal life. He began drinking at the age of 14, around the same time that he began working at the local factory. His father was an alcoholic and Garrincha seemed to have inherited the addiction. At the peak of his career, it wasn't unusual for him to drink a full bottle of Cachaça (a Brazilian spirit) before a game.

The winger's home life was tumultuous too. He married his childhood sweetheart, Nair, who gave birth to eight daughters, before leaving her for Elza Soares, a famous samba singer. He had countless other relationships and in total he fathered at least 14 children, including a son who was conceived during a trip to Sweden. It would be unfair to reduce Garrincha to one piece of trivia, but once you learn that he lost his virginity to a goat, it's hard to forget it.

In the later years of his playing career, Garrincha had to endure the agony of a serious knee injury, getting through games with the aid of pain-killing injections. His pace gone, his powers reduced, he was forced to keep playing because he needed the money. His 60th and last appearance for Brazil came at the 1966 World Cup; a 3–1 defeat to Hungary that saw them eliminated. It was the first time he'd been on the losing side for the national team.

Football had provided a short-term respite from his drinking, but without it he sank further into alcoholism, poverty and tragedy; most appallingly when he drunkenly drove his car into the back of a potato truck, killing one of his passengers, his mother-in-law.

By 1983, Garrincha too was dead, having fallen into an alcoholic coma at the age of just 49, as a result of cirrhosis of the liver. Around 100,000 people are said to have crammed into the cemetery for his burial in his hometown of Pau Grande. His funeral was fittingly chaotic, with the grave being too small for the coffin.

But it was back in 1958 when he'd made a name for himself; the smiling, skipping winger lighting up the World Cup, seemingly playing for his own entertainment.

BRAZIL v USSR, WORLD CUP, GROUP 4, GOTHENBURG 5 JUNE 1958

BRAZIL'S COACHING STAFF WEREN'T SURE ABOUT **GARRINCHA**. DESPITE HIS OBVIOUS AND REMARKABLE TALENTS, HE WAS A MAN IMPERVIOUS TO TACTICAL INSTRUCTION, PLAYING EACH MATCH AS IF IT WERE A KICK ABOUT IN HIS LOCAL VILLAGE. HIS LIFE WAS MIRED IN CHAOS, BUT AT THIS STAGE THERE WERE TWO SAVING GRACES:

Why?

1. FUTEBOL, OBVIOUSLY.

2. THE FACT THAT HE LIVED IN A TIME BEFORE EXPLOITATIVE DAYTIME TELEVISION SHOWS.

You said that we were exclusive, but then I found out that you'd repopulated an entire region

THE CONCERNS OF NATIONAL COACH, VICENTE FEOLA, DEEPENED AFTER BRAZIL'S FINAL FRIENDLY BEFORE THE 1958 WORLD CUP, AGAINST FIORENTINA. GARRINCHA WAS AMAZING, SCORING AT WILL AND HUMILIATING HIS OPPONENTS IN THE PROCESS, BUT HIS SHOWBOATING CAUSED CONSTERNATION IN THE DUGOUT.

Mamma?

FEOLA ENLISTED THE SERVICES OF JOÃO CARVALHAES, A PSYCHOLOGIST WHO WAS USUALLY EMPLOYED TO ASSESS THE MENTAL CONDITION OF PEOPLE WHO WANTED TO BE BUS DRIVERS. HE ADVISED FEOLA TO LEAVE BOTH GARRINCHA AND PELÉ OUT OF THE TEAM.

How did they do?

Dreadfully. I observed them both waiting when some people ran to catch up with them and they showed no aggression when I confronted them with a five pound note.

NEITHER FEATURED IN BRAZIL'S FIRST TWO GAMES, BUT FEOLA RECALLED THEM FOR THE MUST-WIN MATCH AGAINST THE USSR – A TEAM WHOSE SCIENTIFIC APPROACH UNNERVED THE BRAZILIANS.

These guys are like robots! They didn't even drop to their knees and weep praise to sweet merciful Jesus when they were awarded a goal kick.

NOT THAT GARRINCHA WAS FUSSED. HIS KNOWLEDGE OF RUSSIAN ACTIVITIES WAS WORTHY OF A FUTURE AMERICAN PRESIDENT.

Nobody really knows if Russia exists. The experts. Nobody. It's sad. It really is. Do I know Putin? Who can say? Not even the best scientists - who all support me, by the way.

ALTHOUGH, IN GARRINCHA'S CASE THE IGNORANCE WAS LEGITIMATE. ONLY WHEN HE SAW THEM WARMING UP DID HE ASK: MIGHT THESE BE GOOD?

LINING UP BEFORE THE KICK-OFF, NILTON SANTOS REMINDED GARRINCHA HOW IMPORTANT IT WAS THAT HE SHOULDN'T LET HIS TEAMMATES DOWN. GARRINCHA LAUGHED AND REMARKED: 'LOOK AT THE LINESMAN; HE'S JUST LIKE CHARLIE CHAPLIN!'

The only down side to this style of moustache has become painfully clear.

BRAZIL ATTACKED RELENTLESSLY FROM THE START, WITH PELÉ AND GARRINCHA BOTH HITTING THE POST IN THE FIRST MINUTE.

Well this isn't going to do my ulcer any good.

AFTER THREE MINUTES, VAVÁ BROKE THE USSR'S WOOZY RESISTANCE. THE EXALTED L'EQUIPE JOURNALIST GABRIEL HANOT LATER DESCRIBED THIS FLURRY OF ATTACKING PLAY AS THE GREATEST THREE MINUTES IN THE HISTORY OF FOOTBALL.

Alas, I didn't live to see England v Algeria at the 2010 World Cup.

VAVÁ ADDED A SECOND IN THE 77TH MINUTE AND BRAZIL WERE THROUGH. GARRINCHA WAS PERPLEXED AS TO WHY THE SOVIET PLAYERS WERE SO DESPONDENT, AS HE'D ASSUMED (WRONGLY) THERE WAS A SECOND LEG.

We must now face England in a play-off and we all know how formidable they are in high-pressure situations!

CCCP

USSR BEAT ENGLAND 1-0 BUT LOST TO SWEDEN IN THE QUARTER-FINALS.

BRAZIL WENT ON TO WIN THEIR FIRST WORLD CUP AND THEY WOULD RETAIN IT FOUR YEARS LATER, IN CHILE. WHEN GARRINCHA AND PELÉ WERE BOTH IN THE SIDE, BRAZIL NEVER LOST A MATCH.

Pelé! My dear friend! We did it! I believe we shall always stand together, our fortunes shared for ever!

Knife-fighting and Jenga party at my place next Tuesday. You're there, my brother.

THE PLAYERS ALL RECEIVED BONUSES FOR WINNING THE WORLD CUP. GARRINCHA'S WIFE HID HIS UNDER THEIR CHILDREN'S MATTRESS. YEARS LATER, WHEN TIMES WERE HARD, THEY REMEMBERED THE MONEY. CALAMITY NEVER FAR AWAY, THEY DISCOVERED THAT THE CASH HAD BEEN PULPED BY YEARS OF INFANT BED-WETTING.

Bus drivers will still accept this, right? It's legal tender.

This is why you asked me over? You don't even have a Jenga set, do you?

FRANZ BECKENBAUER

Straight back, frizzy hair, pursed lips, Franz Beckenbauer has been a constant presence in football since the 1960s, progressing from player to manager to administrator with the same air of supreme confidence that people always find endearing.

'Der Kaiser' rose from the post-war ruins of working-class Munich. His father, a postal worker, had no time for football and mocked his son's adoration of the national team captain, Fritz Walter, saying that he'd be financially ruined once his career was over. Young Franz wasn't perturbed, and began turning out for SC Munich 1906. Upon learning that the club didn't have the funds to continue the youth team, Franz and his friends vowed to join 1860 Munich. However, at an under-14s tournament in 1959, an 1860 player smacked him in the face, so he decided to join Bayern instead. By the time he left them for New York Cosmos in 1977, Bayern had won the Bundesliga four times and the European Cup three times in succession. That adolescent slap to the chops changed the course of history. Who knows what would have happened if Beckenbauer had taken his precocious talents to 1860 Munich instead? Still, it was probably worth it to see the look on his face, a red hand-print glowing on his cheek.

Whilst he would later come to be seen as an establishment figure, the young Beckenbauer was single-mindedly defiant. In 1963, at the age of 18, he was banned from West Germany's youth team when it was revealed that his girlfriend was pregnant and that he had no intention of marrying her. It took the intervention of coach, Dettmar Cramer, to resolve the situation, with Beckenbauer recalled to the team on the condition that he shared a room with Cramer on away trips. Presumably this would prevent Franz from sneaking off and impregnating the young women of Europe willy-nilly, but it still seems like more of a punishment for Cramer, having to share a stuffy hotel room with a sexually agitated Franz Beckenbauer.

Franz made his full international debut in September 1965 and was one of West Germany's best performers at the following year's World Cup; scoring four goals during the tournament and doing a competent marking job on Bobby

Charlton in the final, which they ultimately lost. Four years later, they went close again, losing a classic semi-final against Italy, 4–3. Beckenbauer played the second half of extra time with his arm in a sling, after picking up a shoulder injury. West Germany had used up all of their substitutions, so he chose to play on. At the end, the Germans felt aggrieved, believing they'd been outdone by the play-acting of the Italians, a low to which no team of Beckenbauer's would ever sink.

However, success was just around the corner. Beckenbauer finally convinced national coach Helmut Schön to allow him to play as a *libero*, launching attacks from defence, as Giacinto Facchetti did for Inter. He captained West Germany to glory in the 1972 European Championships with a 3–0 win in the final against the Soviet Union, but the standout performance came in the quarter-final, with a 3–1 victory against England at Wembley. Beckenbauer's surging runs from deep couldn't have caused more confusion in the England ranks if he'd been trotting forward upon the pink shoulders of a naked and weeping Ted Heath.

Two years later, West Germany would be World Champions, beating the Netherlands 2–1 in Munich, as the celebrated Dutch team laboured under the misapprehension that football matches only last twenty minutes and that you get extra points for dicking around. The atmosphere within the German camp had been turbulent though, and Beckenbauer had to take on the role of de facto manager after Schön finally lost all enthusiasm for spending an extended period of confinement with a large group of cocky twentysomethings arguing about money.

Beckenbauer's leadership skills made him an obvious choice to manage the national team when the job became available in 1984, even though his lack of a coaching licence meant that he had to be given the title of 'team supervisor'. His initial management style of openly insulting his own players was bold, but weirdly effective, as a team of limited quality made it to the 1986 World Cup final, just losing out 3–2 to Argentina.

They went one better in 1990, as Beckenbauer became only the second person, the first being Mario Zagallo – to win the World Cup as a player and a ~~manager~~ team supervisor, after a 1–0 win in the final, again against Argentina. It was his final game in charge of the national team, and after a short spell managing Marseille, he returned to Bayern, first as manager and later as club president, helping to build them into the behemoth they are today.

DESPITE BEING THE MOST DECORATED PLAYER IN GERMAN FOOTBALL HISTORY, **FRANZ BECKENBAUER** STRUGGLED TO WIN A PLACE IN THE HEARTS OF THE PUBLIC, OFTEN SUFFERING UNFLATTERING COMPARISONS TO HIS RIVAL AT CLUB LEVEL, THE DREAMY GÜNTER NETZER.

This was a mistake, Franz.

Oh, please.

THAT NICKNAME DIDN'T HELP — 'DER KAISER'. HE WAS GIVEN IT WHEN HE WAS YOUNG, ON ACCOUNT OF HIS RESEMBLANCE TO LUDWIG II, THE BAVARIAN KING WHO WAS DECLARED 'MAD' DUE TO HIS **QUESTIONABLE FINANCIAL PRACTICES.**

Um, the Cabinet's Ethics Committee wants to talk to you about the bidding process for that big gymnastics tournament you organised.

FRANZ AND GÜNTER BOTH STARRED IN THE 1972 NATIONAL TEAM, THOUGH. IT WAS THE FIRST GERMAN TEAM TO ATTRACT GLOWING INTERNATIONAL PRAISE. L'ÉQUIPE DESCRIBED THEIR HISTORIC 3-1 WIN AGAINST ENGLAND AT WEMBLEY AS 'FOOTBALL FROM THE YEAR 2000', WHICH SOUNDED GREAT UNTIL YOU ACTUALLY SAW GERMANY'S 2000 SIDE.

LINCKER

BECKENBAUER WAS OFTEN CAST AS BEING DEEPLY CONSERVATIVE, BUT HE HAD A REBELLIOUS STREAK. FOR EXAMPLE, DURING THE 1974 WORLD CUP, HE SNUCK OUT OF WEST GERMANY'S HEAVILY-GUARDED TRAINING CAMP TO MEET UP WITH AN ACTRESS FRIEND.

He just strode out from der fence. I've never seen anyone do that before. It was...**graceful.**

Balletic.

You're both idiots.

HE WASN'T THE ONLY ESCAPEE, PLAYERS WERE BREAKING OUT ALL OVER THE PLACE. MANAGER HELMUT SCHÖN PACKED HIS SUITCASES AND THREATENED TO QUIT UNLESS THE DESERTERS WERE THROWN OUT OF THE SQUAD. EVENTUALLY, HE WAS TALKED ROUND.

Fine. I'll stay, but this indiscipline must cease...

Oh, for God's sake.

I wanted to go to the arcade.

West Germany won the competition, but it took its toll on Schön's mental health as his exasperation with the players grew. Beckenbauer stepped up, displaying trademark leadership skills.

We are playing for Helmut Schön!

He's right!

We must do it for the man who wanted to end our international careers last week!

IT WAS INEVITABLE THAT HE WOULD MOVE IN TO MANAGEMENT WHEN HIS PLAYING CAREER ENDED. UPON TAKING CONTROL OF THE NATIONAL TEAM IN 1984, BECKENBAUER CONTINUED TO EXPLORE NEW BOUNDARIES.

He's... standing **up**! How the hell do we counter **that**?

Never mind that, look at the **slacks**.

FRANZ ENDURED A ROCKY START, THOUGH. BEFORE THE MEXICO '86 WORLD CUP STARTED, GOALKEEPER ULI STEIN WAS SENT HOME FOR CALLING THE KAISER A CLOWN, OLAF THON WANTED TO GO HOME VOLUNTARILY AND THE MANAGER CALLED DIETER HOENESS AN IDIOT IN PUBLIC. BELIEVING HE LACKED THE DIPLOMACY TO SUCCEED, BECKENBAUER OFFERED TO RESIGN.

Where does he get the idea that I'm clownish? Let's see how they do without Franzi

Screw this.

HE WAS PERSUADED TO STICK AROUND, THOUGH. SURPRISINGLY, WEST GERMANY REACHED THE FINAL, WHERE THEY LOST 3-2 TO ARGENTINA. THE TWO NATIONS MET AGAIN FOUR YEARS LATER, WITH BECKENBAUER'S TEAM WINNING 1-0 IN THE TETCHIEST WORLD CUP FINAL EVER.

Tonight the world weeps for my brave, referee-bullying boys.

Fucking hilarious.

IT WAS NO SURPRISE WHEN HE LATER TOOK HIS SKILLS TO THE BOARD ROOM AT BAYERN. EVEN AS A CHILD, YOUNG FRANZ HAD DISPLAYED AN APTITUDE FOR BUSINESS.

Pfft. All those posters of football players. They'll all be destitute once their knees give up.

Oh father. Unlike you, they don't have to scrape by on a postman's wage. They'll have invested wisely in future markets and property. I've crunched the numbers. I'd explain it to you, but, y'know... no point.

BECKENBAUER'S UNCOMPROMISING WILL TO WIN DID NOT DIMINISH. ONE TIME, WHEN BAYERN WERE FINED FOR BREACHING BROADCASTING RULES, HE THREATENED TO MOVE THE CLUB TO SERIE A.

That's it, we're off to Italy. Football is far more sensible there.

BUNGA

SILVIO SAYS RELAX

IN 1998, HE WAS APPOINTED AS VICE-PRESIDENT OF THE GERMAN FA AND OVERSAW THEIR SUCCESSFUL BID TO HOST THE 2006 WORLD CUP. HOWEVER, HE HAS SINCE FACED SOME SERIOUS QUESTIONS ABOUT WRONGDOING, SUCH AS WHY THE OFFICIAL MASCOT, 'GOLEO', WAS NUDE FROM THE WAIST DOWN.

Danke.

CRISTIANO RONALDO

There are few sights more uplifting than that of Cristiano Ronaldo sprinting away from goal, the net rippling in his wake, his chest puffed out, the sinews of his tanned neck straining, his mouth screaming his own name. As he reaches the corner flag, he spins in the air, landing with his legs akimbo, arms outstretched; his back to the delighted crowd. Some wave their arms, some clutch their heads, all are astonished that after all this time, after all these celebrations, no one has ever run on and kicked him in the groin.

His supporting cast catch up with him, 'Hooray, you've scored again', they beam through clenched teeth. 'CR7', he roars. Before the day is out, he will stand in his pants and have his photo taken alongside these men: even though they are his subordinates, and in every way lesser-people, he is still capable of great compassion and humility. 'Hooray', they repeat.

If you forget about The Other Bloke, Ronaldo is the most important player of the modern era. Barely a week passes without him breaking another scoring record. He has ingeniously adapted his game throughout the various stages of his career to remain at the very pinnacle of the sport, a global icon unparalleled in terms of success or ability (discarding Him Up The Road, remember).

These days, you might think of Ronaldo as a player wealthy enough to throw a hissy fit when the Spanish authorities have the temerity to ask him to pay tax on his astronomical income; however, he hailed from humble beginnings. His childhood was spent in Madeira, an island whose airport now bears a bust in honour of its most famous son. Yes, the sculpture looks like an advent calendar chocolate that's been sat on for half an hour, but if this book proves anything, it's that creating accurate likenesses is harder than winning four Ballon d'Ors.

Starting out at Sporting CP, Ronaldo came to the attention of Manchester United in 2003, after a dominant performance in a friendly between the two clubs. Alex Ferguson was compelled to sign him by the pleas of his players; one imagines that Roy Keane would have been particularly taken by the young winger's endless step-overs and determined preening.

United's fans and former legends were soon drooling over his performances in the famous number 7 shirt. Under the watchful eye of Ferguson, a more disciplined Ronaldo matured, whilst losing none of his explosive flair. He soon became a prolific and powerful marksman, capable of scoring with astonishing bursts of speed, towering headers and by perfecting an idiosyncratic free-kick technique. This involved him standing with his legs apart for long enough to ensure that the TV cameras zoomed in on his face, which was fixed with a studious look that suggested he was about to disarm a car bomb with a hundred angry scorpions down his shorts, rather than kick a football. A puff of the cheeks, a glance at the big screen and then TWAT, the ball is blasted towards – and sometimes into – the goal.

Critics of Ronaldo have sometimes focused on his moon-sized ego, or the way he does that sardonic laugh when a decision goes against him, or his tendency to throw a tantrum like a git child in a supermarket car park. However, it is the cultivation of this arrogant persona that has helped to make him such a force. Sure, he might remind you of that one kid at school who would never pass the ball, but if you'd been named after Ronald Reagan, you might have a few personality defects too.

Having won three Premier League titles, one Champions League, and established himself as one of the world's greatest – and most marketable – talents, it was no surprise when Real Madrid came calling, eventually capturing Ronaldo's signature for £80 million, a lot of money in 2009.

At the time of writing, Ronaldo's goals, hunger and hissy fits show no sign of abating and have resulted in Madrid winning three Champions League titles in the last four years. As he has entered his thirties, those searing bursts through opposition defences have become less regular; instead he has employed an economy of movement, mostly involving perfectly-timed runs between the 18-yard box and the 6-yard box. The condition of his abdominal muscles alone suggests he could play on for many years to come; Ronaldo does not seem like the kind of man who has ever eaten an entire box of Magnum Mini's in one sitting.

And yet, as he reached the twilight years of his playing career, there was still one achievement that evaded him: success at international level.

IT SEEMED LIKE THE SAME OLD STORY, BUT TWO GOALS, AN ASSIST AND A TRADEMARK HISSY FIT CONTRIBUTED TO A 3-3 DRAW WITH HUNGARY. IT WAS ENOUGH TO SEE PORTUGAL FINISH THIRD IN THE GROUP. THERE COULD BE NO DOUBT AS TO THE IDENTITY OF THE REAL HERO.

AN EXTRA-TIME WIN AGAINST CROATIA, AND A PENALTY SHOOT-OUT SUCCESS AGAINST POLAND PUT PORTUGAL INTO THE SEMI-FINALS WITHOUT WINNING A GAME IN NORMAL TIME. THERE, THEY WOULD FACE WALES, PUTTING RONALDO INTO DIRECT COMPETITION WITH HIS REAL MADRID TEAMMATE AND GREAT BUDDY, GARETH BALE.

Tag. Like. Share.

Lush.

RONALDO HAD BECOME MORE OF AN OUT-AND-OUT STRIKER AS AGE REDUCED HIS ABILITY TO BURN THROUGH DEFENCES. HE'D ALWAYS BEEN A THREAT IN THE AIR, THOUGH. HIS LONG, MUSCULAR NECK AND NATURAL ABILITY TO RISE ABOVE THE CROWD WHEN CAMERAS WERE PRESENT MADE HIM A CONSTANT DANGER. IT WAS WITH A TYPICAL, SOARING HEADER THAT HE GAVE PORTUGAL THE LEAD.

THE GOAL WAS RONALDO'S NINTH AT A EUROPEAN CHAMPIONSHIP, MAKING HIM THE JOINT ALL-TIME HIGHEST SCORER, MATCHING MICHEL PLATINI'S RECORD.

Oh well that's just fucking brilliant.

NANI ADDED A SECOND THREE MINUTES LATER AND PORTUGAL WERE INTO THE FINAL AGAINST HOSTS FRANCE.

HOWEVER, DISASTER STRUCK FOR RONALDO AFTER JUST 25 MINUTES, WHEN A REDUCER FROM THE NOTORIOUS HARD MAN DIMITRI PAYET SAW HIM LEAVE THE FIELD ON A STRETCHER. A CURIOUS-LOOKING MOTH SAT ON HIS TEAR-GLISTENED CHEEK, SLURPING ON HIS ANGUISH.

Oh, sweet ambrosia...

HAVING BEEN SUBSTITUTED, RONALDO COULD SOON BE SEEN HOBBLING ALONG THE TOUCHLINE, HELPING COACH FERNANDO SANTOS BY OFFERING TACTICAL INSTRUCTIONS.

Lads, knock it left

RIGHT! SHIFT IT RIGHT!

WITH FRANCE UNABLE TO BREAK DOWN THE STUBBORN PORTUGUESE UNIT, THE FINAL WENT TO EXTRA-TIME. IN THE 109TH MINUTE, SUBSTITUTE EDER CRASHED IN A LONG-RANGE SHOT TO SEAL THE TITLE. EDER'S PERSONAL STORY WAS REMARKAB

Ahem!

RIGHT, YEAH, SORRY. RONALDO LIMPED UP THE STEPS TO COLLECT THE TROPHY AND WEAR IT LIKE A HAT. HIS MUSEUM WOULD NOW HAVE A NEW ADDITION TO REMIND VISITORS OF THE DRIVING FORCE BEHIND PORTUGAL'S VICTORIOUS SUMMER.

PAOLO MALDINI

The clean-living, symmetrical-faced, ultra-professional Paolo Maldini may not provide the most fascinating of subjects, but you don't get to win seven Scudettos and five European Cups in a 24-year playing career by falling out of Terry Venables' nightclub at five in the morning and using a doner kebab for a pillow. The only indication of any form of excess is the fact that he owns over a hundred pairs of jeans. It's unclear whether he still just wears the same two pairs on rotation until the holes in the groin area become too obvious to wear outside, just like the rest of us, right? *Right?*

Maldini would still have been in stonewash denim when he made his Serie A debut for Milan in 1985. He was still playing at the top level in 2009, by which time he was in his forties. When he did eventually hang up his boots, to spend more time with his tennis court, he was farewelled in the traditional *Milanista* fashion, by being jeered by a small section of Ultras who still harboured a grudge over a molecular-sized slight years before.

Starting out at left-back, Maldini and his ridiculously perfect cheekbones extended their careers by moving to a more central defensive position and forming an imposing partnership with Alessandro Nesta (also handsome enough to have stepped straight out of the pages of the Next Directory). The record books don't show how many opposing players found themselves lost in their captivating eyes, perfect through-balls rolling harmlessly out of play as the sunlight caught the defensive pairing's hair just so. What the record books *do* reveal is that Maldini holds the record for the most Milan appearances (902) and is arguably the greatest player in their history.

BOOOOOOOOOOOOOOOOOO!

WITH A FATHER LIKE CESARE MALDINI - THE DEFENSIVE LINCHPIN OF THE MILAN TEAM THAT WON FOUR SCUDETTOS IN THE 1950s- IT WAS CLEAR THAT YOUNG PAOLO WOULD FOLLOW IN THE FAMILY TRADE.

HE GREW UP WATCHING HIS FATHER PLAY AND TRAIN. EACH PASS, TACKLE AND BLOCK SCHOOLING HIM IN THE ART OF DEFENDING.

SURPRISINGLY, PAOLO WAS A JUVENTUS FAN AS A CHILD AND HAD A POSTER OF ROBERTO BETTEGA ON HIS WALL. HOWEVER, THIS WAS JUST A PHASE AND, AS CESARE LATER OBSERVED: 'HIS SOUL BELONGS TO MILAN'.

EMPLOYMENT CONTRACT
Length: Eternity

PAOLO MADE HIS MILAN DEBUT AT THE AGE OF SIXTEEN AND SOON BECAME A PERMANENT FIXTURE IN DEFENCE, ALONGSIDE BARESI, COSTACURTA AND TASSOTTI. HIS CAREER WOULD SPAN THREE DECADES - OR, ABOUT THE LENGTH OF TIME IT TOOK HIS TEAMMATE FILIPPO INZAGHI TO GRASP THE COMPLEXITIES OF THE OFFSIDE RULE.

Oh for... Pippo, how did you manage to be so far offside when I was only explaining it to you with these condiments?!

I thought the salt cellar was playing me on?

IT WAS UNDER THE COACHING OF ARRIGO SACCHI THAT MALDINI BECAME A WORLD CLASS PLAYER. MILAN BECAME KINGS OF EUROPE, WITH SACCHI TEACHING HIS CHARGES TO THINK ABOUT FOOTBALL ALL THE TIME, SOMETHING PAOLO SAID WAS ACTUALLY QUITE STRESSFUL.

HOWEVER, AFTER TWO EUROPEAN CUP WINS, SACCHI MADE WAY FOR SOMEONE MORE CHILLED OUT.

You broke my heart, Paolo. I know it was you who ate crisps four days before a match.

MORE SUCCESS FOLLOWED WITH A 4-0 HUMPING OF BARCELONA'S DREAM TEAM IN THE 1994 CHAMPIONS LEAGUE FINAL. PAOLO THEN EMULATED THE ACHIEVEMENTS OF CESARE BY LIFTING THE CUP AS MILAN CAPTAIN IN 2003 AFTER A FINAL WITH JUVENTUS THAT WAS APPRECIATED BY PEOPLE WHO HAVE A DEEPER UNDERSTANDING OF THE GAME THAN YOU GOAL-FETISHISING PLEBS.

A masterclass in caution!
An Italian classic!
Drool!

A FIFTH EUROPEAN CROWN FOLLOWED IN 2007 BEFORE RETIREMENT IN 2009. THE MALDINI LEGACY CONTINUES, THOUGH, WITH PAOLO'S SON, CHRISTIAN, COMING THROUGH THE RANKS AT MILAN. HE SEEMS TO BE FOLLOWING A MORE CIRCUITOUS PATH TO WORLD DOMINATION BY SIGN-ING FOR HAMRUN SPARTANS IN THE MALTESE PREMIER LEAGUE.

JIMMY JOHNSTONE

When Jock Stein was appointed as Celtic manager in 1965, he wasn't sure about Jimmy Johnstone. The young winger was undoubtedly talented, but he was small enough to fit in a pouch of tobacco and seemed to enjoy the Glasgow nightlife a little too enthusiastically.

The two men often clashed, but over the next decade they would together win nine league titles in a row – in an age when football in Scotland was actually competitive – and be crowned European Champions, on the greatest night in Scottish football history.

'Jinky' played 505 times for Celtic and is one of its most decorated players, but he got off to a rocky start, making his debut in a 6–0 defeat to Kilmarnock in 1963. However, his ability to entertain the crowd with his darting dribbles and cheeky demeanour soon made him a firm terrace favourite. Stein too would come to see his worth.

Johnstone was in devastating form in the 1967 European Cup final, repeatedly driving at the notoriously mean Inter defence with an energy that sapped the Italians' legs and confidence. Celtic's captain, Billy McNeill, remarked that it was as if he were playing Inter on his own. A green-and-white midgie, with pale legs and red hair, buzzing around the ears of the defenders, ruining their picnic.

After he was released by Celtic, his drinking worsened. The icy fear of sitting in a bar and having Jock Stein phone the landlord to check up on him was gone. Like most players of his generation, he didn't reap the financial benefits of the modern game, and after he retired from playing, he tried his hand at various jobs. For a while, he was employed as a satellite dish installer. The irony that he was fitting the equipment that had helped to make millionaires out of many latter-day footballers wasn't lost on him.

Johnstone fought with characteristic bravery against his alcohol addiction, and did the same when he was diagnosed with motor neurone disease. Sadly, this was one opponent that Jinky was unable to beat, and he passed away in 2006, at the age of 61.

LIKE MANY OF THE GAME'S FINEST SHOWMEN, JIMMY JOHNSTONE DELIGHTED IN BEATING DEFENDERS TIME AFTER TIME.

AS A CHILD, HE'D HONED HIS SKILLS BY DRIBBLING AROUND MILK BOTTLES IN PIT BOOTS. WHEN HE FIRST BROKE INTO THE FIRST-TEAM SQUAD AT CELTIC, THE OTHER PLAYERS ASSUMED HE WAS A BALL BOY. THEY WERE SOON PUT STRAIGHT.

IT WASN'T LONG UNTIL HIS REPUTATION IN GLASGOW GREW. INDEED, THE BUS DRIVER WHO WORKED ON THE ROUTE THAT TOOK JIMMY TO TRAINING EACH DAY WOULD STOP AND WAIT IF THE YOUNG WINGER WAS LATE. THE OTHER PASSENGERS MUSTN'T HAVE MINDED.

JOCK STEIN KNEW HOW TO GET THE BEST OUT OF JINKY, EVEN USING HIS FEAR OF FLYING TO HIS ADVANTAGE. BEFORE A EUROPEAN CUP TIE WITH RED STAR BELGRADE, STEIN TOLD JOHNSTONE THAT IF HE PLAYED WELL IN THE HOME LEG, HE'D BE SPARED FROM FLYING TO THE AWAY LEG.

JOHNSTONE COULDN'T ALWAYS AVOID FLYING, THOUGH. ON ONE OCCASION HE SPRAYED A FLIGHT CABIN WITH HOLY WATER, AS A PRECAUTIONARY MEASURE.

JOHNSTONE WAS AN INSTRUMENTAL COMPONENT DURING THE MOST SUCCESSFUL PERIOD IN CELTIC'S HISTORY, BUT ALL THINGS MUST COME TO AN END. ON THE DAY HE WAS RELEASED BY JOCK STEIN IN 1975, HE SAT IN THE CAR PARK AT CELTIC PARK AND SOBBED LIKE A MAN WHO DIDN'T KNOW THAT HE WOULD ONE DAY PLAY FOR SHEFFIELD UNITED.

HE REMAINED IN THE HEARTS OF THE CELTIC FANS AND WHEN A POLL WAS HELD TO DECIDE UPON THE CLUB'S GREATEST EVER PLAYER, THERE COULD BE ONLY ONE WINNER. HOWEVER, THEY OVERLOOKED WAYNE BIGGINS AND AWARDED IT TO JINKY INSTEAD. A STATUE OF THE GREAT MAN NOW STANDS NOT FAR FROM WHERE HE SAT IN 1975.

GOALKEEPERS ARE DIFFERENT

Modern-day goalkeepers are expected to be part of the team, almost as if they are normal people. Clearly, this is the kind of politically-correct lunacy that can only end with Peter Shilton addressing the Pyramid Stage at Glastonbury, but keepers are no longer selected purely on their ability to fling themselves into a muddy puddle, or shout at defenders until their jaws dislocate; now they are expected to *contribute*.

The role of the goalkeeper really began to change in the early nineties, when the back-pass rule was implemented. For me, this was the golden age of both goalkeeping and slapstick. The reform heralded an era of wild air kicks, frenzied dribbles and a general level of composure usually displayed by antelopes whose afternoon saunter to the watering hole has been interrupted by a leopard with a napkin tied around its neck.

Keepers such as Manuel Neuer are now as competent as outfield players as they are in goal. It seems that the age of the eccentric goalkeeper has passed; we are unlikely to again witness the improvised chaos of René Higuita, or the swivel-eyed fury of Jens Lehmann. The clownish acrobatics of Bruce Grobbelaar would no longer be tolerated for the sake of the occasional breathtaking save.

However, the role of goalkeeper remains a specialist position. Right from childhood, it requires a unique skillset to be the kid who goes in goal, by dint of being the one who owns goalkeeper gloves. It is a tired old cliché that it's usually the people who know their way around a family-sized stuffed crust pizza who get put in goal. However, there was one exception . . .

WILLIAM FOULKE

William 'Fatty' Foulke was born in Derbyshire in 1874, a time before you could call out the blatant body-shaming of such a derogatory and unimaginative nickname. Like most fit and able men of his generation, by the time he was old enough he was working down the pits. However, he loved to play football, turning out for the local village team, Blackwell, on a Saturday afternoon.

Standing at 6ft 4ins, Foulke was a veritable giant compared to his short-arse Victorian contemporaries, and, at least in the early years of his playing career, he had his weight under control, weighing 14st 12lb in 1896. He'd almost doubled in size by the time he was 33. Foulke's story is very relatable.

Derby County were the first professional club to spot Foulke, when he lined up against them in a friendly. He was hard to miss, for as well as being the size of a greenhouse, he'd also knocked out the two front teeth of their centre-forward, John Goodall. That was the other thing about Foulke, as well as being a jolly joker, he also had a terrifying temper. On one occasion he took a swing at a Notts County player, leading to a pitch invasion; another time he picked up Liverpool's centre-forward, George Allan, turned him upside-down and planted him head-first in the mud.

Despite his expanding waistband and wild eccentricities, he was still a talented goalkeeper who let in very few goals. Sheffield United pipped Derby to his signature, and that's where he enjoyed the most successful years of his career, before moving on to Chelsea and inventing ball boys. A man needs a legacy.

THE VICTORIANS HAD A VERY DIFFERENT ATTITUDE TO BODY IMAGE AND WEIGHT ISSUES.

Roll up, roll up, roll up and gaze upon the **grotesque** Walrus Man, with his blubbery throat and vast, undulating bosom.

Are you talking about me? I'm, like, five pounds overweight. I have a desk job!

YET EVEN BY THE MODERN DAY STANDARDS OF CHICKEN DIPPER AND CREME EGG FAD DIETS, **WILLIAM FATTY FOULKE** WAS A BIG LAD. BY THE END OF HIS CAREER, HE WAS SAID TO WEIGH 28 STONES. HE WAS, HOWEVER, ABLE TO DISGUISE THIS BY PULLING HIS SHORTS UP OVER HIS BELLY BUTTON.

Heh, the perfect crime.

AT SIX FEET AND FOUR INCHES, FOULKE WAS AN IMPOSING PRESENCE. HIS FIERCE TEMPER OFTEN SAW HIM COMING TO BLOWS WITH OPPONENTS, AND WHILE CHARGING THE GOALKEEPER WAS STILL ALLOWED, ATTEMPTING TO DO IT TO FOULKE WAS LIKE TRYING TO BUNDLE A FORD DISCOVERY INTO THE NET.

NO MATE

WITH FOULKE IN THEIR SIDE, SHEFFIELD UNITED WON A LEAGUE TITLE AND TWO FA CUPS. IN 1889, THEY BEAT DERBY IN THE FINAL, 4-1. NEWSPAPERS REPORTED THAT THE FANS WERE GREATLY AMUSED BY FOULKE'S SIZE AND ANTICS. HUMOUR WAS LESS SOPHISTICATED BACK THEN.

Sorry...

What is it, Doctor?

I was just thinking about James Corden's Carpool Karaoke again. The roly poly funny man had Chris Martin on this week and... HAHAHAHAHA.

Mother...!

NEVER SHORT OF AN OPINION, UPON COLLECTING HIS WINNER'S MEDAL FROM ASPIRING PRIME MINISTER, A.J. BALFOUR, FOULKE TOLD HIM HE WASN'T UP TO THE JOB.

Fear not, A.J., even if you destroy the whole country, a few well-aimed zingers will ensure a rousing send-off from your fellow Tories.

'KIN USELESS.

THREE YEARS LATER, THE BLADES RETURNED TO THE FINAL, BUT WERE DENIED VICTORY WHEN REFEREE **TOM KIRKHAM** LET A LATE AND CONTROVERSIAL SOUTHAMPTON EQUALISER STAND. AFTER THE MATCH, KIRKHAM HAD TO HIDE IN A BROOM CUPBOARD AS A NAKED FOULKE STALKED THE DRESSING ROOMS, SEEKING JUSTICE.

Come out, damn you! Let us wrestle this out like men: naked as the day we were born and greased to the eyeballs in margarine!

Bloody hell...

SHEFFIELD UNITED WON THE REPLAY, 2-1.

FOULKE WAS SOLD TO CHELSEA FOR £50 IN 1905 AND IMMEDIATELY BECAME SOMETHING OF A CELEBRITY IN THE CAPITAL.

HE WAS BECOMING MORE TEMPERAMENTAL, THOUGH. THERE WERE FREQUENT PHYSICAL ALTERCATIONS WITH OPPONENTS AND HE WOULD SOMETIMES WALK OFF THE PITCH IF HE FELT HIS DEFENCE WASN'T PULLING ITS WEIGHT.

WHILE AT CHELSEA, FOULKE WOULD POSITION A BOY BESIDE EACH OF HIS GOAL POSTS TO RETRIEVE THE BALL AND MAKE HIM APPEAR BIGGER. THUS BEGAN CHELSEA'S LONG AND OCCASIONALLY FRACTIOUS RELATIONSHIP WITH BALL BOYS.

— Eden Hazard has injured one of our own. The global network of ball boys must punish Chelsea by holding onto the ball slightly longer than usual.

BY NOW, HIS SIZE WAS BALLOONING. ON ONE AWAY TRIP, HE SCOFFED ALL OF HIS CHELSEA TEAMMATES' BREAKFASTS BEFORE THEY'D COME DOWN FROM THEIR HOTEL ROOMS. 'I DON'T CARE WHAT YOU CALL ME, JUST DON'T CALL ME LATE FOR DINNER!' HE QUIPPED.

How about I call you a selfish, bircher-muesli-stealing glutton, William? How about that?

Leave it, Simon. There's a place up the road that will do us some demolished avocado on rye toast.

HE SAVED TEN PENALTIES IN HIS SOLITARY SEASON AT CHELSEA, BUT WHEN THEY MISSED OUT ON PROMOTION HE WAS SOLD. HE MOVED TO BRADFORD CITY, WHOSE MANAGER WOULD MOCK HIS SIZE BY MAKING HIM COLLECT HIS WAGES VIA A NARROW GATE.

This is the only reason you signed me, isn't it?

Yep. Now do a little dance for me and we'll talk about your win bonus, Jiggles.

AFTER RETIRING IN 1907, HE FELL ON HARD TIMES. HIS HEALTH DECLINED AFTER BECOMING A PUB LANDLORD IN SHEFFIELD AND HE DIED IN 1916, AT THE AGE OF JUST 42, OF LIVER AND HEART DISEASES.

It was Mr Foulke's express wish that you be a pall bearer.

GIANLUIGI BUFFON

Scientists believe that Gigi Buffon is so old that he would have been practising his long throws at a time when the planet was still populated exclusively by bacteria. Yet, by 2017, he was still playing at the very top level of football, turning out for Juventus in the Champions League final.

Despite a glittering career, in which he'd played over a thousand professional games, become Italy's most capped player, set new records for the most clean sheets in Serie A and for the national team, won every other trophy going, and established himself as the finest goalkeeper of all time, it was a Champions League winners' medal that eluded him. Earlier in the season, he'd stated that he couldn't retire until he'd experienced success in that competition. Buffon is therefore cursed to play on for all eternity, after the remnants of society have crumbled to dust, because of something he said in an interview once.

So invincible was Buffon that he earned the nickname 'Superman', and for a while took to wearing a Superman T-shirt under his goalkeeper top. Buffon is possibly the only man in the world who could get away with this without looking like an IT engineer or an arsehole.

However, his career has not been without controversy; in 2000 he asked to wear the number 88 shirt – a number favoured by Neo-Nazis, as H is the eighth letter of the alphabet, with 88 therefore standing for HH or Heil Hitler. Buffon claimed he liked the number because it represented four balls. Later, he would take to wearing the number 1, which obviously to a suspicious mind looks like A STRAIGHT-ARMED SALUTE. The evidence is damning, but it doesn't seem to have harmed him too much.

RENÉ HIGUITA

There is a scene in *Escobar's Own Goal* (a documentary about the murder of the Colombian captain Andrés Escobar after the 1994 World Cup) in which René Higuita rides a massive motorcycle through his mum's house. Mrs Higuita sits impassively in an armchair, as if this is a regular occurrence – a close-up revealing an air of resignation. It must be exhausting being René Higuita's mum.

Higuita had missed the 1994 World Cup, as he'd not long been released from prison after acting as a go-between to secure the release of a captive in a kidnapping. He was released without charge, but didn't make the squad. There are unconventional goalkeepers, and then there is Higuita.

'El Loco' had come to global attention at the World Cup in Italy four years earlier, with his Rick James hair and fondness for dribbling upfield, positioning himself as one of the original sweeper-keepers. You didn't get this kind of boundary-pushing experimentation with Perry Suckling. It all came horribly unstuck for him in a second-round match against Cameroon, when he was easily dispossessed in the centre circle by a giggling Roger Milla, who sprinted away, rolling the ball into an empty net.

Higuita himself had started out as a centre-forward and even managed to score 44 goals throughout his goalkeeping career, including three for the national team. However, he is best remembered for his signature move, revealed on a cool September evening at Wembley Stadium. Back in Colombia, his mother looks up at the television, rolls her eyes, and goes back to scrubbing motor oil stains from her living-room floor tiles.

RENÉ HIGUITA HAD BEEN PLANNING HIS 'SCORPION KICK' FOR FIVE YEARS; THE IDEA FIRST COMING TO HIM WHEN WATCHING SOME CHILDREN TRYING BICYCLE KICKS IN THE STREET.

Hey, kids, why don't you try something different? Why not do it in reverse? Fling yourselves forward and kick the ball with your heels!

Well he certainly looks like he's full of sensible ideas...!

ONE HOUR LATER...

Open up, Higuita; we know you're in there!

DING-DONG! DING-DONG!

HIS BIG CHANCE CAME ON THE GRANDEST OF STAGES: A FRIENDLY AGAINST ENGLAND IN FRONT OF A QUARTER-FULL WEMBLEY. JAMIE REDKNAPP OVER HIT A LONG BALL INTO THE PENALTY AREA AND 'EL LOCO' UNVEILED HIS NEW MOVE.

Super freak.

Super freaky.

THE MOMENT LIT UP AN OTHERWISE DRAB EVENING, EVEN IF THE LINESMAN HAD ALREADY RAISED AN OFFSIDE FLAG. NOT EVERYONE WAS IMPRESSED. MALCOLM BERRY, SECRETARY TO THE ENGLAND SCHOOL'S FA, DISMISSED IT AS 'CRASS AND STUPID', WHILE POOR OLD JAMIE REDKNAPP WAS CONDEMNED TO SPEND THE REST OF HIS DAYS LOOKING PERMANENTLY STUPEFIED.

AS CLEARANCES GO, IT WAS ARGUABLY LESS PRACTICAL THAN OTHER IMPROBABLE METHODS, SUCH AS:

THE PELVIC THRUST

HUNH!

THE 'SPONSORSHIP OPPORTUNITY'.

YOUR NAME HERE

THE 'GETTING CARLOS VALDERRAMA TO CLOSE DOWN THE SPACE TO PREVENT THE PASS INTO THE BOX'.

Run to your left, Pibe!

HA! You're so crazy, René!

INDEED, HIGUITA CLAIMED TO HAVE A WIDE REPERTOIRE OF SIMILARLY INNOVATIVE KICKS, BUT THERE WAS ONLY EVER ONE PARTY PIECE THE CROWDS WANTED TO SEE.

SCOR-PI-ON, SCOR-PI-ON...

Really? I'm 48 years old. I've got a move where I catch the ball in a big butterfly net and—

SCOR-PI-ON! SCOR-PI-ON!

OK.

NOT THAT HE MINDED. HE WAS HUGELY PROUD OF HIS INNOVATION, CLAIMING IT WAS A GIFT FROM GOD.

Are you gonna sort out that pestilence thing today?

Jesus, there's 20,000 bored football fans at Wembley. I think that's a little bit more important, don't you?

Your heart really isn't in this any more, is it?

BERT TRAUTMANN

What is the most minor injury you'd have to suffer before feeling justified in knocking off work early? A papercut? A headache? A repetitive strain injury caused by years of keeping your jaw clenched as your colleagues spout an endless stream of bollocks? All perfectly valid reasons to sack it off and get home in time for *Pointless*, but Bert Trautmann stayed at work, in his job as goalkeeper for Manchester City in the 1956 FA Cup final, despite suffering A BROKEN NECK.

Trautmann had overcome difficulty before; after years of being brainwashed by the propaganda machine of Nazi Germany, he signed up to join the army a week after his seventeenth birthday, in 1940. He spent the rest of the war as a Luftwaffe paratrooper, until he was captured by the British and sent to a Prisoner of War camp in Lancashire.

Football matches were a regular part of life in the camp, and it was there that he discovered he had a talent for goalkeeping; a path that would lead him to his astonishingly brave performance at Wembley and a date with a spinal specialist.

There was mass outrage when he signed for Manchester City, but their fans soon came to see he was no longer a goose-stepping zombie and that he was also a courageous and intelligent goalkeeper – he was an early pioneer, at least in England, of throwing the ball out, rather than just hoofing it upfield hopefully.

Opposition fans were less quick to forgive. His first match in London was against Fulham – a cauldron of intimidation at the best of times. Their fans hurled abuse at him, but by the end of the afternoon he was applauded from the field by players and supporters of both teams. It was to become a familiar story.

TRAUTMANN SURVIVED MANY NEAR-DEATH EXPERIENCES DURING THE WAR. IT WAS REALLY DANGEROUS. HE WAS ONE OF ONLY 90 MEMBERS OF HIS ORIGINAL UNIT OF 1,000 TO STILL BE ALIVE IN 1945, WHEN HE LEAPT OVER A HEDGE IN FRANCE AND STRAIGHT INTO THE HANDS OF SOME JOVIAL BRITISH SOLDIERS.

Fancy a cup of tea, Fritz?

'Fritz'?

Well, if I'd known there was going to be xenophobia, I'd have never signed up for Hitler's campaign of horror.

HE WAS SENT TO A POW CAMP IN LANCASHIRE, WHERE FOOTBALL MATCHES WERE REGULAR. DURING ONE SUCH GAME, HE WAS INJURED WHILST PLAYING AS A CENTRE-HALF. RATHER THAN LEAVE THE FIELD, HE WENT IN GOAL, THUS BEGINNING HIS CAREER AS A GOALKEEPER.

The thing is, Bernhard, we're actually in the middle of quite a complex escape bid, so...

Gloves.

UPON HIS RELEASE, HE JOINED THE LOCAL AMATEUR TEAM, ST HELENS TOWN. HIS PERFORMANCES EARNED HIM A SHOCK TRANSFER TO MANCHESTER CITY IN 1949, A MOVE THAT WAS SURPRISINGLY MET WITH RESISTANCE.

I'd like to introduce the replacement for our long-serving goalkeeper, Frank Swift; much-loved by our city that still bears the scars of the Luftwaffe's handiwork: FORMER LUFTWAFFE PARATROOPER, BERRRRT TRAUTMANN!

MANCHESTER'S LARGE JEWISH COMMUNITY WAS AGHAST. TWENTY THOUSAND PEOPLE HIT THE STREETS IN PROTEST. HOWEVER, AN OPEN LETTER IN THE LOCAL NEWSPAPER FROM THE COMMUNAL RABBI FOR MANCHESTER CONVINCED PEOPLE TO GIVE TRAUTMANN A CHANCE.

HIS PERFORMANCES AND CHARACTER HAD WON OVER THE PUBLIC BY THE TIME OF THE 1956 FA CUP FINAL, WHERE HIS BRAVERY WOULD BRING HIM WORLDWIDE ACCLAIM. LEADING BIRMINGHAM 3-1, WITH 17 MINUTES LEFT, HE DIVED AT THE FEET OF PETER MURPHY, WHOSE KNEE COLLIDED WITH BERT'S HEAD, KNOCKING HIM UNCONSCIOUS.

Fear not, these smelling salts will bring him back with an invigorating snap.

LITTLE DID HE REALISE, BUT TRAUTMANN HAD ACTUALLY BROKEN HIS NECK. ASTONISHINGLY, HE PLAYED ON, MAKING A NUMBER OF CRUCIAL SAVES TO HELP SEE CITY HOME. HE WAS THEN HELPED UP THE WEMBLEY STEPS TO COLLECT HIS WINNER'S MEDAL FROM THE QUEEN AND PRINCE PHILIP.

Hello, Fritz. Fancy a cup of... um... a cup?

Smooth.

TRAUTMANN'S COURAGE BECAME PART OF FOOTBALL FOLKLORE. THREE DAYS LATER, AN X-RAY REVEALED THAT THE SECOND OF FIVE BROKEN VERTEBRAE HAD SPLIT IN TWO. HE WAS ONLY ALIVE BECAUSE THE THIRD VERTEBRAE HAD SLAMMED AGAINST IT, WEDGING IT INTO POSITION. IT'S UNCLEAR WHAT HE GOT UP TO IN THOSE THREE DAYS BEFORE THE DIAGNOSIS.

You should probably get that looked at.

LEV YASHIN

Lev Yashin endured a tough start to life. His mother died of tuberculosis when he was six and by the time he was 11, he was working alongside his father in a factory that made plane parts. The terrible wartime diet left him with a gastric ulcer and he suffered stomach aches his whole life; he would always carry a bottle of bicarbonate of soda to help alleviate the pain. Despite this discomfort, he was a firm advocate of necking a swig of alcohol and taking a long drag on a cigarette to tone the muscles and soothe pre-match nerves. Thankfully, it was The Sixties, so it wasn't bad for you.

Nobody who saw his early appearances for Dynamo Moscow would have guessed he'd blossom into the greatest goalkeeper of the twentieth century. So calamitous was his debut that his own teammates stood and laughed at him; vomit on his sweater, step-mom's spaghetti. He took some time out from football and honed his skills playing for Dynamo's ice hockey team. His reflexes sharpened and confidence strengthened, he returned a different man; the legend was born.

Yashin was called up for the Soviet national team in 1954 and won gold at the Melbourne Olympics in 1956. He was in goal as the USSR won the first European Championships in 1960 and in 1963 he became the only goal-keeper to ever be awarded the Ballon d'Or. He was even awarded a fridge in recognition of his heroics.

Throughout his career, Yashin kept 209 clean sheets and saved 150 penalties. Sometimes nicknamed The Black Spider, his other nickname of The Black Panther seems more appropriate; a dark imposing presence padding around his penalty area, unlike his goalkeeping contemporaries, who preferred to scuttle crab-like across their goal lines. Along with the celebrated Russian cosmonauts of the era, Yashin was a poster boy for Soviet innovation and progress: the Yuri Gagarin of goalkeeping.

CULT HEROES (PART ONE)

The footballers you remember most fondly are rarely the ones who run the furthest or collect the most bibs at the end of training. They're not always the ones who play for the best clubs, or win the most trophies. They're rarely the kind of person who you'd call upon during a time of crisis, or even entrust with the lowest level of responsibility. Would you, for example, have confidence in Faustino Asprilla holding the bottom of a ladder while you cleared a gutter? Or credit Antonio Cassano with the maturity to feed your cats while you went on holiday? Not bloody likely.

No, the players whose names you chant years after their retirement are the ones who value entertainment above winning; the crowd favourites who accord a deft flick the same status as a goal. Often, they are the underachievers; the ones who show their talents only in flashes – those who burn brightly, but briefly. These are the mavericks, the rock stars. If Pelé was The Beatles, these players are The Rolling Stones (if you imagine that they weren't still touring at the age of 132, and that Mick Jagger had written a decent record since 1972).

The first player in this section is something of an exception to the rule, as he trained hard, lived cleanly, and, eventually, made the most of his talents. He even defies the definition of a cult hero, the awkward bugger.

ÉRIC CANTONA

British football had never experienced anything like Éric Cantona before. An enigmatic rebel, a brooding anti-authoritarian genius, sticking it to the man by wearing his collar in an unconventional manner, lobbing the Sunderland goalkeeper and doing Nike adverts. Hell, *Britain* had never seen anything like Éric Cantona before.

Right from the start, Cantona was different; he grew up in a cave, for God's sake. His family's dwelling was dug into the hills in the Les Caillols area of Marseille. However, one suspects it was a stylish pop-art cave, rather than a Fred Flintstone arrangement with dinosaur-powered white goods.

Cantona actually started out as a goalkeeper, likely in a knowing nod to Albert Camus, but he was not a man whose creative energy could be repressed by the button-downed confinements of a penalty area. Set free, Éric would soon be spraying passes as if he were throwing paint at a canvas, smashing goals as if they were verses at a poetry slam, and assaulting opponents as if they were south London racists in tight trousers and bad leather jackets.

It was, of course, at Manchester United, where his reputation was forged: his five years at the club showcasing every aspect of his personality and talents. It was a period punctuated by a lengthy ban, from which he returned a more influential player and, eventually, a leader; the impetuous days of his youth soothed by the responsibilities of captaincy. Even a non-conformist like Cantona knew that a certain level of restraint was called for when entrusted with the power to call the coin toss and distribute complimentary tickets.

ERIC CANTONA'S CAREER WAS TYPIFIED BY SPECTACULAR BRILLIANCE AND PERIODS OF ENFORCED ABSENCE. RIGHT AT THE OUTSET, HIS PROGRESS AT AUXERRE WAS INTERRUPTED BY THE NEED TO DO NATIONAL SERVICE.

ANTI-AUTHORITY AND BROODINESS CORPS.

Excellent, Private!

Shut up.

MARCEL PROUST

HIS FIRST DISCIPLINARY PROBLEMS CAME IN 1987, WHEN HE PUNCHED HIS TEAMMATE BRUNO MARTINI IN THE FACE. THE NEXT YEAR HE RECEIVED A THREE-MONTH BAN FOR A FLYING KICK ON NANTES PLAYER, MICHEL DER ZAKARIAN.

I'm just saying that if you read Sartre, you'll see his work is littered with contradiction.

HIS ABILITY WAS NEVER IN DOUBT, HOWEVER. HE SHONE AS FRANCE WON THE UNDER-21 EUROPEAN CHAMPIONSHIP IN 1988, BUT HIS RELATIONSHIP WITH THE NATIONAL TEAM WAS COMPLICATED. AT ONE POINT, HE INSULTED COACH HENRI MICHEL, WITH A PHRASE THAT SUGGESTED HIS SOUL ALREADY SANG FOR MANCHESTER.

Sac de merde.

LAGER

AFTER TEMPESTUOUS SPELLS AT MARSEILLE, BORDEAUX AND MONTPELLIER, HE WOUND UP AT NÎMES, WHERE HE WAS BANNED FOR FOUR MATCHES FOR THROWING A BALL AT A REFEREE. THE SUSPENSION WAS EXTENDED TO TWO MONTHS WHEN HE INSULTED EACH MEMBER OF THE DISCIPLINARY PANEL.

Ignoramus. Philistine. Moron. Dog molester.

Oi!

DECIDING HE'D HAD ENOUGH, CANTONA ANNOUNCED HIS RETIREMENT, AT THE AGE OF 25. HOWEVER, MICHEL PLATINI CONVINCED HIM TO RECONSIDER, SUGGESTING THAT HE MOVE TO ENGLAND. PLATINI EVEN SPOKE TO GRAEME SOUNESS ABOUT SIGNING CANTONA, BUT THE LIVERPOOL BOSS DECLINED.

Why would I want Cantona when I have Ronnie Rosenthal and Dean Saunders?

AFTER A TRIAL WITH SHEFFIELD WEDNESDAY, HE SIGNED FOR LEEDS IN EARLY 1992. HE ONLY PLAYED 15 GAMES, BUT WAS KEY TO THEM WINNING THE LEAGUE TITLE. AT A CIVIC RECEPTION IN THE CITY CENTRE, CANTONA TOLD THE ECSTATIC LEEDS FANS: 'I DON'T KNOW WHY I LOVE YOU, BUT I DO'.

ERIC CAN

Like all the classic French romances, this one is destined to end in blissful monogamy!

SEVEN MONTHS LATER HE WAS GONE, HIS RELATIONSHIP WITH MANAGER HOWARD WILKINSON HAVING BROKEN DOWN. AT ONE POINT, WILKINSON, POSSIBLY READING FROM HIS DIARY, TOLD JOURNALISTS:

Eric does what he likes, when he likes — and then fucks off.

WHAT MADE MATTERS WORSE FOR LEEDS FANS WAS THAT CANTONA LEFT FOR HATED RIVALS, MANCHESTER UNITED. ALEX FERGUSON MADE A CHEEKY BID FOR HIM DURING A PHONE CHAT ABOUT ANOTHER PLAYER AND TO HIS SURPRISE THE OFFER WAS ACCEPTED. HOWEVER, WILKINSON WOULD HAVE THE LAST LAUGH.

Why do I need Cantona when I've already lined up a summer deal for Brian Deane?

CANTONA ARRIVED WITH A REPUTATION THAT MADE SOME OF UNITED'S SENIOR PLAYERS WARY. BRYAN ROBSON, STEVE BRUCE AND GARY PALLISTER ALL EXPRESSED CONCERN AND EVEN PARTY BOY LEE SHARPE WAS WORRIED.

Flippin' eck, he's madder than one of Giggsy's legendary barbecues!

THOSE ANXIETIES MELTED AWAY WHEN THEY SAW HIM PLAY. ROY KEANE WAS PARTICULARLY IMPRESSED BY CANTONA'S WINNING MENTALITY AND SWAGGER, LATER WRITING:

'Collar turned up, back straight, chest stuck out, he glided into the arena as if he owned the fucking place.'

UNITED LOST ONLY TWO MORE GAMES THAT SEASON AND CLAIMED THEIR FIRST LEAGUE TITLE IN 26 YEARS. THERE WAS LITTLE DOUBT ABOUT WHICH PLAYER HAD BEEN THE CATALYST FOR THE SUCCESS.

All hail King Clayton Blackmore!

Sac de merde!

THEY RETAINED THEIR CROWN THE FOLLOWING SEASON, WINNING THE DOUBLE, WITH CANTONA SCORING TWICE IN A 4-0 FA CUP FINAL WIN AGAINST CHELSEA. THEY WERE ON TRACK FOR ANOTHER TITLE IN 1995, WHEN THE MOMENT CAME THAT WOULD DE-RAIL THEIR CAMPAIGN AND DEFINE CANTONA'S CAREER: A FLYING KUNG-FU KICK ON A RACIALLY ABUSIVE CRYSTAL PALACE FAN.

What did you say?

A MAN REGRETTING EVERY SINGLE LIFE CHOICE THAT HAS LED HIM TO THIS POINT.

CANTONA WOULD LATER DESCRIBE IT AS HIS PROUDEST MOMENT, BUT AT THE TIME HE WAS IN AS MUCH DOO-DOO AS THE MOUNDS THAT FILLED MATTHEW SIMMONS' GREY SLACKS WHEN CANTONA TURNED ON HIM. CANTONA'S CASE WAS NOT HELPED WHEN HE COMMITTED A FURTHER VIOLENT CRIME, AGAINST KNITWEAR, THE NEXT DAY.

HE RETURNED AFTER AN EIGHT-MONTH BAN IN OCTOBER, MARKING HIS COMEBACK WITH A GOAL AND AN ASSIST AGAINST LIVERPOOL, WHILST CANTONA STRUGGLED FOR FORM AT FIRST, HIS POST-CHRISTMAS PERFORMANCES INSPIRED UNITED TO OVERHAUL NEWCASTLE TO WIN ANOTHER TITLE, AN OUTCOME THAT SEEMED TO BREAK SOME-THING IN THEIR MANAGER, KEVIN KEEGAN.

What do you think? Smart isn't it? Designer.

THE DOUBLE WAS COMPLETED WITH A CUP FINAL WIN AGAINST LIVERPOOL, CAPTAIN CANTONA THREADING AN 86TH-MINUTE VOLLEY THROUGH A CROWD OF DESPAIRING DEFENDERS FOR THE GAME'S ONLY GOAL.

A rare mistake from David James! Chances like this don't come along every single game. Make it count, Éric!

KING ÉRIC RETIRED AT THE END OF THE NEXT SEASON, AFTER YET ANOTHER LEAGUE TITLE. HE WAS STILL ONLY 30, BUT WANTED TO PURSUE OTHER INTERESTS LIKE BEACH SOCCER, ACTING AND DOING ADVERTS, HIS GOD-LIKE STATUS AT OLD TRAFFORD REMAINS UNDIMINISHED BY TIME.

It's him, it's really him!

Saul from Homeland, here at The Theatre of Dreams!

SÓCRATES

A free-thinking intellectual with a doctorate in medicine, whose abilities as a footballer were only matched by his passion for social activism; in many ways Sócrates was the Ray Parlour of Brazilian football.

The midfielder's inclusion in the Brazil team that graced the 1982 World Cup means he'll always be remembered fondly by a certain generation of fans. Taking his place in the centre of the pitch alongside Zico, Falcão and Cerezo, Sócrates was a striking presence. He even looked like a marble statue of an ancient philosopher, with his curly hair, impressive beard and upright posture. A player of great vision and technique, he was renowned for his fondness for backheels (Pelé said he could play better backwards than most players did forwards).

This was the last Brazil team to truly adhere to the ideology of '*jogo bonito*'; there was no Dunga in the side. Sócrates took Brazil's chances so seriously that he even quit beer and cigarettes for the tournament. This sacrifice had been made at the behest of national team coach Telê Santana, who'd given up smoking in 1965 and encouraged Sócrates to also quit, with the restrained modesty of all reformed smokers.

Sócrates scored Brazil's first goal of the tournament, a 25-yard screamer against the USSR; a strike he later described as being like 'an endless orgasm', which sounds both unhygienic and impractical. Brazil would fall at the quarter-final stage to Italy, thus becoming the latest glorious failure in World Cup history.

Sócrates was more than just a footballer, though; he had bigger targets in his sights.

IF THE MODERN DEMOCRATIC PROCESS HAS TAUGHT US ANYTHING, IT'S THAT PEOPLE WOULD APPARENTLY VOTE FOR PIG IN A TOP HAT IF THEY BELIEVED IT WOULD GIVE THEM A FEW EXTRA PENNIES IN THEIR BACK POCKET.

The pig will stop immigration and make everything like it was in the good old days!

Polio! Segregation! PIG! PIG! PIG! PIG!

YET DESPITE ITS FLAWS, DEMOCRACY IS PREFERABLE TO THE ALTERNATIVES, SUCH AS MILITARY DICTATORSHIPS, LIKE THE ONE THAT SEIZED POWER IN BRAZIL IN 1962 - AN EVENT THAT HAD A PROFOUND IMPACT ON THE TEN-YEAR-OLD SÓCRATES

SPIDER-MAN

Filhos da puta!

FOOTBALL IN BRAZIL WAS ALSO ORGANISED IN AN AUTHORITARIAN STYLE. PLAYERS WERE NOT TRUSTED TO BEHAVE, SO WERE MADE TO ENDURE THE DREADED 'CONCENTRAÇÃO' - A PERIOD OF ENFORCED CONFINEMENT IN A TEAM HOTEL PRIOR TO MATCHES. THIS DID NOT SIT WELL WITH THE FREE-SPIRITED SÓCRATES

Think of it like a camp. A big old concentration camp!

BOOKS, YEAH.

TOGETHER WITH HIS CORINTHIANS TEAMMATE WLADIMIR, SÓCRATES FORMED 'CORINTHIANS DEMOCRACY' TO RECLAIM POWER FROM THE CLUB'S MANAGEMENT.

Brothers, we will vote on every decision that affects us, no matter how trivial.

That sounds like a lot of work. Can we vote on it?

No.

THE FOCUS OF CORINTHIANS DEMOCRACY SOON MOVED TO POLITICS. THE TEAM WORE SHIRTS BEARING THE GROUP'S NAME AND, IN 1982, ENCOURAGED PEOPLE TO VOTE IN ELECTIONS BEING HELD ON 15 NOVEMBER.

He's good at football. We should do what he says.

Definitely.

DIA 15 VOTE

IN 1984, SÓCRATES ADDRESSED A PRO-DEMOCRACY RALLY OF HALF A MILLION PEOPLE...

I promise that, if Congress passes a constitutional amendment to re-establish free presidential elections, then I won't move to Italy, with its famously laid back attitude to training that will perfectly fit my lifestyle.

HOWEVER, THE AMENDMENT WAS VOTED DOWN AND SÓCRATES LEFT FOR FIORENTINA, SIGNALLING THE END OF CORINTHIANS DEMOCRACY.

BUT BRAZIL WAS NOW ON THE PATH TO DEMOCRACY AND FREE PRESIDENTIAL ELECTIONS WERE HELD IN 1989. SÓCRATES' PASSION FOR POLITICS NEVER WANED AND DURING A VISIT TO LIBYA IN 1996 HE ACTUALLY MET WITH COLONEL GADDAFI, WHO OFFERED TO SUPPORT AND FINANCE THE DOCTOR IF HE DECIDED TO RUN FOR PRESIDENT.

That sounds like a lot of work. It's great that you dig democracy, though. The people of Libya must really love you to keep voting you in, Col.

SÓCRATES HELD FIRMLY TO HIS FAITH IN DEMOCRACY. IN LATER LIFE HE TOLD THE WRITER ALEX BELLOS THAT HE BELIEVED THE JOB OF BRAZIL'S NATIONAL TEAM MANAGER SHOULD BE VOTED FOR VIA A PUBLIC REFERENDUM.

Well, it's better than Dunga...

PIG! PIG! PIG! PIG!

YMAR JR

MATTHEW LE TISSIER

There are some things that are quintessentially English. The gentle smattering of applause echoing around a village cricket match, the flying fists of a high-street brawl after two-for-one shots night at The Lava Lounge, and, of course, an enduring distrust of flair players who refuse to fit conveniently into analogies about trench warfare.

It was against such a backdrop that Matt Le Tissier forged a long and entertaining career. Throughout the 1990s he was a staple in Goal of the Season competitions and his touch, vision and shooting prowess were without parallel. He was also lethal from the spot, scoring 47 out of 48 penalties (Nottingham Forest's Mark Crossley being the only goalkeeper to keep one out). Given England's record in this area, you'd think he would be a useful asset, yet he made only eight appearances for the national team (although, in fairness, they did have David Batty). Even Glenn Hoddle – one of the great creative players of his generation – left him out of his squad for the 1998 World Cup; a rejection that Le Tissier believes he never really got over.

It was at club level where he thrived, though, the adoring Southampton fans nicknaming him 'Le God'. His decision to spend his entire career at the club was broadly interpreted as showing a lack of ambition, but Southampton is close to his native Guernsey and, it should be noted, is quite nice. Even there, he was forced to see off managers such as Ian Branfoot, who preferred a more utilitarian approach. One his most memorable goals, against Newcastle, which involved an astonishing piece of ball control, a flick over a defender's head and a side-foot, half-volley finish, came as Branfoot was preparing to substitute him for Paul Moody. Sit down, Paul.

It was fitting that Le Tissier would score the last ever goal at Southampton's old ground, The Dell; firing in a late winner in a 3–2 win against Arsenal in 2001. It also turned out to be the last goal of a scintillating career that had brought joy to millions. Not that you'd want him in the trenches with you, though; because, as we have established, he was a professional footballer in the late twentieth century and was unlikely to have experienced any combat training.

IT'S HARD TO STAY NONCHALANT IN TODAY'S FAST-PACED WORLD, SO TRY TO RELAX THE MIND BY FINDING A LARGE, OPEN SPACE AND WATCHING THE CLOUDS FLOAT BY.

You're fired-up today, Matt. I've never seen you work so hard!

NEXT, MAKE SURE YOU'RE A FAIR DISTANCE FROM GOAL. ABOUT EIGHT MILES SHOULD DO IT.

One large gastro meal, with a bucket of carbonated syrup and a side of reconstructed chicken slush. Better take it easy – it's a match day.

OH NO, HERE COME SOME GENERIC MID-NINETIES DEFENDERS TO HARSH YOUR VIBE. TIME TO TEACH THE FUN POLICE A LESSON OR TWO.

FLICK THE BALL DEFTLY OVER THEIR HEADS, LEAVING THEM IN A STATE OF BAFFLEMENT AND HUMILIATION.

Mummy.

PHEW, THIS IS EXHAUSTING; THAT'S ENOUGH EFFORT FOR ONE DAY. THERE'S JUST ENOUGH TIME FOR A CASUAL GLANCE TOWARDS THE WATCHING ENGLAND MANAGER...

1001 OFFENSIVE THEORIES ABOUT DISABLED PEOPLE

...BEFORE WELLYING HOME YET ANOTHER CONTENDER FOR GOAL OF THE SEASON.

BASK IN THE ADULATION OF THE STUNNED SPECTATORS, ENGLAND MANAGER INCLUDED.

NOW GET YOURSELF HOME FOR A CELEBRATORY FISH SUPPER (A NICE BIG ONE, CAUGHT FROM A SMALL POND) IN FRONT OF YOUR FAVOURITE DETECTIVE SERIES.

BERGERAC

Still half an hour of the game left? Hah, not for me, boss.

ROGER MILLA

The British reggae artist Macka B probably summarised the events surrounding Cameroon's 1990 World Cup quarter-final defeat to England more succinctly than anyone else, in his record 'Pam Pam Cameroun':

> They were lucky, lucky, very lucky, lucky; against the Cameroun,
>   England were lucky, lucky.
> They were lucky, lucky, very lucky, lucky; against the Cameroun,
>   they were lucky, lucky.

Cameroon provided the most compelling story of that tournament, especially as their most dangerous attacking threat was posed by a semi-retired journeyman striker who was a month younger than my dad. With his pencil moustache, gap-toothed grin and swinging hips, Roger Milla (not my dad), became the most famous centre-forward in the world.

Milla was of course already a legend in Cameroon, and was also well-known in France, where he'd earned a solid reputation as a goal-scorer, banging them in for Saint-Étienne and Montpellier in the 1980s. As a youngster in Cameroon, he impressed people with his dribbling skills, earning pocket money as local sides hired him to play on a game-by-game basis. Eventually, at the age of 15, he made his debut for L'Éclair de Douala on the grassless pitches of Cameroon's second division. As confident as he was in his own ability, even Milla wouldn't have thought that international stardom would descend upon him by the time he was a middle-aged man with a mortgage and a scar on his head from a DIY accident when he was trying to demolish an airing cupboard. No, wait; that *was* my dad.

ROGER MILLA HAD ENJOYED A LONG CAREER IN FRANCE, BUT BY THE TIME 1990 ROLLED AROUND HE WAS PLAYING IN LA RÉUNION (A HOLIDAY DESTINATION IN THE INDIAN OCEAN) AND WINDING DOWN FOR RETIREMENT.

SO WHEN THE 38-YEAR-OLD WAS DRAFTED INTO CAMEROON'S WORLD CUP SQUAD, AT THE BEHEST OF PRESIDENT BIYA, THE REST OF THE PLAYERS WERE UNIMPRESSED. AS WELL AS BEING CLEARLY UNFIT, MILLA HAD SUCH A FIERCE TEMPER THAT HIS TEAMMATES GAVE HIM A SPECIAL NICKNAME.

Where's 'Gaddafi'?

Hiding in that drainpipe to avoid the cross-country run.

HOPES FOR SUCCESS WEREN'T HIGH. EVEN THEIR COACH, THE RUSSIAN VALERI NEPOMNIACHI, WAS AS GLOOMY AS A MAN WHOSE JOB HAD BEEN UNDERMINED BY A PRESIDENT. HE SPOKE NO FRENCH AND TEAM TALKS WERE GIVEN VIA AN INTERPRETER.

Stay close to Maradona and cut off the supply to Caniggia.

kick the crap out of Maradona and take Caniggia apart like a freakin' Duplo set.

BUT, ASTONISHINGLY, THE INDOMITABLE LIONS BEAT REIGNING CHAMPIONS ARGENTINA IN THEIR FIRST GAME AND THEN BACKED IT UP WITH A 2-1 WIN AGAINST ROMANIA. MILLA CAME OFF THE BENCH TO SCORE BOTH GOALS; IN THE PROCESS BECOMING THE OLDEST MAN TO BOTH SCORE AT A WORLD CUP AND TO DO A SEXY DANCE WITH A CORNER FLAG.

Did you tell him to do that?

MILLA REPEATED THE TRICK IN THE NEXT ROUND, SCORING TWICE IN EXTRA-TIME AGAINST COLOMBIA TO SEND THEM THROUGH. HIS SECOND, AND MOST MEMORABLE, GOAL SAW HIM ROB THE BALL FROM COLOMBIA'S WACKY GOALKEEPER, HIGUITA, ON THE HALFWAY LINE AND RACE AWAY, BEAMING, TO SCORE.

The Colombian people will forgive a genuine mistake, right?

HAHAHAHAH

CAMEROON WERE NOW THE FIRST AFRICAN NATION TO REACH A WORLD CUP QUARTER-FINAL. HOWEVER, IF THERE'S ONE GROUP OF PEOPLE YOU CAN RELY UPON TO POOP ON A PARTY, IT'S THE NATIONAL FOOTBALL TEAM OF ENGLAND.

Look, I hate to be a pedant, but it's not really a party without a Black Lace mixtape and some little pieces of cheese and pineapple on cocktail sticks.

I'm not sure you do hate to be a pedant.

CAMEROON LED 2-1 WITH 25 MINUTES LEFT; MILLA HAVING PLAYED A PART IN BOTH GOALS, BUT TWO GARY LINEKER PENALTIES RESCUED ENGLAND. CAMEROON WERE OUT, BUT THE TEAM, AND ESPECIALLY MILLA, HAD LEFT A LASTING IMPRESSION IN ITALY.

This is going to sound crazy, but I think all of our corner flags are...pregnant.

FOUR YEARS LATER, CAMEROON CALLED ON MILLA AGAIN. NOW 42, HE WOULD BREAK HIS OWN RECORD FOR BEING THE OLDEST WORLD CUP SCORER WITH A CONSOLATION GOAL IN A 6-1 DEFEAT TO RUSSIA. ALAS, CAMEROON WERE UNABLE TO REPEAT THEIR EXPLOITS AT ITALIA '90, AS THEIR CAMPAIGN WAS SCUPPERED BY...

IN-FIGHTING OVER BONUS PAYMENTS!

9

TOMAS BROLIN

Nowadays, Tomas Brolin plays poker for a living and has the weathered appearance of a police informer in a Scandinavian crime drama. However, with his button nose, chubby cheeks and mop of blond hair, at the height of his career, Brolin looked more like a child prince than a professional footballer. For a while, in the 1990s, the world doted as he frolicked merrily through the defences of Europe, skipping and leaping with a *joie de vivre* more commonly associated with the unwavering sense of entitlement that comes with inherited economic freedom.

Prince Brolin made his professional debut at the age of 14 for Näsvikens IK in the Swedish fourth division, but had to wait until he was 20 before being called up to the national team. He scored two goals within six minutes of his debut, against Wales, and was selected for Sweden's squad for the 1990 World Cup. Sweden lost all three of their games at the World Cup, but Brolin scored against Brazil and impressed enough to earn a transfer to Parma, who'd just been promoted to Serie A. Brolin scored seven goals in his first season and Parma's bright, attacking football saw them finish fifth and qualify for Europe. His goals helped them to win the Coppa Italia the following year.

It was at Euro '92 where Brolin really made a name for himself. As hosts, Sweden made it to the semi-finals, with Brolin scoring a memorable goal in a 2-1 win against England, which he celebrated with a trademark spinning leap. Two years later, Sweden also reached the semi-final stage at the World Cup in the United States. Brolin formed an effective partnership with striker Martin Dahlin and scored three goals, the pick of which came against Romania, when he slipped behind a defensive wall and lifted a shot into the roof of the net.

However, life was becoming harder at club level. First-team opportunities were limited by Serie A's restrictions on foreign players, and the arrival of Gianfranco Zola at Parma further reduced his playing time. A serious injury in November 1994 sidelined him for much of that season, and he realised that it was time for a change. Enter Leeds . . .

WHEN HOWARD WILKINSON SIGNED TOMAS BROLIN FOR LEEDS, HE PROBABLY THOUGHT HE WAS GETTING THE PIROUETTING PLAYMAKER WHO'D LIT UP EURO '92 AND USA '94.

HOWEVER, IF THERE WAS ONE MAN WHO COULD WHIP HIM INTO SHAPE IT WAS WORKRATE'S 'SERGEANT WILKO'.

HE STARTED MODERATELY AND SCORED THE OCCASIONAL GOAL, INCLUDING ONE AGAINST SHEFFIELD WEDNESDAY, WHEN HE WAS LYING ON THE GROUND AND A CLEARANCE REBOUNDED OFF HIS HEAD AND INTO THE NET.

BUT AFTER A 5-0 DEFEAT AT LIVERPOOL, HE FELL OUT WITH WILKINSON AFTER AN ARGUMENT ABOUT THE SWEDE'S DEFENSIVE RESPONSIBILITIES.

BROLIN'S FORTUNES APPEARED TO HAVE IMPROVED WHEN WILKINSON WAS REPLACED BY THE FAR MORE LAID BACK GEORGE GRAHAM.

BROLIN FAILED TO TURN UP FOR PRE-SEASON TRAINING IN 1997, CLAIMING THAT A BIRD HAD FLOWN INTO HIS CAR WINDSCREEN, FORCING HIM TO MISS HIS FLIGHT FROM SWEDEN TO ENGLAND. WHEN HE DID EVENTUALLY SHOW UP, A FURIOUS GRAHAM CONFISCATED HIS PASSPORT AND REFUSED TO LET HIM JOIN THE TEAM ON A PRE-SEASON TOUR.

HE NEVER GOT BACK INTO THE LEEDS SIDE AND HIS CONTRACT WAS TERMINATED A FEW MONTHS LATER. HOWEVER, STEVE COPPELL SIGNED HIM FOR CRYSTAL PALACE, INITIALLY FOR THE COST OF HIS BED AND BREAKFAST ACCOMMODATION.

BROLIN CAME UP AGAINST HIS OLD CLUB IN HIS THIRD GAME FOR PALACE. AFTER SUFFERING A HEAD INJURY, HE PLAYED ON IN A COMEDICALLY LARGE BANDAGE, UNTIL IT WAS KNOCKED OFF BY A CLEARANCE IN FRONT OF THE DELIGHTED LEEDS FANS. PERHAPS IT WAS THEN THAT HE CONCEIVED OF THE IDEA FOR HIS POST-RETIREMENT BUSINESS VENTURE.

ANTI-HEROES

Every successful team needs a player who is willing to cross the line of acceptable behaviour; someone with an uncompromising determination to win at all costs. If that means leaving a few stud marks on that nippy winger's thigh, then fine. If the chances of claiming three points are improved by chatting up a teammate's girlfriend while he's off recovering from a hernia operation, even better.

These are the anti-heroes; adored by supporters of the clubs they play for, loathed by fans of other teams, with a passion that only dissipates when he later signs for them too. 'Oh yeah, I might have quit my job to dedicate my life to being the first person to reply to his tweets with a stream of bile, but I've always respected him, you know!'

The players included in this section are not merely the thuggish self-proclaimed hard men, the kinds of sociopaths who, without football, would be low-level street enforcers, organ harvesters or *Daily Mail* columnists. No, these are the ones who can *play*. Sure, in some cases their personalities might be so toxic that you'd rather crucify your cat than spend five seconds in their company, but when they pull on your team's shirt, all is forgiven.

GIORGIO CHINAGLIA

Giorgio Chinaglia was a complete nutter who used to carry a .44 Magnum around with him. Not only was he a bastard, he was an *armed* bastard: the worst kind.

Born in Tuscany in 1947, he moved to Cardiff in 1955, following his father, who'd left Italy to work in a steel factory. Young Giorgio travelled on his own, with his destination address sewn into the back of his jumper. Imagine the ecstatic look on his father's face upon opening the door to see the scowling face of a contemptuous eight-year-old he thought he'd seen the back of.

However, it was his father who convinced him to play football, rather than rugby. In later life, Chinaglia would proclaim that rugby is a sport 'only played by ugly people'; cauliflower ears and pancake noses not fitting into his conventional view on the nature of beauty.

The young centre-forward started his playing career at Swansea, but was let go, in part because of his winning personality. On one occasion, he was tasked with helping to paint the main stand at the Vetch Field, at which point he picked up a bucket of paint and threw it at the stand. Before he left, he told the other Swansea players that they would one day beg him for his autograph. Ok, mate. They could barely believe their eyes when Italy played England at Wembley in 1973 and there was Giorgio, tearing up the English defence and setting up Fabio Capello to score the winning goal.

Chinaglia had returned to Italy in 1966 to complete his military service, which provided a legitimate reason to play with guns. He kicked around at clubs in Serie C, before being picked up by Lazio in 1969. A poll held by its fans at the end of the century declared Chinaglia to be their greatest player of all time, possibly out of fear that he would come round their houses if they voted for Pavel Nedvěd.

THE LAZIO SIDE OF THE EARLY SEVENTIES CONTAINED SO MANY UNHINGED, GUN-TOTING, FAR-RIGHT SYMPATHISERS THAT IT MADE THE AVERAGE TRUMP RALLY LOOK LIKE ONE OF THOSE CLUBS WHERE ADULTS GATHER TO DO COLOURING-IN BOOKS.

Lovely, Donald.

EVEN THE PLAYERS DESPISED EACH OTHER, TO THE EXTENT THAT THEY WERE DIVIDED INTO TWO SEPARATE DRESSING ROOMS. YET, SOMEHOW, TOMMASO MAESTRELLI WAS ABLE TO COACH THEM TO THE CLUB'S FIRST SCUDETTO IN THE 1973-74 SEASON.

Coach, please tell Mario that if he wants me to head his crosses, he might try keeping them within Earth's atmosphere.

Coach, please inform Gino that he might be able to get off the ground more easily if his arse wasn't the size of a static caravan.

THIS FEAT WAS AIDED BY THE 24 GOALS OF THE BRASH, ARROGANT, ARSEHOLE-IN-CHIEF, GIORGIO CHINAGLIA.

HE WAS LOATHED BY OPPOSITION FANS THROUGHOUT ITALY, ESPECIALLY AFTER HE ANNOUNCED HIS INTENTION TO VOTE FOR A NEO-FASCIST PARTY IN 1972. THIS DIDN'T SEEM TO PERTURB LAZIO FANS, CURIOUSLY.

HOWEVER, IT'S POSSIBLE THAT CHINAGLIA DIDN'T MEAN IT, AS HE WAS PRIMARILY MOTIVATED BY WINDING PEOPLE UP.

Where'd you get your trainers?

They're shit.

Give me your shit trainers, Shit Trainers.

Look, I rate Giorgio; I just think he's a bit too left wing.

Finally, someone said it!

PUTTING THE SS INTO SS LAZIO

AAAAAAAAAAAAAAAAHHH! I made you all hate me.

I can't even leave my own house anymore. One-nil!

ONE THING THAT UNITED THE LAZIO TEAM WAS THEIR LOVE OF A GOOD SCRAP, SOMETIMES AGAINST OTHER SIDES. THERE ARE TWO NOTABLE EXAMPLES, BOTH OF WHICH INVOLVE ENGLISH OPPONENTS:

• A MASSIVE PUNCH-UP WITH THE ARSENAL TEAM IN A RESTAURANT IN 1970. IT ALL KICKED OFF WHEN THE ARSENAL PLAYERS WERE RUDE ABOUT THE MAN BAGS THE LAZIO TEAM HAD GIVEN THEM AS GIFTS.

English footballers mocking foreign cultures and being casually homophobic? This is 1970, damnit! Let's get them!

• A HUGE RUCK WITH IPSWICH IN 1973. LAZIO FANS PEPPERED THE PITCH WITH MISSILES, WHICH THE LAZIO PLAYERS THEN THREW AT THEIR OPPONENTS. IPSWICH RACED TO THE DRESSING ROOM AT FULL-TIME, BUT GOALKEEPER DAVID BEST WAS TOO SLOW.

Lads, let me in; they haven't caught up yet.

Sorry, Dave; too risky.

I think they're armed!

We'd better step back from the door then. See you back in Suffolk, probably.

THAT INCIDENT SAW LAZIO BANNED FROM EUROPE FOR A YEAR, DENYING THEM THE CHANCE TO HAVE A CRACK AT THE EUROPEAN CUP. FRANKLY, THE LESS TIME THEY SPENT ON PLANES, THE BETTER. SO MANY OF THE TEAM CARRIED GUNS THAT, ON ONE OCCASION, A PILOT REFUSED TO TAKE OFF WITH THE LAZIO PLAYERS ONBOARD.

This cool?

Mm.

PRACTICAL DETECTIFIER

SECURITY

THIS CASUAL RELATIONSHIP WITH FIREARMS WOULD HAVE TRAGIC CONSEQUENCES THAT NO-ONE COULD HAVE SEEN COMING A MILE OFF. IN 1977, ON A TRIP TO A JEWELLERY SHOP, MIDFIELDER AND PRACTICAL JOKER LUCIANO RE CECCONI PULLED OUT HIS GUN AND DID AN IMPRESSION OF AN ARMED ROBBER THAT WAS SO CONVINCING THAT THE SHOPKEEPER PULLED A GUN OF HIS OWN AND SHOT HIM IN THE CHEST. HE DIED LATER THAT DAY.

AAAAAAAAAAAAAAHH! Made you think you were going to be robbed. Sucker!

Cough

One-nil.

CHINAGLIA HAD LEFT BY THEN; THE HOSTILITY IN ROME BECOMING TOO MUCH EVEN FOR HIM. THE FINAL STRAW CAME WHEN ROMA SUPPORTERS ATTACKED HIS NEW JEANS SHOP.

Not 'The Jean Pool'! I'd only just finished writing the sickeningly matey marketing text. Everyone would have hated it. My elaborate trolling masterpiece in ruins!

HE'D MOVED TO THE NEW YORK COSMOS, WHERE HE'D BECOME A HUGE SUCCESS. LAZIO WERE FIGHTING TO AVOID RELEGATION WHEN HE LEFT, WITH THREE GAMES OF THE SEASON REMAINING. HE'S SAID TO HAVE GIVEN THE FANS A FASCIST SALUTE AFTER HIS LAST MATCH.

What is he doing with his arm, father?

Ah. Well, young Paolo, it's, um, just his way of saying that he likes Lazio very much, but has to fly away on a big aeroplane... that only has one wing, apparently.

CHINAGLIA WOULD RETURN IN 1983, SPENDING HUGE AMOUNTS OF HIS OWN MONEY TO BUY THE CLUB.

WITH HIS ICE COOL TEMPERAMENT, HE WAS PERFECTLY CUT OUT TO BE

A CLUB PRESIDENT, ONLY ONCE ATTACKING A REFEREE WITH AN UMBRELLA, AFTER A 2-2 DRAW WITH UDINESE.

What is he doing to that referee, father?

Ah. Well, young Paolo; he's assaulting him. Referees are more verminous than footballers who eat ketchup. Never forget it, son.

HE RECEIVED AN EIGHT-MONTH BAN FOR THAT, BUT WORSE WAS TO FOLLOW. IN HIS SECOND YEAR, LAZIO AMASSED JUST 15 POINTS AND FINISHED BOTTOM OF SERIE A. HE FINALLY STEPPED DOWN IN 1986, WHEN HE WAS CHARGED WITH FRAUDULENT BANKRUPTCY AND FALSE ACCOUNTING. NOT EVERYONE, IT SEEMS, IS PRESIDENT MATERIAL.

LAZIO

Lovely, Giorgio.

Where'd you get your trainers?

ACCOUNTS

AUDIT

JOHN TERRY

Captain. Leader. Legend. Where do you start? The four-match ban for racially abusing QPR's Anton Ferdinand? The accusations of affairs with teammates' girlfriends? The massive drinking binge at a Heathrow hotel and flinging himself down the lanes of a bowling alley in front of a group of grieving and stranded American tourists on 11 September 2001? John Terry managed to fit a lot into his Chelsea career.

Terry is undoubtedly one of the most divisive players in Premier League history, with opinions on the dominant central defender broadly falling into two camps:

1. Chelsea Fans, who consider him to be an unfairly maligned leader and one of the best players in English football history; and
2. Everyone Else, who think he's a shit.

There is an element of truth to both arguments. Terry was the most successful captain in Chelsea's history, a commanding presence during a period that saw the club win five league titles and emerge as one of the new superpowers of world football. However, it is self-evident that his defensive capabilities and leadership skills were underpinned by an abundant reservoir of shititude.

Terry's career was not without setbacks. After he missed a penalty during the shoot-out at the 2008 Champions League final in Moscow, millions wept with him; some of us wondering whether we'd ever be able to stop laughing. His chance at personal redemption was then cruelly denied in 2012, when he was forced to sit in the stands and watch Chelsea win the trophy. Terry was suspended for the game, having been red-carded in the semi-final for kneeing Barcelona's Alexis Sánchez up the bum for no reason whatsoever. 'I would not do that,' protested Terry. He would, and did, do that.

Not playing in the final did not prevent Terry from joining in with the trophy presentation, wearing full kit and shin pads, an image that launched a million memes. His farewell at Chelsea, five years later, was typically understated: a pre-ordained substitution after 26 minutes allowing him to soak in the adulation of the Blues supporters, manager Antonio Conte presumably agreeing to the whole charade, knowing it would at least mean that Terry was definitely leaving.

PLAY THE 'J.T.' WAY

Jog on.

GET TO THE GROUND NICE AND EARLY, IN ORDER TO NAB ONE OF THOSE SWEET PARKING SPOTS NEAR THE ENTRANCE.

AS CAPTAIN, IT'S YOUR JOB TO REMIND YOUR SUBORDINATES OF THEIR RESPONSIBILITIES.

Work for each other, yeah. Keep the lines tight. We can't be having no sloppiness when you form the guard of honour when I get substituted.

ROLL YOUR SOCKS UP OVER YOUR KNEES, LIKE A JAPANESE SCHOOL GIRL.

PRE-MATCH RITUALS CAN BE MORE BORING THAN ONE OF AVRAM GRANT'S WINE AND CHEESE EVENINGS, BUT YOU CAN HURRY THINGS ALONG BY COMMITTING ACTS IN YOUR PRIVATE LIFE THAT ENSURE YOUR OPPONENTS DON'T WANT TO SHAKE YOUR HAND.

Rude. Whatever. Bothered. Next.

TACKLE

HEAD

POINT

LEAD

AH. SOMEONE THINKS YOU'VE DIRECTED SOME RACISM AT THEM...

What the...?

RESOLVE ANY CONFUSION BY LOUDLY REPEATING THE ALLEGED SLUR, WITH ADDED EFFS AND CEES FOR EMPHASIS. THAT OUGHT TO CLEAR THINGS UP.

HAVING THOROUGHLY ANTAGONISED EVERYONE, POP UP AND NOD ONE IN FROM A SET-PIECE.

Bosh!

PEOPLE NEED REMINDING THAT THE WORLD IS A COLD, UNJUST PLACE. THIS IS THE PREMIER LEAGUE, NOT THE CHELSEA FLOWER SHOW, YOU MUG.

TWENTY-SIX MINUTES. TIME FOR YOUR PRE-ARRANGED, SELF-AGGRANDISING SUBSTITUTION. THE MEMORY SUPPRESSANT YOU'VE PUMPED INTO THE PRESS BOX WILL ENSURE NO ONE DISCUSSES YOUR RELENTLESS SHITEHOUSERY.

Stand up for him, you dogs.

JOB DONE. NOW YOU CAN HEAD OFF TO A LOCAL RESTAURANT OF INTERNATIONAL CUISINE AND DEMAND THAT THEY MAKE YOU BURGER AND CHIPS THE WAY YOU LIKE IT.

Sweet.

HRISTO STOICHKOV

It's important for centre-forwards to show some aggression. That might be what Hristo Stoichkov told himself when the then 38-year-old DC United player discovered he was being sued by an 18-year-old American University student whose leg he had destroyed in a 'friendly'. In fairness to Stoichkov, no one could ever accuse him of mellowing with age. Within a few months of starting his professional career at CSKA Sofia, the teenage Hristo had received a life ban for his involvement in a massive fight at the 1985 Bulgarian Cup final. The ban was later reduced to a one-year suspension, but didn't exactly reform his behaviour.

For the early part of the 1990s, Stoichkov was among the most feared strikers in world football, and not just because, with one glance, he could make your blood run as cold as a bowl of Bulgarian cucumber soup. Fast, powerful and perennially furious, Stoichkov was a supremely gifted player. The three goals he scored for CSKA against Barcelona were enough to convince Johan Cruyff that this was the man who should spearhead his attack. As well as his obvious goal-scoring ability, Cruyff was impressed by Stoichkov's nastiness, having previously been concerned that his Barcelona team were too nice.

Whilst at Barça, Stoichkov won La Liga four years in a row (1991–94) and helped the club win its first European Cup. During this period, Stoichkov also captained Bulgaria to their best ever performance at the World Cup. They'd never even won a game at the finals before, yet they made it as far as the semi-final of the 1994 tournament, knocking out the reigning champions, Germany, along the way. The legend of Hristo was written . . .

LUIS MONTI

Luis Filipe Monti is the only man to have kicked people up in the air at two consecutive World Cups, for two different countries. Born in Buenos Aires, Monti enjoyed early success at Huracán and San Lorenzo, which earned him a regular spot in the Argentina team. He was to become their most influential player at the 1930 World Cup. As well as contributing two goals and unpicking defences with his intelligent range of passing, he also:

- Busted the ankle of the French goalkeeper, Lucien Laurent, within two minutes of kick-off.

- Booted Chile's Arturo Torres in mid-air, provoking a near-riot involving players, officials, supporters and mounted police officers.

- Contributed to a catalogue of foul play against the United States that so incensed their trainer, Jack Coll, that he ran onto the pitch, tripped and inhaled some chloroform that had spilled in his medical bag, and had to be helped back to the sideline.

This is the kind of slapstick you just don't get with the modern game. It's hard to imagine Paul Pogba clinging on to the hands of a stadium clock, or Leroy Sané and Kevin De Bruyne struggling to get a grand piano up some steps to the camera gantry.

Argentina eventually lost the 1930 final to Uruguay; with Monti cutting a subdued figure, his enthusiasm perhaps dampened by receiving death threats before the game. It was to be his last appearance for Argentina, and the following year he left San Lorenzo for Juventus, with whom he'd win four league titles in a row. His Italian heritage meant he was eligible to play for the national team and he was selected for Vittorio Pozzo's squad for the 1934 World Cup. Monti's hard, physical approach would come in handy during the semi-final, when he effectively subdued Austria's delicate artist Matthias Sindelar; squishing him into the thick mud of a sodden San Siro.

Italy went on to edge the final against Czechoslovakia, 2–1. Monti later revealed that before the game a message had been passed down from Benito Mussolini that there would be consequences for failure, but by now, Monti was used to playing under the cloud of threats from nut-jobs.

ARGENTINA BOASTED A WORLD-CLASS NATIONAL TEAM IN THE 1920s. THEIR MOST EXPLOSIVE PLAYER WAS THE GIFTED BUT FEARSOME MIDFIELDER, **LUIS FELIPE MONTI**. HIS EXPANSIVE PLAY AND TIRELESS WORK ETHIC EARNED HIM THE NICKNAME 'DOBLE ANCHO' (OR, 'DOUBLE WIDE').

Hey, check out Double Wide.

U wot.

On account of your ability to cover both sides of the pitch, Luisito!

And the middle.

Oh yes, and the middle.

AN EXAMPLE OF MONTI'S UNIQUE TAKE ON SPORTSMANSHIP CAME WHEN CHELSEA TOURED SOUTH AMERICA. UPON INTRODUCTION TO THE VISITING TEAM'S CAPTAIN, MONTI OFFERED HIS HAND, BEFORE KICKING HIS OPPONENT FIRMLY IN THE SHINS.

Tidy little ground, this. Amazing what a bit of British engineering can achieve, even in the most... basic of settings. Here, you're not as wide as I'd heard...

SADLY, AT THE TIME OF MONTI'S DEATH IN 1983, CRYOGENIC SCIENCE WAS NOT SUFFICIENTLY ADVANCED TO PERMIT HIS REANIMATION AT A LATER DATE, IN ORDER TO MEET FUTURE CHELSEA CAPTAINS.

Alright, Steptoe.

MONTI SURVIVED DEATH THREATS, SCORED GOALS, INSTIGATED BRAWLS AND GENERALLY INSPIRED ARGENTINA TO THE WORLD CUP FINAL IN 1930. WHILE THEY LOST 4-2 TO HOSTS URUGUAY, MONTI WAS SURE THAT GLORY LAY AHEAD.

We may have lost today, but our spirit will never be cowed. We shall return even stronger, for we are Argentinians and our hearts are as mighty as the Andes—

KNOCK KNOCK KNOCK

There's a man from Juventus out here. He wants to speak to Luis.

Tell him to do one. It'll take more than a wedge of cash and a new Fiat to tempt our Luis. Right, Luis?

Luis?

HE SWITCHED NATIONALITIES IN 1931, BECOMING ONE OF THREE 'ORIUNDI' (FOREIGNERS OF ITALIAN DESCENT) WHO HELPED ITALY TO WIN THE 1934 WORLD CUP. MUSSOLINI'S REGIME HAD PROMOTED THE USE OF THE ORIUNDI, BUT THEY WERE EXCLUDED WHEN THE STATE AWARDED SPECIAL MEDALS TO THE NEW WORLD CHAMPIONS.

SADLY, AT THE TIME OF MONTI'S DEATH IN 1983, CRYOGENIC SCIENCE WAS NOT SUFFICIENTLY ADVANCED TO PERMIT HIS REANIMATION AT A LATER DATE, IN ORDER TO MEET FUTURE FASCIST ARSEHOLES. **OR WAS IT...?**

Not you.

Hmm. It's almost as if these guys don't like foreigners at all.

It's Pepe; it's become kind of a symbol—

LUIS SUÁREZ

By rights, Luis Suárez shouldn't be in this section at all, as there has never been another footballer – nay, *person* – who has ever been so remorselessly and unjustly persecuted.

The oppression really began at the 2010 World Cup, when a flying Suárez save denied Ghana's Dominic Adiyiah a late, winning goal in a quarter-final clash with Uruguay. In any reasonable society, his lightning-fast cheat reflex would be celebrated; instead, Luis was shown the red card. The vision of Suárez celebrating in the tunnel as Ghana fluffed the resultant penalty kick was a sad one indeed.

The next year, Suárez again found himself being smashed by THE MACHINE, when the FA found him guilty of making repeated and insulting references to Patrice Evra's skin colour during a game between Liverpool and Manchester United. If Suárez was guilty of anything, it was of being ahead of his time. Just a few years later, racially abusing strangers in public would become the fun new craze sweeping Britain. Would they have given the inventor of fidget spinners a nine-match ban and a £40,000 fine? We all know the answer to that one.

Then there is the biting. Cruel fate has seen Suárez receive draconian punishments by three separate authorities during his career (to date), which can only suggest a coordinated assault. On each occasion, Suárez has been innocently chewing the air, when footballers have strayed into his path. (Deliberately? Who can say?) Yet successive regimes have chosen to punish the victim: Luis. Uruguay's national team manager, Óscar Tabárez, was in no doubt as to who was culpable when Suárez was banned for 'biting' Italy's Georgio Chiellini at the 2014 World Cup: The British Press. Suárez was forced to console himself with a £65 million transfer to Barcelona.

THE ANATOMY OF LUIS SUÁREZ

MUCH LIKE A DOG, SUÁREZ IS INCAPABLE OF SEEING COLOUR. HIS GOAL RECORD PROVES THAT HE IS INCAPABLE OF RACISM, SO YOU'RE THE RACIST FOR THINKING HIS RACISM IS RACIST, YEAH.

EARS - STRANGE, AREN'T THEY.

EACH SUMMER SOLSTICE, THE PEOPLE OF URUGUAY GATHER AROUND SUÁREZ'S TEETH AND PARTICIPATE IN AN ANCIENT CELEBRATION THAT INCLUDES DANCING AND MUSIC AND THE RITUAL CANNIBALISATION OF A FULL-BACK.

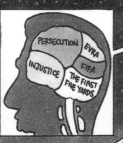

PERSECUTION

EVRA

INJUSTICE

FIFA

THE FIRST FIVE YARDS

ACID TONGUE.

WRIST STRAPPING - OFFERS SUPPORT WHEN PUNCHING GOAL-BOUND EFFORTS OFF THE LINE. THERE'S NO ROOM FOR WEAKNESS WHEN YOU'RE CRUSHING THE DREAMS OF AN **ENTIRE CONTINENT.**

LION TATTOO ON INDEX FINGER - A PERMANENT REMINDER OF THE LUXURIANT MANE OF HIS FORMER COLLEAGUE, ANDY CARROLL.

SUÁREZ'S TWITCH MUSCLES ARE LEGENDARY; THE SPEED WITH WHICH HE IS ABLE TO PULL OUT OF A HANDSHAKE IS UNPARALLELED. A MASTER OF MIME, SUÁREZ IS ALSO ABLE TO USE HIS HAND TO CALL FOR A RED CARD IN ANY GIVEN SITUATION.

SUÁREZ'S INCREDIBLE LUNG CAPACITY ALLOWS HIM TO SCREAM AS IF HE'S TRAPPED HIS LITTLE PISTOLA IN A LATHE, EVERY TIME AN OPPONENT INVADES HIS PERSONAL SPACE. THIS COTTON T-SHIRT OFFERS THE DUAL BENEFIT OF KEEPING HIS CHEST WARM AND SHOWING ZERO CONTRITION AFTER BEING ACCUSED OF RACIAL ABUSE. GOOOAAAL!

HIS LEGS ARE SOMEHOW STILL INTACT, DESPITE SUFFERING DOZENS OF FOULS EACH GAME, ALL OF WHICH APPEAR TO BE CAREER-ENDING, GIVEN HIS REACTION. SUÁREZ REMAINS A MIRACLE OF NATURE AND SETS AN EXAMPLE OF BRAVERY FOR US ALL.

IT CAN TAKE UP TO FIVE YEARS TO FULLY DIGEST THE SINEWY REMNANTS OF AN ITALIAN DEFENDER'S SHOULDER.

ANDONI GOIKOETXEA

The foul was no different to the kind of physical assault that Diego Maradona suffered dozens of times a game. It was common for him to end matches by sitting in the dressing room with torn socks, bruised legs and knees like pin cushions, spiked with pain-killing injections.

However, on this occasion, Athletic Bilbao's Andoni Goikoetxea had caught the Barcelona star with enough force to break his ankle. It was one of the most brutal fouls in football history and would come to define the defender's career. The incident earned him the nickname 'The Butcher of Bilbao', which became a source of pride for the six-foot column of aggression. Barcelona's manager, César Luis Menotti, was less impressed, describing Goikoetxea as 'belonging to a breed of anti-footballers'.

Despite his brutal reputation, Goikoetxea was an accomplished player; you don't make nearly 40 appearances for one of Europe's leading national teams without being a handy footballer (just ask Stewart Downing). As well as winning a couple of La Liga titles with Athletic, Goikoetxea also represented Spain at the 1984 European Championships and the 1986 World Cup; accomplishments that would have been impossible if he were just an Easter-Island-faced hacker.

MUCH LIKE THE SERIAL KILLER IN A HOLLYWOOD THRILLER, **ANDONI GOIKOETXEA** LIKED TO COLLECT TROPHIES FROM THE SCENES OF HIS BRUTAL CRIMES. THE BOOT THAT HE WORE TO SNAP DIEGO MARADONA'S ANKLE IN 1983 SITS IN A PERSPEX DISPLAY CASE IN HIS LIVING ROOM.

It rubs the lotion on its leather uppers...

THE ASSAULT ON MARADONA HAD BEEN TWO YEARS IN THE MAKING. BACK IN 1981, GOIKOETXEA HAD SMASHED THE KNEE OF BARCELONA'S BERND SCHUSTER. AFTER NINE MONTHS OUT, HE WENT LOOKING FOR REVENGE. THE NEXT TIME HE FACED ATHLETIC BILBAO, HE GOT IT. WITH BARÇA LEADING 3-0, HE HACKED DOWN GOIKOETXEA. UNINJURED BUT FURIOUS, THE DEFENDER SOUGHT RETRIBUTION. MARADONA SAYS HE TRIED TO SOOTHE HIM WITH THE FOLLOWING WORDS:

Take it easy, Goiko, chill out. You're losing 3-0 and will just get booked for nothing.

Also, this definitely sounds like the kind of measured thing I'd say.

THIS MERELY SERVED TO ENRAGE HIM FURTHER, AND THE NEXT CHANCE HE GOT, HE LAUNCHED AT MARADONA, BREAKING HIS ANKLE. THE AGONISED MARADONA COULD AT LEAST TAKE CONSOLATION FROM BEING RIGHT ABOUT GOIKOETXEA GETTING HIMSELF BOOKED.

Why do the bad things always happen to me?

BARCELONA'S COACH, CÉSAR MENOTTI CALLED FOR GOIKOETXEA TO BE BANNED FOR LIFE, BUT A WEEK LATER HE WAS SCORING IN A 4-0 EUROPEAN CUP WIN AGAINST LECH POZNAN AND BEING CARRIED FROM THE PITCH UPON THE SHOULDERS OF HIS ADORING BILBAO TEAMMATES.

GOIKO! GOIKO! GOIKO! GOIKO! GO

All's well that ends well.

BILBAO WON THE LEAGUE THAT SEASON, AND RETAINED IT IN 1984. ALL THAT STOOD BETWEEN THEM AND AN HISTORIC LEAGUE AND CUP DOUBLE WAS BARCELONA. CONSCIOUS OF THE BAD BLOOD BETWEEN THE CLUBS, AND THE SIMMERING POLITICAL CONTEXT, BILBAO COACH JAVIER CLEMENTE EXERCISED DIPLOMATIC CAUTION IN THE RUN UP TO THE COPA DEL REY FINAL.

Diego Maradona is stupid and castrated.

He has no human qualities whatsoever.

SOME BILBAO FANS SET THE TONE FOR THE EVENING BY BOOING DURING A MINUTE'S SILENCE FOR TWO BARÇA FANS WHO'D DIED IN A CAR CRASH ON THEIR WAY TO THE FINAL.

BOOooooooooOoooooooo

Um. This is fine, right?

Yes, because they came from a different place to us and liked a football team different from the one we like.

ENDIKA OF BILBAO SCORED THE GAME'S ONLY GOAL, BUT BEFORE THEY COULD COLLECT THEIR PRIZE THEY HAD TO PARTICIPATE IN ONE OF THE GREAT PUNCH-UPS.

MARADONA LATER CLAIMED HE'D BEEN PROVOKED BY A V-SIGN FROM BILBAO'S JOSÉ NÚÑEZ...

BUT THAT DOESN'T REALLY EXPLAIN WHY HE THEN DID THIS TO THEIR SUBSTITUTE, MIGUEL SOLA.

GOIKOETXEA RETALIATED IMMEDIATELY, WITH A FLYING KICK TO MARADONA'S CHEST.

DISPLAY-CASE SPECIAL.

...WHICH SIGNALLED A FLURRY OF WILD KUNG-FU KICKS OF VARYING DEGREES OF COMPETENCE.

MARADONA NEVER PLAYED FOR BARCELONA AGAIN. MIRACULOUSLY, HIS TORN SHIRT WAS THE ONLY CASUALTY OF THE BRAWL.

Come on, Miguel; eat your green mush.

PAOLO DI CANIO

Remember when the only fascist you had to worry about was Paolo Di Canio? If you were a fan of a mid-ranking club who had a managerial vacancy, there was always a chance you'd have to compromise your morals in order to accept a manic-eyed man with extreme political opinions.

Still, Di Canio was hugely popular at most of the clubs he represented; conducting himself with the passion of a fan – one who you'd change your season ticket seat to avoid sitting near. The first half of his playing career was spent in Italy, a phase that ended when he told Fabio Capello, his manager at Milan: 'I'm not going to hang around here and look at your ugly penis face any longer.' True to his word, he signed for Celtic.

As a player, Di Canio was gifted, but unpredictable; as likely to smash in a volley from an impossible angle as to sit on the ground and rant like a childish dictator. He didn't moderate his behaviour once he moved into management. He won the League Two title at Swindon, but his tenure was typified by lavish spending and wild behaviour. When the club's owners decided to pull the financial plug, Di Canio resigned (later breaking into the club's offices to retrieve some photos).

In March 2013, he was appointed by Sunderland and given the brief to keep them in the Premier League, which he accomplished, thanks in part to a 3–0 win at Newcastle, a victory he celebrated with a touchline knee-slide. However, he would last only 13 matches, sacked after a revolt from the players, who'd grown tired of his harsh disciplinarian regime (he'd banned coffee, condiments, mobile phones, joking and singing; which was all a bit, well, totalitarian).

He was widely viewed as a colourful eccentric until he started waving about the straight-armed salutes at Lazio. Up to then, the most significant moment of his playing career came in September 1998, when Arsenal visited Hillsborough for a Premier League game with Di Canio's Sheffield Wednesday . . .

THE GAME ERUPTED FROM THE MOST UNLIKELY OF SOURCES: A DIRTY TACKLE FROM PATRICK VIEIRA, SOME SNIDENESS FROM MARTIN KEOWN, AND A WILD REACTION FROM PAOLO DI CANIO, BUT IT WAS WHAT FOLLOWED THAT WOULD STAY IN THE MEMORY. KEOWN AND DI CANIO WERE SHOWN RED CARDS AND, IN A FIT OF RAGE, THE COMBUSTIBLE ITALIAN SHOVED THE REFEREE, PAUL ALCOCK, IN THE CHEST. ALCOCK STAGGERED BACKWARDS, RETAINING HIS DIGNITY IN AN UNDERSTATED FASHION.

AS DI CANIO STOMPED TOWARDS THE TUNNEL, ARSENAL'S NIGEL WINTERBURN STEPPED FORWARD TO BRAVELY SHARE HIS OPINION.

DI CANIO TURNED, RAISING A CLENCHED FIST A FRACTION OF AN INCH.

WINTERBURN'S LIFE FLASHED BEFORE HIS EYES, PERHAPS TO THE SOUNDTRACK OF THE BYRDS' 'TURN, TURN, TURN'.

WIMBLEDON
NIGEL WINTERBURN

DI CANIO WAS GIVEN AN 11-MATCH BAN AND WAS FINED £10,000. HIS CAREER WAS IN TATTERS. SENSING AN OPPORTUNITY TO GET A TOP, TOP PLAYER AT A BARGAIN PRICE, HARRY REDKNAPP SNAPPED HIM UP FOR £1.5 MILLION FOR WEST HAM. COINCIDENTALLY, THE HAMMERS WOULD LATER SIGN WINTERBURN TOO.

DI CANIO REPAID REDKNAPP BY PRODUCING THE FORM OF HIS CAREER, HELPING WEST HAM TO QUALIFY FOR EUROPE AND SCORING ONE OF THE BEST GOALS OF THE PREMIER LEAGUE ERA – A GOOSE-STEPPING VOLLEY AGAINST WIMBLEDON. THE TURBULENT DAYS WERE BEHIND HIM, FROM NOW ON, DI CANIO WOULD BE THE PICTURE OF RESTRAINT.

THE BOSSES

In the early part of the twentieth century, the job of the football manager, particularly in Britain, mostly involved making sure that the players were able to catch a medicine ball, complete the requisite number of star jumps, and drag themselves out of the bookmakers in time for kick-off on a Saturday afternoon. Responsibilities such as team selection, transfers, and tactics (such as they were) were largely overseen by committees of men, gathered in smoke-stained boardrooms.

This situation really began to change with the arrival of Herbert Chapman. Here was a man who challenged his superiors at Huddersfield Town and Arsenal, demanding a more direct say in both team affairs and the running of the club. Soon it would be commonplace for managers to take on more of a dictatorial role, having oversight of everything from team strategy to kit design.

There developed a cult of personality around many of these men, and while in recent years the scope of their roles has scaled back to reflect a more Continental model, the intense media interest remains. Nowadays, it is usual once more for a manager to be charged primarily with getting the best out of the squad of players they've been lumbered with by people with job titles that look more impressive on LinkedIn. This allows them more time to focus on being rude to journalists, talking about penalty decisions, and complaining about not being able to reveal their true feelings, for fear of being fined, before going on to say exactly what they were going to anyway.

ALEX FERGUSON

A furious Scottish man stands over you. His hot spittle rains down on your vacant, blinking face; his violent, sexual swearwords pin you against the wall. At least his breath smells nice – a classic cocktail of Cabernet Sauvignon and spearmint chewing gum. On the face of it, his bullet-point sermon on your failures as a human seems harsh; after all, your team won 4–0. However, in the 84th minute you didn't track the run of the opposition's left-back and Alex Ferguson has had enough of your bullshit. Your name is Ashley Young and deep down you know he is right. He's always right.

Ferguson's managerial career began at East Stirlingshire, at the age of 32. He was there only a few months before leaving for St Mirren, whom he led to the First Division title in 1977; the first trophy of 49 he would win throughout his career (if you count the Community Shield and the Drybrough Cup, which you obviously should). From there, it was on to Aberdeen, where he would win three Scottish Premier League titles, four Scottish FA Cups and, in 1983, the European Cup Winners' Cup. For most people, that would already be enough for one career, but in 1986, he took over at Manchester United, where he would become the most successful manager in English football history.

It wasn't all plain sailing at Old Trafford, though. He started with a 2–0 defeat at Oxford United and was seemingly on the verge of being sacked in early 1990. A late, winning goal from Mark Robbins at Nottingham Forest kept United in the FA Cup and saved Ferguson's famously beautiful skin. They went on to win the cup that year, and he never looked back.

OVER THE COURSE OF 27 YEARS, ALEX FERGUSON BUILT AN ALL-CONQUERING DYNASTY AT MANCHESTER UNITED, THE LIKES OF WHICH ARE UNLIKELY TO EVER BE SEEN AGAIN. ESPECIALLY AS HE FAILED TO WIN A TROPHY UNTIL THREE AND A HALF YEARS INTO HIS REIGN.

I'm sick of this. He's spent millions and hasn't achieved a thing.

I think **someone's** forgetting a little matter of finishing as runners-up in the 1987 **Guinness Soccer Sixes.**

FERGUSON'S IDIOSYNCRATIC METHODS BECAME AS FAMOUS AS HIS TEAMS THEMSELVES. OVER TIME, THOSE BEHAVIOURS WERE WOVEN INTO THE VERY LANGUAGE OF THE SPORT IN BRITAIN. THERE WAS...

'FERGIE TIME'

The scoreboard clock is for me, not for you. We finish when I say.

sorry...

'SQUEAKY BUM TIME'

And you a knight of the realm, sir...

AND, OF COURSE, THE DREADED 'HAIRDRYER TREATMENT'.

LISTEN TO ME, YOU FILM PREMIERE SEAT-FILLING, SARONG-WEARING, COCKNEY MR BEAN; IF YOU DON'T STAY ON THE WING, I'LL NAIL YOUR FEET TO THE GROUND – WHICH, INCIDENTALLY, MIGHT GIVE YOU AN EXTRA YARD OF PACE. YOU MIGHT HAVE RUINED THE SPICE GIRLS, BUT I'LL NO LET YOU RUIN THIS FOOTBALL CLUB, YOKO!!

Just to the left a bit.

WHEN THAT DIDN'T WORK, HE HAD OTHER WAYS OF GETTING HIS MESSAGE ACROSS TO HIS PLAYERS.

WEE PEROXIDE BASTARD

Vicky...!

THEN THERE WERE THE INFAMOUS **MIND GAMES**; CUNNING PSYCHOLOGICAL TRICKS THAT DROVE MANY A MANAGERIAL RIVAL TO ABJECT DESPAIR:

KEVIN KEEGAN

I'll tell you this: if you wear these ear protectors, he can't poison your head with his brain powers!

RAFA BENÍTEZ

I want to talk about facts.

Ferguson uses chemtrails to numb the minds of disciplinary panels. Also, Michael Carrick did 9/11.

ARSÈNE WENGER

HE COULD BE FIERCELY LOYAL TO HIS PLAYERS. WHEN THE PRESS CRITICISED JUAN SEBASTIAN VERON, HE EXPLODED: 'I'M NO FUCKIN TALKING TO YOU. VERON'S A GREAT PLAYER. YOUSE ARE ALL FUCKING IDIOTS!' HOWEVER, HE WAS UNSENTIMENTAL ABOUT MOVING PLAYERS ON WHEN THE TIME WAS RIGHT.

Morning, Incey.

'The Guvnor.' You've got to call me 'The Guvnor'.

Get me the phone.

FERGUSON'S GREATEST TRIUMPH WAS WINNING THE TREBLE IN 1999, WITH A CORE GROUP OF PLAYERS WHO'D COME THROUGH THE YOUTH SYSTEM. THIS WAS A FEATURE OF HIS MANAGEMENT AND HE TOOK A FIRM HAND WHEN IT CAME TO DISCIPLINE, OFTEN SHUTTING DOWN PARTIES INVOLVING HIS YOUNG PROTÉGÉS.

Chocolate cake? Sunny Delight? Jenga?! You boys are on a slippery slope to the Sunderland first team; a slippery slope!

Ooh, good, the clown's here...

OF THOSE YOUNG FOOTBALLERS, RYAN GIGGS AND PAUL SCHOLES WERE TWO OF ONLY FOUR PLAYERS WHO FERGUSON CONSIDERED TO BE TRULY WORLD CLASS DURING HIS TIME AT OLD TRAFFORD. THE OTHER TWO WERE ÉRIC CANTONA AND, OF COURSE, A CERTAIN PORTUGUESE GENIUS...

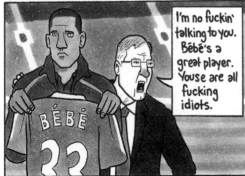

I'm no fuckin' talking to you. Bébé's a great player. Youse are all fucking idiots.

BÉBÉ 33

NO, IT WAS RONALDO, OBVIOUSLY, BUT THE WEIRD SIGNING OF BÉBÉ DOES SHOW THAT FERGUSON'S TENURE WASN'T WITHOUT CONTROVERSY. FOR EXAMPLE, HE FELL OUT WITH ONE OF UNITED'S MAJOR SHAREHOLDERS, JOHN MAGNIER, OVER A JOINTLY-OWNED RACEHORSE. A FURIOUS MAGNIER THEN SOLD HIS SHARES TO THE GLAZER FAMILY.

Oh, we're gonna run this place like a big organised family. Our debt is your debt!

See. This is fine!

FERGUSON'S RELATIONSHIP WITH THE GLAZERS PUT HIM AT ODDS WITH SOME FANS, WHO WERE CONCERNED ABOUT THE FINANCIAL HEALTH OF THE CLUB AND THE ASTRONOMICAL RISE OF TICKET PRICES...

Sweet mother of Eric! Have you seen this?

Yeah, it's a disgr—

SEASON TICKET FINANCE PLAN

... BUT OTHERS WERE PLACATED BY THE STEADY STREAM OF SILVERWARE THAT FERGUSON CONTINUED TO DELIVER IN THE FINAL PHASE OF HIS CAREER.

Ooh, shiny.

WHEN HE EVENTUALLY CALLED IT A DAY IN 2013, FERGUSON'S UNPARALLED SUCCESS WAS REWARDED WITH THE ULTIMATE PRIZE: A RETIREMENT SPENT SITTING BACK, WATCHING A LINE OF SUCCESSORS FAILING MISERABLY TO MEET HIS STANDARDS.

Football... Bloody hell.

BOOOOOO

MARÍO ZAGALLO

Marío Zagallo was the first man to win the World Cup as both a player and a manager. He may even have won it twice as a manager if Ronaldo hadn't suffered a seizure a few hours before Brazil's appearance in the 1998 World Cup final.

As a player, 'The Little Ant' was industrious. Not for Zagallo the insouciant flick or the showy dribble; here was a man who knew the value of running up and down the line like a metronome, of teamwork, of carrying tiny morsels of food back to the colony to nourish the queen.

As is common with many of the coaches contained in this section, Zagallo was famed for his fiery temper; almost as if spending a lifetime shouting at recalcitrant immature men has a long-term effect on a person's emotional well-being. However, Marío was as Zen as a Pilates instructor in comparison to his predecessor as Brazil's national coach, Joáo Saldanha. When Saldanha was sacked, just weeks before the start of the 1970 World Cup, he walked into a hotel lobby with a loaded pistol, looking for his critics.

Zagallo had little time to work with the squad, but Brazil returned from Mexico as World Champions. Whilst he was blessed with a unit of exceptionally talented players, the history of football is littered with examples of brilliant sides who choked with glory in sight: Hungary in 1954, the Netherlands in 1974, and, of course, Brazil in 1950.

Zagallo's skill as a motivator should not be underestimated; his impassioned team talk at half-time of their semi-final against Uruguay helped to assuage the fears of the players, who believed that their South American opponents had a hex over them. An impudent second-half showing saw them through to the final, where they would overwhelm their wilting Italian opponents, 4–1, and put their insect-human hybrid coach into the record books.

MARÍO ZAGALLO ENJOYED A LONG AND HAPPY RELATIONSHIP WITH THE WORLD CUP, WINNING IT TWICE AS A PLAYER AND ONCE AS A MANAGER. HE FIRST SET EYES ON IT IN 1950, WHILE HE WAS ON MILITARY SERVICE AND WORKING AS PART OF THE SECURITY OPERATION AT THE MARACANA STADIUM.

HE STARTED OUT AS A PLAYMAKER, BUT SWITCHED TO BECOME A WINGER WHEN HE REMEMBERED THAT HE LIVED IN BRAZIL AND OPPORTUNITIES WOULD BE LIMITED OTHERWISE.

IT WAS PLAYING THIS ROLE FOR FLAMENGO THAT EARNED HIM A PLACE IN THE NATIONAL TEAM. HOWEVER, IN THE LEAD-UP TO THE 1958 WORLD CUP, SPECULATION WAS RIFE THAT ZAGALLO WOULD BE CUT FROM VICENTE FEOLA'S SQUAD, SO HE STOPPED LISTENING TO THE RADIO, WATCHING TV AND READING THE NEWS; STILL A SMART MOVE.

HIS WORKMANLIKE APPROACH EARNED HIM THE NOD THOUGH, AND HE TOOK HIS PLACE IN MIDFIELD ALONGSIDE DIDI, ZITO AND GARRINCHA, WITH VAVÁ AND THE NEWCOMER PELÉ UP FRONT. BRAZIL CLAIMED THEIR FIRST WORLD CUP WITH A 5-2 WIN OVER HOSTS SWEDEN. ZAGALLO SCORED ONE AND SET ONE UP, LEAVING NO DOUBT AS TO WHO WAS THE HERO OF THE DAY.

THEY RETAINED THEIR TITLE FOUR YEARS LATER, ZAGALLO PLAYING EVERY MINUTE. HIS STANDOUT PERFORMANCE CAME IN THE SEMI-FINAL, WHEN HE DRIBBLED AROUND SEVERAL CHILE PLAYERS BEFORE CROSSING TO VAVÁ TO GIVE BRAZIL AN UNASSAILABLE 4-2 LEAD.

JUST EIGHT WEEKS BEFORE THE START OF THE 1970 WORLD CUP, ZAGALLO WAS CALLED UPON TO REPLACE THE VOLATILE JOÃO SALDANHA AS BRAZIL'S COACH. SALDANHA HAD COMMITTED THE ULTIMATE SIN: CRITICISING PELÉ - HE PUT ABOUT A RUMOUR THAT HE WAS GOING BLIND. STILL, THE VANQUISHED COACH TOOK HIS DISMISSAL TYPICALLY WELL.

ZAGALLO DRAFTED RIVELINO INTO THE TEAM AND ALSO PICKED TOSTÃO AS CENTRE-FORWARD, DESPITE THE FACT HE WAS SUFFERING A SERIOUS RETINA COMPLAINT. MEDICAL STAFF ASSURED ZAGALLO THAT HE WAS FINE, SO HE JUST MADE SURE HE LOOKED TOSTÃO IN HIS NON-GAMMY EYE.

THE SIDE HE GUIDED TO GLORY IN MEXICO IS COMMONLY REGARDED TO BE THE GREATEST TO HAVE EVER PLAYED THE GAME, AS ZAGALLO HIT UPON THE NOVEL IDEA OF SELECTING ALL HIS BEST PLAYERS AND LETTING THEM DO WHAT THEY LIKED.

BRIAN CLOUGH

'Have you ever been hit before?' enquired the Nottingham Forest manager of his striker, Nigel Jemson. Before the bemused youngster could answer – wallop – Clough had punched him in the guts. 'Well, you have now.' It's fair to say, Brian Clough had some unorthodox methods.

Clough was a riddle of contradictions. He ruled by fear, but was a great motivator. His involvement with players was kept to the bare minimum, yet they seemed to adore him (Leeds United aside). He had an aversion to the term 'tactics', yet his teams played to an obvious strategic plan. Pass and move, keep the ball on the ground, each player with specific instructions, disobey and you'll find yourself clutching your belly on the changing-room floor.

In the 1970s, Clough was a force of nature; as much a national celebrity as a football manager. His intelligent, funny, acerbic views were devoured by the general public and producers of light entertainment television shows alike. Yet his endless quotes would have counted for little if he had not also been a hugely successful football manager.

Key to his success was his partnership with Peter Taylor. They'd met when they were both players at Middlesbrough, and when Clough became manager of Hartlepool, Taylor left his job at Burton Albion to join him. They went on to work together at Derby County (where they won a league title), Brighton (where they didn't), and most fruitfully at Nottingham Forest. You don't get to win a championship and two European Cup finals with a squad of journeymen at a provincial club from the East Midlands just by bantering with Michael Parkinson.

The incident with Jemson occurred in the latter years of Clough's career, when his behaviour was becoming increasingly erratic. He'd fallen out with Taylor in the mid-eighties and their relationship was never repaired. Without Taylor, his alcoholism worsened. Forest went into decline and were relegated in his final season at the club, in 1993, with Clough cutting a tragic figure. However, he is best remembered as a coaching virtuoso in a scruffy green sweatshirt, who for a while made Nottingham Forest the best team in Europe.

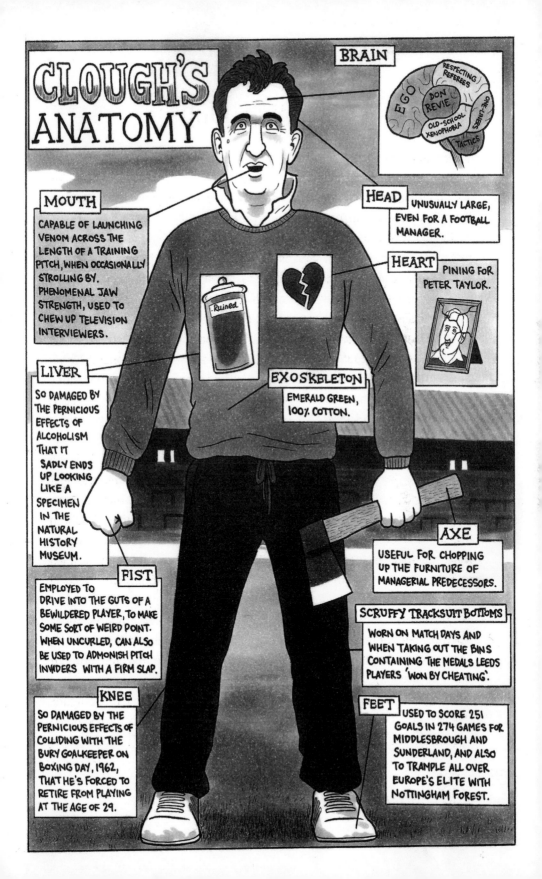

HELENIO HERRERA

Visionary tactician, master motivator, uncompromising disciplinarian, Helenio Herrera can't have been much fun to work for. Some believe that he worked Roma's Giuliano Taccola to death – continuing to make him train and play after he had suffered a heart murmur. Another time, he decided against telling Aristide Guarneri that his father had died until after he'd put in a 90-minute shift for him in Inter's defence. Still, the man got results. Two Spanish titles with Atlético Madrid, another pair with Barcelona, and three Scudettos with Inter, with whom he also won two European Cups.

The headstone of Herrera's grave is in the shape of the European Cup; this was a man who dedicated his life to football. The actual date of Herrera's birth remains a mystery, not helped by the fact that he's rumoured to have died his hair jet black until the day he died, meaning he must have looked 23 his whole life. Born in Argentina to Spanish parents (his father was an exiled anarchist), Herrera was raised in Casablanca, before moving to France, where he became naturalised in 1934. His career as a footballer was unspectacular, but it was as a coach that he would leave a lasting legacy.

Herrera is famed for his employment of the *catenaccio* system, which brought huge success to Inter, and his vast presence as a coach led to a change in the way people viewed managers, making them the focal point of a team's success or failure and enabling them to command larger salaries. Next time you see José Mourinho carping his way through a post-match interview, you can thank the genius of Helenio Herrera.

One of Herrera's favoured methods was the *ritiro* – an enforced, pre-match training camp, where players could focus on the task at hand. When the English forward Gerry Hitchens left Inter, he remarked that it was like 'coming out of the bloody army'. Now if that doesn't sound like a fun development experience, I don't know what does.

ALF RAMSEY

Alf Ramsey was as English as a stale cheese and pickle sandwich. He was the physical embodiment of post-war austerity, all stiff-lipped stoicism and clipped vowels. However, what he lacked in gregariousness, he more than made up for in tactical acumen. After all, this was the man who achieved the impossible: turning England's opinion of itself as a genuine football power into reality.

Sir Alf was appointed as England manager in 1963, having transformed Ipswich Town from Third Division also-rans to national champions. One of his first acts as manager was to stand up to the Football Association's selection committee. Alf would pick the team and if they tried to interfere, he would speak to them as harshly as he would any player, colleague, journalist or member of the service industry who stepped out of line. Despite his famed use of elocution lessons, Ramsey was still fond of using industrial language when the situation fucking well called for it.

While at Ipswich, Ramsey experimented with putting a team out that didn't contain wingers. In the early sixties, this was the tactical equivalent of Bob Dylan 'going electric'. At the 1966 World Cup, Ramsey introduced his 'Wingless Wonders' at the quarter-final stage. A hard-fought 1–0 win against Argentina was followed by victory against Portugal and a historic win against West Germany in the final.

Simply, Ramsey picked the best players for the system. This is how Jack Charlton came to be making his England debut when he was nearly 30 years old; and Ramsey's lack of sentimentality meant that he didn't hesitate to leave Jimmy Greaves out of the team for the World Cup final, even though the striker had recovered from an injury sustained earlier in the tournament.

Ramsey took an even better side to the Mexico World Cup in 1970, but his team wilted in the heat of Léon and threw away a two-goal lead to lose 3–2 to West Germany in the quarter-final. When they failed to even qualify for the 1974 World Cup, Ramsey was sacked. An indication of the lack of gratitude shown to him by his employers can be seen in his salary. In his final year as England manager, Ramsey was on just £7,200 per annum. His eventual replacement, Don Revie, was paid £25,000 a year.

WITH WOLFGANG WEBER HAVING SCORED A LAST-MINUTE EQUALISER FOR WEST GERMANY, ENGLAND MANAGER **ALF RAMSEY** RALLIES HIS TEAM BEFORE EXTRA TIME IN THE 1966 WORLD CUP FINAL...

Come along, stand up. Pull those stockings up, Cohen; the Queen don't want to see your sweaty shins, man.

I've done all I can for you, providing instruction on everything from your diet and sleeping patterns, to the correct way to conduct your ablutions, simplifying it for your 'basic working-class brains.

Aren't you from Dagenham?

'It's up to you now. This game is there to be won; won like the way I've won the respect of my superiors at The Football Association.'

'I admit that over the years, I've been hard on you, gentlemen...'

Morning, Sir Harold!

Yes, yes.

What's the blasted window cleaner so chipper about?

Well played, Gordon; see you next time.

Sure, Alf.

Sure are you? Picking the team are you? Let me tell you, it'll be a cold day in Margate before any player holds more sway than the England manager!

... but it's all been for your benefit, to toughen you up. Just look at the Germans; they're exhausted, beaten. Physically and emotionally drained, as if they've been denied the chance to even play in the biggest game of their lives.

Um, that's Jimmy Greaves.

It's a shitty old game.

You've won it once, now go out there and make it an albatross around the neck of every footballer who ever pulls on an England shirt again.

Now, who do I have to reprimand in an affected, haughty fashion to get a decent cup of tea round here?

ENGLAND

JOSÉ MOURINHO

Whether you dislike him, or simply loathe him, there's no ignoring José Mourinho. There he is, sliding along the touchline on his knees; there he is sticking his finger in the eye of an opposition coach; there he is publicly castigating a medical professional for doing her job. Oh, José.

Since the turn of the century, the Portuguese coach has been a constant presence at the top of the game, like a beautiful, scowling wart. He has won every competition going, not allowing the tyranny of success to either cheer him up, or apparently make him like football much

José first achieved prominence with Porto, whom he led to Champions League glory in 2004. Porto's defeat of Manchester United earlier in the competition really brought him to the attention of English football fans and there was much excitement when he was appointed as the manager of the newly oil-rich Chelsea. Mourinho arrived in England as an exotic, brooding figure, exuding a confidence that made supporters and journalists swoon. The general public were infatuated with The Special One; a fascination that lasted literally weeks, until his pragmatic Chelsea started to monotonously grind out results, with José settling into a now familiar routine of constantly moaning in a fashion that was frankly alien to English people.

Having won two Premier League titles at Chelsea, Mourinho was then dumped after a series of disagreements with the club owner and real life Bond-villain, Roman Abramovich. Having survived being cut in half by a laser, Mourinho found employment at Inter, where he won two Scudettos and another Champions League title. From there, it was off to Real Madrid, where he won another league title and explored new areas of bastardry. This would come in handy when he returned to Chelsea; two successful seasons being followed by the bizarre episode with the club physio and, eventually, again, the sack.

However, this had all just been the build-up for Mourinho landing his dream position as Manchester United manager. It was a role he leapt into with relish: a whole new José, finally in the job he had long coveted. There would be no more complaining now.

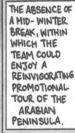

BILL SHANKLY

When Bill Shankly arrived at Liverpool in 1959, the second division club was in a state of malaise. The training ground was in disrepair, there was little money available for transfers, and the board of directors had a habit of meddling in team affairs. Shankly initiated a complete overhaul, but crucially retained the services of the backroom staff, including Joe Fagan, Reuben Bennett and Bob Paisley; a brains trust who would come to be known as 'The Boot Room'. Paisley was also a trained bricklayer, which came in handy when it was time to renovate the decrepit training ground. Imagine a video montage of middle-aged men in red tracksuits, painting fences, banging nails and teaching clumsy apprentices to gradually be better at football. Try downloading the *Top Gun* soundtrack, if that helps.

Before his first game in charge, Shankly famously told the media that he wanted to build a side so invincible that they'd have to send a team from Mars to beat them. However, Cardiff City had only come from Wales and they thrashed Liverpool 4-0. Within five years, though, Liverpool would be champions of England.

Liverpool was changing in the sixties. Shankly often spoke of the football club's place in a city that was undergoing a cultural revolution; adding to the sense of excitement generated by the music of The Beatles and Cilla Black and the comedy of Jimmy Tarbuck and Ken Dodd. Shankly himself was also an entertainer; a charismatic, quick-witted lyricist whose catalogue of quotes stood in stark contrast to the dry, monotone oration of his managerial peers. Shankly was not a man who took each game as it came.

Liverpool won the FA Cup in 1965 and another league title the year after. Shankly's second great team, of 1972-4 laid the foundations for the success that would follow, as the Reds became the most dominant club side of the decade under Bob Paisley, who took over the reins after Shankly's shock resignation in 1974. It was a decision he would regret bitterly, but at the time he seemed to be tired of just *being* Bill Shankly and the associated pressure of firing out an endless stream of sharply observed quips.

THE GODS (PART TWO)

STANLEY MATTHEWS

The ashes of Stanley Matthews are buried beneath the centre circle of Stoke City's Bet365 Stadium; a more dignified resting place for one of English football's all-time greats, it's harder to imagine. I was present on the day the stadium was officially opened, in 1997. Naturally, as Stoke's most famous son, Sir Stanley was guest of honour, and the occasion was marked by the great man lashing a penalty kick into a vacant goal. Sadly, by this stage, he was a frail old man, and the ball barely rolled over the line. Finally, age had caught up with the Wizard of Dribble, a man who had cheated it for so long, continuing to play at the top level until he was 50.

In his pomp, Matthews was a devastatingly quick winger. Though his signature move was simple, it was brilliantly effective: giving the defender a tantalising glimpse of the ball, before whipping it away and zipping into space, leaving only a whiff of Brylcreem as evidence he'd been there at all. Opponents who tried to blunt his menace by marking him more tightly discovered that he was also capable of swinging in accurate crosses from distance; no mean feat on days when a wet leather ball took on the weight and consistency of a dead badger.

The majority of his club career was spent at Stoke, but his only trophy was won at Blackpool, with whom he won the FA Cup in 1953. Blackpool found themselves 3–1 down to Bolton Wanderers, with just over 20 minutes remaining, but Matthews inspired one of English football's most famous comebacks, creating mayhem on the right wing, flinging in crosses for Stan Mortensen to pull one back and then, in injury time, for Bill Perry to crash in a winning goal.

Matthews also enjoyed a 23-year international career and was involved in some of the most famous moments in the history of the England team. He was on the pitch for the 'Battle of Highbury' against Italy in 1934, and again when the British government forced the England players to give Nazi salutes before a friendly with Germany in Berlin in 1938. England won 6–3 that day – a result that infuriated the onlooking Hermann Göring. Matthews was also present when Hungary took apart England by the same score-line in 1953, and in typical fashion, he shared some frank opinions about the FA and its team selectors, whom he felt were responsible for the result.

Insanely, he was already in his forties by the time he was named European Footballer of the Year in 1956. *I'm* in my forties. THERE'S STILL TIME*. How did he enjoy such a long and successful career?

---

*There isn't.

FERENC PUSKÁS

I have always held in high regard those most talented of footballers who completely let themselves go once their playing days are over. It shows that they are as fallible as the rest of us; those years invested in training the body and mind insufficient to equip some with the discipline to ignore the packet of chocolate digestives in the kitchen cupboard. Perhaps they're human after all.

Ferenc Puskás was no stranger to the biscuit barrel, but so what; he was Ferenc Puskás, for flip's sake. Among the various things that have been named in his honour are: an annual FIFA award for the goal of the year, the national stadium in Budapest, and, tellingly, a sausage factory in Madrid. There's also a statue of him in Budapest and another one in South Melbourne, where he enjoyed greatest success as a coach. So who are you to judge him if he wants a Custard Cream?

In the time-old tradition of exceptionally gifted footballers mastering the game by teaching themselves with objects other than footballs, the young Puskás developed his skills by playing with a tennis ball. He signed for his local club, Kispest, at the age of 12, making his full debut four years later, in 1943. When the Hungarian Ministry of Defence took control of Kispest in 1949, their name was changed to Budapest Honvéd. As the official team of the Hungarian Army, each Honvéd player was issued with a military rank. Puskás was made a major, which he must have been pretty pleased with. It's also how he came to be known as 'The Galloping Major' in the international football press. Honvéd used conscription to acquire the best players in Hungary and, as a result, dominated the domestic scene. The majority of their squad also represented the national side, who, for a period in the early fifties, were the best team on the planet.

In addition to Puskás, 'The Aranycsapat' ('The Golden Squad') contained talent such as Nándor Hidegkuti, Zoltán Czibor and Sándor Kocsis; world-class players in their own right. Over the course of six years, the team enjoyed a 32-game unbeaten run, during which time they became Olympic champions, in 1952. With half of the Continent shrouded in secrecy, there was still an air of mystery about teams from behind the Iron Curtain, this also being an age before televised European football or blogs.

However, following victory at the Helsinki Olympics, the world was becoming more aware of the quality of this Hungary team. In 1953 they breezed past Italy, 3–0, in the opening game at Rome's Stadio Olimpico, but it was in November of that year that they really announced themselves, with a mesmerising 6–3 win at Wembley against a shell-shocked England. Hidegkuti scored a hat-trick and Puskás bagged two, the pick of which included a drag-back that left the England captain, Billy Wright, flat on his arse; the perfect visual metaphor for the gulf in class between Hungary's progressive, free-flowing football and the old-fashioned stodge served up by England.

Hungary went to the 1954 World Cup in Switzerland as favourites, but it was the tournament at which their incredible run would end. It all started so well, cruising through the group stage with thumping wins against South Korea (9–0) and West Germany (8–3); though in the latter game Puskás received a hairline fracture to his ankle after a hefty challenge from Werner Liebrich. Though half-fit, he was hurried back into the team for the final – a re-match with the Germans – and opened the scoring. Czibor doubled their lead shortly afterwards, but then the Hungarians eased off, allowing West Germany back into the game; by the 19th minute, the scores were level. The Germans survived a Hungarian bombardment in the second half and stole the match with a Helmut Rahn goal, five minutes from time. Puskás had an equaliser ruled out for offside, correctly. They'd never reach these heights again.

FERENC PUSKÁS WAS THE FINEST PLAYER HUNGARY HAS EVER PRODUCED, EVEN IF YOU INCLUDE GOALKEEPER GÁBOR KIRÁLY, WHOSE EXPLOITS AT EURO 2016 LEGITIMISED THE WEARING OF GREY TRACKSUIT BOTTOMS IN A WORKPLACE ENVIRONMENT.

As you can see, we offer a range of caskets to suit all budgetary requirements.

AS WELL AS CAPTAINING THE GLORIOUS NATIONAL TEAM OF THE EARLY FIFTIES, PUSKÁS ALSO STARRED FOR HONVÉD, THE CLUB OF THE MINISTRY OF DEFENCE. EACH PLAYER WAS GIVEN A MILITARY RANK AND AS SUCH, PUSKÁS BECAME A MAJOR.

Well you can't play in that.

Can and will. You know how much paper maché it took me to make this?

HONVÉD ENTERED THE EUROPEAN CUP FOR THE FIRST TIME IN 1956 AND IT WAS AFTER AN AWAY GAME AGAINST ATHLETIC BILBAO THAT THE NEWS BROKE THAT SOVIET TANKS HAD ROLLED IN TO BUDAPEST TO VIOLENTLY CRUSH A POPULAR UPRISING. HONVÉD TOOK EVASIVE ACTION.

I wonder how my players would feel about an impromptu tour of South America?

UPON THEIR EVENTUAL RETURN TO EUROPE, SEVERAL PLAYERS — PUSKÁS INCLUDED — DECIDED AGAINST GOING BACK TO HUNGARY. AFTER ALL, THEY WERE NO STRANGERS TO HOSTILITY — AFTER HUNGARY LOST THE 1954 WORLD CUP FINAL, THEIR TRAIN BACK TO BUDAPEST HAD TO BE DIVERTED IN ORDER TO AVOID AN ANGRY MOB.

MAGYAR FANS' TV

Our first defeat in six years? A 32-game unbeaten run ended by an erroneously-disallowed goal? A team to be cherished for the ages? The universal respect of the football community? **GET THEM!!**

UEFA AND THE HUNGARIAN FA PUNISHED THE DEFECTORS WITH LENGTHY BANS. PUSKÁS USED THE TWO YEARS WELL, LETTING HIMSELF GO WITH THE SAME ABÁNDON HE'D SO OFTEN DISPLAYED ON THE PITCH.

The elasticated waist in these grey tracksuit bottoms really help me to go the extra mile at the all-you-can-eat buffet.

SOLD OUT

WHEN THE BAN ENDED IN 1958, HE SET ABOUT FINDING A NEW CLUB. HOWEVER, HE WAS 31 BY THEN AND 18 KILOGRAMS OVERWEIGHT. FINALLY, REAL MADRID TOOK A CHANCE ON HIM AND HE WORKED TO LOSE THE EXTRA KILOS.

Can't I just saw my right leg off?

It's not like I use it.

AT FIRST, MADRIDISTAS WERE UNCONVINCED...

RM FANS' TV

He's as big as a cow!

...BUT HE WOULD BECOME ONE OF THE MOST SUCCESSFUL PLAYERS IN THE CLUB'S HISTORY, WINNING COUNTLESS (NINE) TROPHIES OVER THE NEXT EIGHT YEARS.

MONTAGE:

HE WAS A SELFLESS PLAYER AND A GENEROUS MAN. AFTER SCORING FOUR GOALS IN THE 1960 EUROPEAN CUP FINAL, HE HANDED THE MATCH BALL TO FRANKFURT'S ERWIN STEIN, WHO'D SCORED TWO. THIS MAY HAVE SURPRISED ALFREDO DI STÉFANO, WHO'D BAGGED A HAT-TRICK OF HIS OWN.

Where the **hell** is that ball? Oh, President Bernabéu will hear about this; isn't that right, Ferenc?

Yep.

PUSKÁS REPRESENTED SPAIN AT THE 1962 WORLD CUP AND ONCE HIS PLAYING DAYS WERE OVER, HE BECAME SOMETHING OF AN INTERNATIONAL MAN, COACHING TEAMS ALL OVER THE WORLD. ACCORDING TO HIS FORMER DRINKING COMPANION, JIM BAXTER, PUSKÁS ONLY KNEW TWO WORDS OF ENGLISH:

Whisky.

Jiggy-jiggy.

Look, mate; if you're not gonna buy one then piss off, yeah.

Mr Floppy

Jiggy.

PRESUMABLY, HE DIDN'T TRY TO LEARN THE LOCAL LANGUAGE WHEN HE MANAGED THE SAUDI NATIONAL SIDE IN THE MID-SEVENTIES.

PUSKAS

Start the engines!

START THE ENGINES!

THE HUNGARIAN GOVERNMENT PARDONED PUSKÁS FOR HIS DEFECTION IN 1993. HE RETURNED HOME TO TAKE CHARGE OF THE NATIONAL TEAM, BUT THEY NO LONGER BOASTED THE WEALTH OF TALENT OF THE GALLOPING MAJOR'S HEYDAY.

You know what's underrated?

Thirty-seven years of political exile.

BOBBY CHARLTON

It was from watching Stanley Matthews play that Bobby Charlton learned the importance of being able to burst into space over short distances. Whenever Matthews played at Newcastle's St. James' Park, local lad Bobby would stand in awe, taking mental notes as the winger swivelled past defenders, finding room to create havoc. Though not a winger himself, these principles stayed with him and he would use them to become arguably the greatest English footballer of all time, emulating even his childhood hero.

The distinctive sight of Bobby Charlton thundering a shot towards goal was replicated in playgrounds throughout England in the sixties and seventies. How was he able to stay suspended in mid-air, holding his shooting pose, as the ball rocketed past a succession of helpless goalkeepers? His gravity-defying, otherworldly aura was accentuated by a long, thin strand of blond hair, which stretched upwards from the side of his head like an antenna.

His talent aside, Charlton's physical appearance made him stand out from the crowd; male pattern baldness being a blight that even those who enjoy the status of a national treasure cannot avoid. These days, if you suffer from this affliction, there are at least a variety of options at your disposal. You can shave it all off (Jason Statham-style), you can leave a neatly combed bit at the sides (Jason Alexander-style), or you can cover it up with one of those 'baseball caps' all the teenagers are wearing now. For the brave or wealthy, there is even the choice of a painful scalp weave (handy tip: you can achieve the Wayne Rooney look without the need for expensive surgery by gluing four Weetabix to the top of your dome). Alas, none of these routes were available to Bobby Charlton, so he had to construct a cunning optical illusion. He conned the world into believing he had a full head of hair by wearing it with a parting that started just above his left ear and stretched over his head to the top of his right ear. The architects won't admit it, but it was this feat of engineering that was the inspiration for the arch at the renovated Wembley Stadium.

It was at the famous old ground where Charlton enjoyed the two crowning moments of his long career: winning the World Cup final in 1966, and then returning in 1968 to lift the European Cup as captain of Manchester United. The second achievement had a deeper meaning; it signified the end of a journey that he had begun as a callow teenager, one that had seen him overcome the physical and emotional trauma of the Munich air disaster.

His international career saw him attend four world cups, his final appearance coming in England's ill-fated quarter-final against West Germany in 1970. England were leading 2–1 when Alf Ramsey made the bold decision to substitute Charlton. They went on to lose, 3–2, with Charlton later saying that he still felt 'full of running'. His last start in a Manchester United shirt – his 758th – came against Chelsea at Stamford Bridge on 28 April 1973. The home fans gave Charlton a standing ovation and their chairman presented him with a silver cigarette case, which was actually a useful gift, as he smoked like a bastard.

Charlton's peers were sometimes slow to grasp how profoundly the tragedy of Munich had affected him; football being an unforgiving environment for anyone unwilling to indulge in the endless procession of epic banter. However, Charlton's ability to hammer the ball in from 30 yards, his capacity to run until that strand of hair stuck to his forehead like a string of spaghetti, and his general air of *decency* meant he was loved by football fans the world over.

IN THE FIRST HALF OF THE TWENTIETH CENTURY, THE NORTH-EAST OF ENGLAND WAS A FOOTBALL HOTBED. **BOBBY CHARLTON** WAS BORN INTO HIS FAMILY'S TRADE. FOUR OF HIS UNCLES WERE PROFESSIONALS AND THE FAMOUS JACKIE MILBURN WAS A RELATIVE. FOR BOBBY AND HIS BROTHER JACK, THERE WAS NO ESCAPE.

Robert! Get that pit worker outfit off. There will be no namby-pamby coal mining in **this** house, for in this family we are **footballers.** Now, go and wash up and practise your short corners, lad.

Naw!

HIS MOTHER, CISSIE, WAS THE MATRIARCH OF THE FAMILY AND A FOOTBALL OBSESSIVE. A LOCAL LEGEND, SHE PASSED HER LOVE OF THE GAME ON TO HER CHILDREN.

CISSIE, NOT CISSÉ

CHARLTON SIGNED FOR MANCHESTER UNITED AT THE AGE OF 15. HE WAS TOLD THAT THEY PLAYED AT TRAFFORD PARK, WHICH HE ASSUMED TO BE AN IDYLLIC, GREEN, OPEN SPACE.

Chin up, son; there's a tree just over there...

Mm~

HE WORKED FOR HOURS TO BECOME EQUALLY ADEPT WITH BOTH FEET, BOTH OF WHICH COULD UNLEASH A POWERFUL SHOT. DESPITE BEING A HEAVY SMOKER, HE WAS INCREDIBLY FIT; A FACT IN NO WAY DIMINISHED BY THE ACCEPTANCE THAT EVERYONE ELSE WAS PROBABLY SMOKING LIKE JOHAN CRUYFF AFTER A DUTY-FREE TROLLEY DASH.

HE WAS PART OF THE JUNIOR TEAM THAT WON THE FA YOUTH CUP FIVE YEARS IN A ROW, TRAVELLING BACK FROM NATIONAL SERVICE DUTY TO PLAY FOR UNITED AT THE WEEKENDS. THEY SHOULD BRING THAT SYSTEM BACK FOR WASTREL MODERN PLAYERS WHO HAVE PROBABLY NEVER EVEN SHOT AN ISIS.

WHAT IS YOUR MAJOR MALFUNCTION, NUMBNUTS?

Infrequent nights out after work?

CHARLTON MADE A SMOOTH TRANSITION TO THE FIRST TEAM, PLAYING A STARRING ROLE AS 'THE RED DEVILS' WON CONSECUTIVE LEAGUE TITLES IN 1956 AND 1957.

UNITED WERE ALSO PIONEERS IN EUROPE, DEFYING THE WILL OF THE CONSERVATIVE ENGLISH FOOTBALL AUTHORITIES TO PARTICIPATE ON THE CONTINENT.

It's about securing our football borders and protecting our sovereignty, yeah. We don't want **Johny Schnitzel** regulating the length of our goal kicks!

You're out of gin again, sir.

THE MUNICH AIR DISASTER CHANGED HIM – AS IT WOULD ANYONE. HE WAS DRAGGED FROM THE WRECKAGE BY HARRY GREGG, LUCKY TO ESCAPE WITH CUTS AND BRUISES. EIGHT OF HIS TEAMMATES DIED IN A CRASH THAT CLAIMED 23 LIVES. CHARLTON'S GRIEF WAS SOMETIMES CONFUSED FOR ALOOFNESS, WITH HIS STATUS AS 'A GOOD BLOKE' OFTEN CALLED INTO QUESTION BY **FOOTBALL MEN** WHO MAY HAVE FORGOTTEN THAT **HE NEARLY DIED IN A PLANE CRASH.** HE WROTE OF AN ENDURING PAIN IN HIS BOOK 'MY MANCHESTER UNITED YEARS'...

'Sometimes I feel it quite lightly, a mere brush stroke across an otherwise happy mood. Sometimes it engulfs me with a terrible regret and sadness – and guilt.'

CHARLTON BORE THE WEIGHT OF RESPONSIBILITY FOR MAKING UNITED SUCCESSFUL, FOR THE PLAYERS WHO HAD DIED. HIS PROFESSIONALISM DIDN'T ALWAYS MAKE HIM POPULAR, THOUGH. DENIS LAW CALLED HIM 'SIR BOBBY' YEARS BEFORE HIS KNIGHTHOOD AND GEORGE BEST ONCE THREW EGGS AT A PORTRAIT OF HIM IN A PUB.

I think I left my lighter in here, has anyone seen...oh.

EGG! EGG! EGG! EGG!

HE RETURNED TO THE FIRST TEAM LESS THAN A MONTH AFTER MUNICH AND MADE HIS ENGLAND DEBUT SOON AFTER, SCORING THE FIRST OF 49 INTERNATIONAL GOALS. THIS REMAINED A RECORD FOR AN ENGLAND PLAYER UNTIL 2015, WHEN IT WAS SURPASSED BY WAYNE ROONEY, WHO WOULD ENJOY A SIMILAR LEVEL OF PUBLIC ADULATION.

I think I left my army hat in here, has anyone seen...oh.

HE WENT ON TO PLAY 106 TIMES FOR HIS COUNTRY. AFTER ENGLAND WON THE WORLD CUP (ENGLAND!) IN 1966, HE TEARFULLY ASKED JACK, 'WHAT ELSE IS THERE TO ACHIEVE NOW?'

Well, you could have a disappointing dalliance with management at Preston, open some soccer schools and then return to United as a scowling director.

Forget I asked.

BUT THERE WAS MORE. HE RETURNED TO WEMBLEY TWO YEARS LATER, LEADING UNITED TO AN EMOTIONAL EUROPEAN CUP FINAL WIN AGAINST BENFICA. CHARLTON OPENED THE SCORING AND CELEBRATED WITH A EUPHORIC, UNCHOREOGRAPHED LEAP. IN THAT MOMENT, THERE WAS NOTHING THAT COULD KEEP HIM DOWN.

Three skips and one jump? No, no, no, this won't do at all.

J. SCHNITZEL

LIONEL MESSI

Are you Team Leo or Team Ronnie? You have to be one, it's the law. To simply appreciate both players for their astonishing individual talents and be grateful to be living in a time when you can enjoy the thrill of seeing them at the peak of their powers is to miss the point completely. YOU HAVE TO CHOOSE.

For the last decade, the escalating power struggle between Messi and Ronaldo has dominated the football narrative. Messi breaks a goal-scoring record, Ronaldo matches it. Ronaldo dyes one bit of hair, Messi dips his whole head in a bucket of peroxide and grows a massive orange beard. Messi is found guilty of tax evasion, the Spanish authorities hit Ronaldo with a huge bill for unpaid taxes. The sense is that this epic struggle will only end when one of them either develops long-range nuclear capabilities or they both retire peacefully to their castles.

Messi arrived at FC Barcelona as a shy, underdeveloped teen. The other young hopefuls were told to go easy on him in training, but they soon found he was a giant on the pitch; even if they'd wanted to, they couldn't have got close enough to rough him up. He would grow to become the creative fulcrum of Pep Guardiola's great Barcelona side of the early 2010s: the unpredictable element who would provide variety and excitement to the relentless procession of passing.

Without question he is Barcelona's greatest ever player. The statistics speak for themselves. As well as scoring the most goals in La Liga history, Messi's name sits at the top of the tables of almost all of Barcelona's individual records. At the time of writing, he's their highest all-time goal-scorer, by a margin of nearly 300; he's bagged over 100 goals in the Champions League; he's won the most trophies; and he holds the record for the player most frequently linked with a move to Manchester City whenever his contract is up for renewal. The man is a machine.

Inevitably, comparisons are made with his countryman, Diego Maradona, but Messi's accomplishments at club level have, as yet, not been replicated at international level. This has come with some unfair criticism (some of it from Maradona himself), which suggests that Messi plays only for himself when wearing the Argentina shirt. However, he remains adored in his homeland.

During the 2007 Copa América in Venezuela, an over-exuberant spectator threw herself from the top tier to give the bemused Messi a kiss and a cuddle.

Messi's biggest vice appears to be his predilection for bland food; his favourite post-match meal being cheese pizza and a bottle of Sprite. His poor diet has often been commented on, but, like many modern professionals, Messi has been incubated in Football World since he was a teenager; is it any wonder that his palette is as sophisticated as that of a 13-year-old boy? This is clearly preferable to the self-destructive addictions that ruined the lives of so many creative superstars of previous generations.

Now in his thirties, Messi is entering the final phase of his playing career. There are few medals or accolades that still elude him. Winning a trophy with Argentina, after near-misses in the 2014 World Cup and multiple versions of the Copa América, would enable him to finally silence those who doubt his demi-god status (*cough*-DIEGO-*cough*). Other than that, he could try to beat Joan Gamper's record of scoring nine goals in one Barcelona game (which Gamper managed on three occasions), or maybe he could have a go in goal, to try and set a new benchmark for clean sheets. Really, though, overhauling Cristiano Ronaldo's tally of Champions League goals is the achievement that will enable him to retire happily to the paradise of an Iberian hilltop mansion, crafted from the recycled boxes of Dr. Oetker four-cheese frozen pizzas.

IN EARLY 2016, PHOTOS EMERGED OF A YOUNG AFGHAN BOY, MURTAZA AHMADI, PLAYING FOOTBALL, WEARING A HOMEMADE MESSI SHIRT, CRAFTED FROM A PLASTIC BAG.

UPON SEEING THE IMAGES, LIONEL MESSI SENT HIM A SIGNED SHIRT, IN THE LAST NICE THING TO HAPPEN THAT YEAR. MESSI HIMSELF HAD GROWN UP IN THE ECONOMICALLY DEPRIVED SUBURB OF GRANDOLI, IN ROSÁRIO. MUCH LIKE MURTAZA, HE WAS OBSESSED WITH FOOTBALL.

BY THE AGE OF SIX, MESSI WAS ALREADY ENTERTAINING THE CROWDS AT NEWELL'S OLD BOYS GAMES, WITH HALF-TIME DISPLAYS OF BALL SKILLS. HE WAS EVEN ON THE PITCH ON THE DAY IN 1993 THAT DIEGO MARADONA MADE HIS DEBUT FOR THE CLUB. IT WAS NOT THE LAST TIME THAT THEIR PATHS WOULD CROSS.

That boy! I swear that one day I will publicly criticise his commitment to the national team!

ALTHOUGH GIFTED, LEO WAS SMALL; SO SMALL THAT HE HAD TO UNDERGO GROWTH HORMONE TREATMENT, PAID FOR OUT OF HIS FATHER'S OWN POCKET.

Hmm. I may need to tweak the recipe.

This soup tastes funny

PAPA'S OLD-TIME GROWTH FORMULA

FERTILIZANTE

HIS FATHER ALSO RECORDED A VHS TAPE OF LEO JUGGLING VARIOUS ITEMS.

TAP   TAP   TAP

THE TAPE ENDED UP IN FRONT OF BARCELONA'S DIRECTOR OF FOOTBALL, CARLES REXACH, WHO AGREED TO PAY FOR LEO'S HORMONE TREATMENT AND FIND HIS DAD A JOB IN RETURN FOR HIS SIGNATURE.

HE MOVED TO SPAIN IN 2000, AT THE AGE OF 13. HE WAS NERVOUS AT FIRST, PREFERRING TO GET CHANGED IN THE CORRIDORS OF LA MASIA, RATHER THAN IN THE CHANGING ROOM WITH THE OTHER YOUTH PLAYERS.

There's no way I'm getting my Newell's Old Boys out in front of these strangers!

THIS NERVOUSNESS NEVER FULLY LEFT HIM AND EVEN WHEN HE REACHED THE PINNACLE OF HIS PROFESSION, HE WOULD OFTEN VOMIT ON THE PITCH. HOWEVER, THIS MAY ALSO HAVE BEEN A RESULT OF HIS POOR DIET. IN HIS EARLY DAYS AT BARCELONA, THE COACHING STAFF HAD TO TELL HIM TO EASE UP ON THE FIZZY DRINKS.

That's all we need, another sawn-off Argentinian genius with a massive coke habit.

MESSI'S TALENT SHONE THROUGH AND HIS LACK OF HEIGHT SOON BECAME AN IRRELEVANCE. HE MADE HIS COMPETITIVE DEBUT AGAINST ESPANYOL AT THE AGE OF 17; AT THE TIME HE WAS THE YOUNGEST BARCELONA PLAYER TO DO SO.

THE CHANCES THAT YOU'RE UNFAMILIAR WITH THE REST OF THE MESSI STORY ARE AS UNLIKELY AS THE IDEA THAT THIS CARTOON HAS OVERPLAYED THE HEIGHT THING. HIS TALE IS ONE OF DAZZLING SUCCESS, WHICH HAS SEEN HIM BECOME ONE OF THE MOST ICONIC AND DECORATED SPORTS PEOPLE OF THE 21ST CENTURY. BY THE TIME YOU READ THIS, HE'LL NO DOUBT HAVE ADDED TO HIS LIST OF ACHIEVEMENTS, BUT SOME OF HIS BEST MOMENTS HAVE INCLUDED...

A RIDICULOUS SLALOM THROUGH THE GETAFE TEAM TO SCORE A GOAL THAT LOOKED LIKE A TALENT-SHOW TRIBUTE TO MARADONA'S SOLO EFFORT AGAINST ENGLAND IN 1986.

2007

Tonight, I'll be... Mr Diego Maradona.

HIS FIRST HAT-TRICK, AGAINST REAL MADRID OF ALL TEAMS. HE WAS ALSO IMPERIOUS IN BARCELONA'S 5-0 DEMOLITION OF REAL, IN JOSÉ MOURINHO'S FIRST CLÁSICO AS MADRID BOSS, IN 2010.

GRIND GRIND

ANOTHER MARADONA TRIBUTE, WITH HIS OWN 'HAND OF GOD' GOAL, AGAINST ESPANYOL IN 2007.

Més que un club!

Oh, this is getting ridiculous. It's like a breathy, folksy cover version of a rock classic, used in an advert for car insurance. Hey, kid, get your own act!

HEADING A GOAL IN THE 2009 CHAMPIONS LEAGUE FINAL AGAINST MANCHESTER UNITED, TO CONCLUSIVELY SETTLE ONE OF FOOTBALL'S NEVER TIRESOME DEBATES.

I must concede that you are the superior player, Lionel.

That's very gracious of you. Let's never speak of this again.

SCORING 91 GOALS IN A CALENDAR YEAR IN 2012, BREAKING GERD MÜLLER'S RECORD, WHICH HAD STOOD SINCE 1972. THIS HELPED MESSI TO SECURE HIS THIRD CONSECUTIVE BALLON D'OR; AN ACHIEVEMENT HE MARKED BY DRESSING LIKE A MAGICIAN, WHICH IN A WAY HE WAS, YEAH.

NOTCHING UP HIS 500TH CLUB GOAL WITH A 90TH-MINUTE WINNER AT THE BERNABÉU; AN ACHIEVEMENT HE MARKED BY REMOVING HIS SHIRT AND HOLDING IT UP TO THE FURIOUS REAL MADRID FANS.

HE EVEN GOT TO MEET HIS YOUNG AFGHAN FAN, IN A HEART-MELTING MOMENT BEFORE A BARCELONA FRIENDLY IN DOHA, A REMINDER OF THE POSITIVE POWER OF SPONSORSHIP OBLIGATION. ♥

Mate, the hair. Talk me through the hair.

KENNY DALGLISH

Players and managers come and go, some even spend their whole careers at one club, but it's hard to think of an individual who has had such a long and profound relationship with a club as Kenny Dalglish has enjoyed with Liverpool. His union with the city itself was forged in the shared experiences of joy, triumph and grief.

Yet Liverpool fans were far from convinced when Bob Paisley splurged a record £440,000 on the Celtic forward in 1977. Kenny's quiet Glaswegian mumble hardly radiated the confidence of a goal-scorer. This was in stark contrast to the man he was signed to replace: Kevin Keegan, the garrulous idol of the Anfield terraces. However, any misgivings about Dalglish's ability quickly evaporated.

By the end of the season, he would be scoring the winning goal against Club Brugge to clinch the European Cup final at Wembley. It was a hard-fought victory, with Liverpool overcoming the disruption of losing influential defender Tommy Smith to injury in the build-up to the final. Smith had dropped a pickaxe handle on his foot in his garage, thus becoming part of an exclusive group of players who have been sidelined through non-football-related injuries.*

Dalglish would win two more European Cup winner's medals as a Liverpool player. First, in 1981, with a 1–0 victory against Real Madrid at the Parc des Princes, and again in 1984, with AS Roma beaten on penalties on their own turf amidst a hostile atmosphere. They reached the final again the following year. However, it was a match that would become an insignificant sidenote to a dreadful human tragedy. The lack of segregation and the woeful disorganisation within Brussels' decaying Heysel Stadium would have dire consequences. Thirty-nine people, mostly Juventus fans, were crushed to death when a cluster of Liverpool fans breached the small chain-link fence that separated the two groups of supporters.

Accounts vary as to how much the players knew about the unfolding horror, but the decision was made to play the final, in the belief that it would quell

---

* My favourite story of footballers suffering domestic injuries involved lower-league journeyman Sammy Igoe. In the middle of recuperating from a broken arm (a recovery which had already been impeded when he'd cut the plaster cast off and returned to training prematurely), the Swindon Town midfielder managed to glue one of his eyes shut whilst making a model aeroplane for his son, thus earning himself the nickname 'Sammy Eye-glue'.

further violence. Earlier that day, it was announced that the match would be Joe Fagan's last as Liverpool manager, and that Kenny Dalglish would be taking over as player-manager. Dalglish's first duty was to attend a press conference in the aftermath of the tragedy; his second was to try and talk a distressed Bruce Grobbelaar, Liverpool's goalkeeper, out of quitting football.

It took some time for Dalglish to adapt to his new role, but his players were mostly accepting of him. Liverpool won an historic double in his first season, extending their period of near-total domination. To be a schoolchild in England at this time was to be surrounded by a sea of kids wearing shiny red shirts, conditioning you to buy Crown paints and Candy electrical goods.

Dalglish remained a key player during the first couple of years of his new role, but it was once he took a step back that he was able to create one of the best teams in English football history. The addition of John Barnes, Peter Beardsley and John Aldridge to the squad left the Reds with the most exciting forward line in the country, as they cruised to the league title in 1988. They were well on course for another double in 1989, when they arrived at Hillsborough for an FA Cup semi-final against Nottingham Forest.

Within minutes of the kick-off, it became clear that horror was unfolding in the enclosure behind Grobbelaar's goal. With thousands of Liverpool fans funnelled into two sections of terracing, an appalling human crush claimed the lives of 96 people, the innocent victims of criminally negligent policing and a pervasive attitude that football supporters were to be treated like cattle. One of the many enduring images from that day is of a glassy-eyed Dalglish staring towards the Leppings Lane end; confusion and concern etched across his face. He and his players bore the weight of the tragedy, attending scores of funerals for the victims, including four in one day. Unsurprisingly, the disaster and its aftermath would affect them deeply. Liverpool surrendered the league title with a dramatic 2–0 defeat to Arsenal in their last game of the season, but nobody bore any ill-will towards the manager or his players.

Liverpool reclaimed the title the following year, Dalglish being the last person to deliver a league championship to Anfield (he even returned as manager of Blackburn Rovers in 1995 to lift the Premier League trophy in front of the home fans, a reminder of the good times). His shock resignation in early 1991 resembled that of another former club legend, Bill Shankly, but his status as a son of Liverpool was ensured; for ever entwined with the city and its people.

KENNY DALGLISH HAD A MASSIVE ARSE.

ACCORDING TO BRIAN CLOUGH, 'IT CAME DOWN BELOW HIS KNEES AND THAT'S WHERE HE GOT HIS STRENGTH FROM.' DALGLISH USED THIS NATURAL GIFT TO DEVASTATING EFFECT, STRIKING FEAR INTO THE HEARTS OF DEFENDERS EVERYWHERE.

Oh gog!

KING KENNY GREW UP AS A RANGERS FAN IN GLASGOW, BUT WHEN CELTIC'S ASSISTANT MANAGER, SEAN FALLON, CAME KNOCKING AT HIS PARENTS' DOOR, HE RACED UP TO HIS ROOM AND TOOK DOWN HIS RANGERS MEMORABILIA.

Ah, you'll fit in just fine, laddie.

AS A YOUNGSTER, DALGLISH PLAYED IN CELTIC'S LAUDED RESERVE TEAM, DUBBED 'THE QUALITY STREET GANG', ALONGSIDE FUTURE CLUB IDOLS, LOU MACARI AND DANNY McGRAIN.

Another trophy, eh? I can't wait until I'm 18, so I can celebrate with something stronger.

Aye, right, Danny.

LIFE WAS TOUGH IN GLASGOW IN THE 1960s.

DALGLISH WAS SOON SCORING GOALS FOR THE FIRST TEAM (39 OF THEM IN 1972-73) AND WAS SNAPPED UP BY LIVERPOOL TO REPLACE THE DEPARTING KEVIN KEEGAN IN 1977. HE WOULD TAKE POSSESSION OF THE FABLED NUMBER 7 SHIRT, LATER WORN BY SUCH LUMINARIES AS:

PETER BEARDSLEY

JOHN ALDRIDGE

I'm Ian Rush.

DAVID SPEEDIE

LUIS SUÁREZ

FREE LUIS

THE LIVERPOOL FANS QUICKLY ADOPTED HIM AS ONE OF THEIR OWN AND IMMORTALISED HIM IN THE TERRACE CHANT 'KENNY DALGLISH IS COOLER THAN THE FONZ'. THEY HAD CORRECTLY IDENTIFIED THE 'HAPPY DAYS' CHARACTER AS THE EPITOME OF SUAVE.

What's cooler than a middle-aged man who wears a leather jacket and hangs around in a cafe with a load of teenagers all day?

Apart from King Kenny, literally nothing.

DALGLISH CAPPED OFF HIS FIRST SEASON BY SCORING THE WINNING GOAL IN THE EUROPEAN CUP FINAL AGAINST BRUGES. IN TYPICAL STYLE, HE DARTED ON TO A GRAEME SOUNESS PASS AND DINKED THE BALL INTO THE NET BEFORE HURDLING THE ADVERTISING BOARD IN DELIGHT.

Ey!

HIS TIME AT LIVERPOOL COINCIDED WITH A PERIOD OF UNPRECEDENTED SUCCESS. AS A PLAYER, HE WON FIVE LEAGUE TITLES AND THREE EUROPEAN CUPS, BEFORE TAKING OVER AS PLAYER-MANAGER IN THE WAKE OF THE HEYSEL DISASTER. HE FOUND THE TRANSITION HARD AT FIRST. ON HIS FIRST DAY, HE FOUND HIMSELF STARING AT THE TELEPHONE, WAITING FOR IT TO RING.

If only there was a way that computers could talk to each other. I could use this time to discover the alarming political opinions of people I haven't seen since primary school.

HE WOULD WIN THE DOUBLE AT HIS FIRST ATTEMPT AND EVEN SCORED THE WINNING GOAL AT CHELSEA THAT SECURED THE LEAGUE TITLE ON THE LAST DAY OF THE SEASON.

You think I look happy now? Wait until I come back here in 25 year's time and fleece them for £50m for a busted Fernando Torres.

DALGLISH'S 1988 TEAM IS WIDELY REGARDED AS BEING THE BEST LIVERPOOL SIDE OF ALL TIME. THEY ENJOYED A 29-GAME UNBEATEN RUN AND WON THE LEAGUE BY THE DISTANCE OF GARY GILLESPIE'S NECK. ONLY A SHOCK DEFEAT TO WIMBLEDON IN THE FA CUP FINAL DENIED THEM ANOTHER DOUBLE.

It could have all been so different, if only you'd been able to score that penalty, Aldo.

For the last time, I'm... oh, forget it.

THE HILLSBOROUGH DISASTER CHANGED EVERYTHING: THE CLUB, THE CITY AND BRITISH FOOTBALL AS A WHOLE WOULD NEVER BE THE SAME AGAIN. FOR DALGLISH, WHO HAD ATTENDED THE FUNERALS OF SO MANY INNOCENT PEOPLE, THE EMOTIONAL TOLL WOULD BE HEAVY.

NO-ONE WOULD HAVE BLAMED HIM IF HE'D QUIT FOOTBALL THEN; INDEED, HE FOUGHT THE DESIRE TO DO SO. YET IT STILL CAME AS A HUGE SHOCK WHEN HE EVENTUALLY ANNOUNCED HIS RESIGNATION IN THE WAKE OF A CRAZY 4-4 DRAW WITH EVERTON IN THE FA CUP NEARLY TWO YEARS LATER. DALGLISH LEFT LIVERPOOL AS REIGNING CHAMPIONS; A SUCCESSION OF MANAGERS HAVE SINCE FAILED TO WIN A LEAGUE TITLE FOR LIVERPOOL.

GRAEME SOUNESS

ROY EVANS

GÉRARD HOULLIER

RAFA BENITEZ

ROY HODGSON

BRENDAN RODGERS

JÜRGEN KLOPP

UM, KENNY DALGLISH

YES, HIS RETURN IN 2011 FAILED TO RECAPTURE THE GLORY DAYS, BUT GIVEN THE ENDURING BOND BETWEEN DALGLISH AND THE CLUB, FEW FANS WERE WILLING TO JUDGE HIM TOO HARSHLY. NOT EVEN WHEN HE SIGNED CHARLIE ADAM.

ALFREDO DI STÉFANO

The discovery of one of the most influential players in the history of the game appears to have been a complete accident.

'My Alfredo likes playing football,' said Mrs Di Stéfano to a visiting electrician, gesturing towards her teenage son. 'Oh yeah?' he replied casually, hoisting up his tool belt, 'I play for River Plate; I'll take him along to training if you like?' Astonishingly, this wasn't a lie. It was also, arguably, more impressive than saying you'd once had a trial with Luton Town.

Di Stéfano would go on to become a forward whom Diego Maradona claims was even better than Pelé. Indeed, 'The Blond Arrow' had strength, pace, stamina, skill, a powerful shot and phenomenal heading ability, so maybe Maradona's endorsement wasn't just designed to antagonise the Brazilian legend.

Having built a formidable reputation at River, and then at the Colombian club Millonarios, Di Stéfano became the subject of an epic tussle between Barcelona and Real Madrid. Eventually, it was the Madrid club who prevailed, making him perhaps the most important player acquisition in their history. At the time of his arrival in 1953, Real Madrid hadn't won the Spanish championship in 20 years, but his 11 seasons there would yield eight league titles. However, it was in the nascent European Cup where his legend would really be forged. Real Madrid lifted the trophy in each of the first five years of the competition, with Di Stéfano scoring in each of the finals, a record that still stands today.

Di Stéfano's international fame did have some drawbacks though, and he was briefly kidnapped during a summer tour of Venezuela in 1963. As the news spread across the world, somewhere in Buenos Aires an electrician adjusted his overalls and nonchalantly informed his colleagues in the break room, 'I discovered him, you know.' Course you did, mate; course you did.

CARACAS, 1963

The National Liberation Army Front needs to show the people of Venezuela that we are serious about overthrowing the vile and corrupt government. Who did you kidnap?

This guy. He won't shut up.

You fool, that's...

THE BLOND ARROW

It's more mousey than blond, but yeah, hi.

THE BLOND ARROW TRAVELS THE WORLD, GETTING IN ADVENTURES, SCORING GOALS, AND RECOVERING PRECIOUS ARTEFACTS.

Start the engine! Start the engine!

FASTER THAN A SPEEDING POST-WAR CENTRE-HALF, HIS CHIEF WEAPONS ARE STRENGTH, STAMINA, HEADING, SHOOTING AND ELASTICITY.

Real Madrid saw him first!

Oh you fibber! FC Barcelona liked him ages before you lot!

THE BLOND ARROW LEADS AN INCREDIBLE DOUBLE LIFE; AN INSPIRATIONAL GOAL-MACHINE CAPABLE OF GREAT WARMTH AND HUMOUR BY DAY...

Yes, I scored four, but none of them would have been possible without you, my dear friend.

A DESPOTIC EGOIST ALSO BY DAY (THIS BEING A TIME BEFORE THE WIDESPREAD USE OF FLOODLIGHTS).

Who knows, maybe I'd have scored five if you didn't have a right foot like a frikkin' sandwich toaster.

EVEN IF YOU STOP HIM, THERE'S STILL HIS TRUSTY BAND OF SIDEKICKS.

I'm just not sure the outfit is necessary...

Stop complaining, Ferenc.

AND, LIKE ALL THE BEST SUPERHEROES, HE'S A POWERFUL PROPAGANDA TOOL FOR A FASCIST DICTATORSHIP.

NOT TODAY ¡BASTARDOS SOCIALISTAS!

So, we should probably release him then?

Yes, I think that's a— WHERE DID HE GO?!

EUSÉBIO

The Portugal side that reached the semi-finals of the 1966 World Cup is regarded by many in that country as the most talented in its history; even more so than the one that bored Europe into submission at Euro 2016. The driving force behind the 'Os Magriços' team was Eusébio da Silva Ferreira, the blisteringly fast virtuoso from Mozambique.

The core of the Portuguese national team around this time came from the East African nation, then a colony of Portugal. As well as Eusébio, there was the captain, Mário Coluna (who later became Mozambique's minister for sport), the forward Matateu, his brother Vicente Lucas (named by Pelé as the greatest defender he'd ever faced), left-back Hilário and goalkeeper Alberto da Costa Pereira. This generation of players could have made Mozambique World Cup contenders.

Eusébio's performances captivated England during the World Cup, where he won the golden boot with nine goals in six matches. His most crucial intervention came in the quarter-final against North Korea, who had successfully tested their long-range offensive capabilities with three quick goals within the first 25 minutes at Goodison Park. However, there was barely time to organise a celebratory procession of military hardware in Pyongyang before Eusébio had cracked a shot past the goalkeeper without breaking his stride. He'd add three more goals before the afternoon was out, as Portugal ran out 5–3 winners. The final result was a real kick in the balls for the North Korean leadership, but sadly it wasn't hard enough to render them infertile, which is why we now get to worry about the nuclear arsenal of a tubby virgin who looks like his mum cuts his hair in his kitchen.

Anyway, Eusébio . . .

A CONVERSATION IN A LISBON BARBER'S SHOP CHANGED THE COURSE OF A YOUNG EUSÉBIO'S LIFE. IT WAS THERE THAT BENFICA'S COACH, BÉLA GUTTMANN WAS TOLD OF AN EXTRAORDINARY TALENT PLAYING CLUB FOOTBALL IN MOZAMBIQUE.

I must visit South America immediately!

Um...

LEGENDARY COACH MONTHLY

GUTTMANN TRAVELLED TO AFRICA AND USED SUBTLE NEGOTIATION SKILLS TO CONVINCE EUSÉBIO'S MOTHER TO LET HER SON SIGN FOR BENFICA.

Eusébio, pack your bags.

BENFICA'S GREAT RIVALS, SPORTING, WERE FURIOUS, AS EUSÉBIO HAD BEEN PLAYING FOR THEIR FEEDER CLUB IN MOZAMBIQUE. AS THE LEGAL BATTLE UNFOLDED, GUTTMANN HID THE YOUNGSTER IN AN ALGARVE HOTEL AND TOLD HIM TO STAY IN HIS ROOM.

When will this torment end? Footballers aren't supposed to spend endless hours just loafing around hotels!

Bit to the left...

Oh yeah.

HE SCORED A HAT-TRICK ON HIS DEBUT, AGED 18, THEN HIT ANOTHER IN A FRIENDLY AGAINST SANTOS, IMPRESSING PELÉ.

Pelé predicts that Eusébio will become one of the finest goalkeepers in the world!

HE WON THE EUROPEAN CUP IN HIS FIRST FULL SEASON AT BENFICA, SCORING TWICE IN THE FINAL TO HELP BEAT REAL MADRID, 5-3. AFTERWARDS, THE ILLUSTRIOUS FERENC PUSKÁS GAVE HIM HIS SHIRT; A SYMBOLIC GESTURE THAT RECOGNISED EUSÉBIO'S ALREADY LOFTY STATUS.

You'll grow into it.

hm.

'THE BLACK PEARL' WOULD SCORE 41 GOALS IN 64 GAMES FOR PORTUGAL, INCLUDING NINE AT THE 1966 WORLD CUP. THEY REACHED THE SEMI-FINALS, BUT LOST TO ENGLAND. EUSÉBIO WAS MARKED OUT OF THE GAME BY NOBBY STILES; THE DEFEAT WOULD HAUNT HIM FOR YEARS.

HE WAS FAMED FOR HIS SPORTSMANSHIP, AS EVIDENCED WHEN HE CONGRATULATED ALEX STEPNEY AFTER THE MANCHESTER UNITED GOALKEEPER DENIED HIM A WINNING GOAL IN THE 1968 EUROPEAN CUP FINAL.

Well done. Really. Bra-vo!

Ow! You're ...hurting... me...!

UPON HIS DEATH IN 2014, COUNTLESS TRIBUTES ATTESTED TO HIS BRILLIANCE AS A PLAYER AND DECENCY AS A MAN. AMONG THE EULOGIES WAS ONE FROM JOSÉ MOURINHO, WHO TOLD OF HOW, AS A CHILD, HE WOULD RECEIVE YEARLY BIRTHDAY AND CHRISTMAS PRESENTS FROM THE GREAT MAN.

DR. EVA

ACTION FIGURE

UNDERSTANDS INSULTS IN FIVE LANGUAGES!

WON'T PUT UP WITH YOUR SHIT!

Did he send receipt?

GERD MÜLLER

On the occasion of Gerd Müller's fiftieth birthday, his old friend and teammate, Franz Beckenbauer, toasted the great man. 'Without Gerd Müller,' he roared, 'Bayern would probably still be in the wooden hut that was once our clubhouse.' It was a bit rough to blame him for that, especially at his birthday party, but Beckenbauer was right.

Müller scored 365 goals in 427 Bundesliga matches for the club and was instrumental in them winning three consecutive European Cups between 1974 and 1976. It was said that when it came to goal-scoring he was gifted with a '*fingersputzengefuhl*', or sixth sense. However, his potency in front of goal was more down to an absolute dedication to training, learning and improvement, than it was some innate knack for knowing where the ball would land; although, yes, it may have helped that he left the penalty area about as regularly as Paul Breitner got a haircut.

Gerhard's talents extended beyond just planting the ball in the net. At the 1974 World Cup, he was named as West Germany's emergency goalkeeper; a role he took typically seriously. In fact, he managed to injure a finger while playing in goal during a training session, meaning he had to wear a bandage for the group match against East Germany.

Crucial playing talent wouldn't be put at such risk these days, nor would they be likely to record a cheesy pop record, as Müller also did in 1969: 'Dann macht es bumm' ('Then it goes boom'). Footballers generally seem less inclined to make records in the modern era. Being a grime MC doesn't count, unless it includes an oompah band, or Chris Waddle spitting rhymes.

THE NOTED PENTATHLETE, HEIDE ROSENDAHL, WASN'T HAPPY ABOUT THE PROSPECT OF GERD MÜLLER BEING AWARDED WEST GERMAN SPORTS PERSONALITY OF THE YEAR.

All he does is hang around the penalty area and score goals.

AS YOU WOULD EXPECT FROM SOMEONE WHO WAS BOTH EUROPEAN AND BESPECTACLED, THIS WAS AN INCISIVE OBSERVATION, FOR MÜLLER WAS A MACHINE, CAPABLE OF SCORING WITH EVERY PART OF HIS BAVARIAN BEER KEG BODY.

SHIN! KNEE! NECK! HIP! TIT! BELL!

MÜLLER WAS FAMOUS FOR HIS ENORMOUS THUNDER THIGHS AND ATTRIBUTED HIS PHENOMENAL STRENGTH TO HIS MOTHER'S POTATO SALAD.

That's right, Gerhard; eat it up...

Eat it all up.

'MEIN KLEINER CHERUB' BAVARIA'S FATTEST CHILD CONTEST. CASH PRIZE

HE BEGAN HIS CAREER AT 1861 NÖRDLINGEN, BUT SIGNED FOR BAYERN MUNICH IN 1964. THEIR COACH, ZLATKO CAJKOVSKI WAS SCEPTICAL AT FIRST, QUIPPING: 'WHAT AM I SUPPOSED TO DO WITH A WEIGHTLIFTER?'

Actually, that is quite handy.

HE SOON SAW MÜLLER'S BENEFIT, AS THE STRIKER BEGAN JUST HANGING AROUND THE PENALTY AREA AND SCORING GOALS AT AN ASTONISHING RATE. IT WAS A GLASWEGIAN NEWSPAPER THAT GAVE HIM THE MEMORABLE NICKNAME, 'DER BOMBER'.

Hmn. This nickname. Might be a bit insensitive. What else have you got?

Golditz; The Alt-Right Footer; Fruit Corner Fritz; Joseph Goalballs; Gerd, Gerd, Gerd is the Word, Everybody's Heard About the Gerd; and The Final Solution.

Der Bomber it is then.

HIS RECORD AT INTERNATIONAL LEVEL WAS JUST AS IMPRESSIVE, SCORING A FREAKISH 68 GOALS IN 62 MATCHES. HIS MOST IMPORTANT STRIKE CAME IN THE 1974 WORLD CUP FINAL, WITH A TYPICAL TURN AND SCUFF PAST HOLLAND'S JONGBLOED.

I'm rooted here.

AFTER SCORING 398 FOR BAYERN, HE TOOK HIS SIXTH SENSE FOR GOAL-SCORING TO FORT LAUDERDALE STRIKERS AND THE RICHES OF THE NASL.

I see bread, people.

HE WAS NO LESS PROLIFIC IN THE STATES, WHERE HE TOOK GLEEFUL ADVANTAGE OF THE NASL'S 35-YARD OFFSIDE LINE.

Surprised he strayed that far away from the goal, right?

LET IT GO, HEIDE; LET IT GO.

ZINEDINE ZIDANE

As a coach, Zinedine Zidane exudes a quiet authority, seemingly more placid and less prone to self-destructive moments of violence than he was as a player. At the time of writing, he has just led Real Madrid to back-to-back Champions League final victories and he hasn't once attempted to crush anyone's breastplate with the top of his head. Zidane's success appears to be partly based on the awe his reputation inspires. While some of his predecessors at Madrid, such as Rafa Benítez, may have been more experienced as coaches, none was never able to command the respect that comes with having your face projected onto the Arc de Triomphe after scoring two goals in a World Cup final.

In the period between the 1998 and 2002 World Cups, France were the most feared team in the world. Central to that was the explosive midfield presence of Zidane; a muscular, monk-like figure, whose incomparable first touch, hawkish vision and ability to crack in a volley from 30 yards also made him an invaluable asset at club level, most notably for Juventus and Real Madrid.

The French-Algerian playmaker grew up in the tough northern suburbs of Marseille, where he learned to play the game in the main square of his local housing estate. This was also where he learned how to look after himself and not back down when some bigmouth started trash-talking his family.

Zizou's range of skills were captured in the beautiful film, *Zidane: A 21st Century Portrait*, a 92-minute study of his performance for Real Madrid in a La Liga match against Villarreal in 2005. His delicate touches, sharp turns and physical dominance* are set to the haunting guitar melodies of Mogwai, an artistic concept that should be applied to other football personalities ('Hi, we're Mumford & Sons and we're here for the recording of *Michael Owen: Interesting!*'). Seeing as Zidane has now moved into the next phase of his career, it is perhaps time for the filmmakers to consider a sequel.

---

* SPOILER ALERT: he gets sent off at the end after getting involved in a brawl.

ZIDANE

A 21st CENTURY PORTRAIT
PART I: THE DUGOUT YEARS

- Don't call Gareth 'English'

GRIM NEWS NOTIFICATION

BRONZER · MAHOGANY

'OH GOD, WHAT NOW?' ALERT.

RONALDO

To see him in full flight was a beautiful, terrifying vision. His devastating pace and agility was aesthetically countered by the round shoulders and uncompromising dentistry of a deranged farmhand. Ronaldo Luís Nazário de Lima, known to billions as simply 'Ronaldo', and then later as 'No, the Brazilian one', was a colossus. If it wasn't for the terrible knee injuries that blighted his career, he would unquestionably be spoken about in the same breath as luminaries such as Pelé, Maradona, Messi and, confusingly, Ronaldo.

By the age of 20, Ronaldo had already been voted World Player of the Year. He'd scored 30 goals in his first season at PSV Eindhoven, at the age of just 17. A record transfer to Barcelona followed in 1996, where he plundered 47 goals in 49 matches *and* still found time to fly back to Rio for an unsanctioned trip to the Mardi Gras. *O Fenômeno*'s spell at Barcelona lasted just one season, with Inter paying another record fee, of $27 million, to sign him. If he wanted, he was now rich enough to have hosted the Rio Carnival in his own garage.

It was at Inter where he really established himself as one of the greats. Between 1997 and 1999, when a cruciate ligament injury kept him sidelined for nearly two years, Ronaldo became the complete forward; creating more chances for teammates, while continuing to terrorise defences with his supersonic charges towards goal. He was football's answer to Jonah Lomu: a thunder-thighed blur, scattering opponents in his path. For a while, they even had the same haircut: shaved all over with a merkin-like tuft at the front.

By rights, Ronaldo should have won the World Cup in 1998. Still only 21, he was player of the tournament, scoring four goals and setting up three to earn Brazil a place in the final against hosts France. Mystery still surrounds the events in the hours leading up the final, but what is known is that after Ronaldo suffered a convulsive fit, his name was replaced on the starting team-sheet by that of Edmundo. However, as the world's media processed this announcement, the decision was then reversed and short straws were pulled to determine who would tell Edmundo. A ghostlike Ronaldo drifted through the game and Brazil lost 3–0.

Redemption came four years later, when Ronaldo lined up alongside Rivaldo and Ronaldinho to help Brazil win their nation's fifth World Cup. He'd barely played in two years, and missed the entire qualification campaign, but he contributed eight goals in Japan and South Korea, including the two decisive strikes in the final against Germany.

At club level, Ronaldo was on the move again; this time to be recruited as one of Real Madrid president Florentino Pérez's famous Galácticos. Pérez had sold Real Madrid's training ground to the local government for €480 million, allowing them to clear their debts, build a replacement training complex (at a fraction of the cost), and splash out on the world's top playing talent. It was the kind of arrangement that helped make Real Madrid loved universally. In came Luís Figo and Zinedine Zidane for record transfer fees, followed in 2002 by Ronaldo. His best moment in a Real Madrid shirt came in his first season at the club, with a hat-trick in the second leg of their Champions League quarter-final triumph against Manchester United at Old Trafford. Ronaldo was substituted after 80 minutes and was given a standing ovation by both sets of supporters. It seemed everyone enjoyed watching Manchester United get steamrollered.

Real Madrid lost to Juventus at the semi-final stage, but won the league title, and the following year Ronaldo finished as La Liga's top scorer. However, it was to be his last great season. Injuries became more frequent and he struggled to keep his weight in check. Even the presence of Fabio Capello barking at him to lay off the Kit-Kats didn't seem to help. Eventually he moved on to AC Milan, where he played sporadically for two seasons, before returning to Brazil with Corinthians in 2009.

An emotional Ronaldo announced his retirement in early 2011, the cumulative pain of so many injuries finally becoming too much to bear. However, it was his performances in the first phase of his career, particularly at Inter, that linger in the memory. A burst of speed, more dummies than Mothercare, a goalkeeper in a lurid mid-nineties top providing as much resistance as a wet square of toilet tissue, the ball in the net. His goal against Lazio in the 1998 UEFA Cup final was a prime example of the genre.

THEN IT'S INTO A PSYCHEDELIC VORTEX FOR A SUMMARY OF RONALDO'S WORLD CUP RECORD.

1998 PLAYER OF THE TOURNAMENT, BUT SUFFERS A SEIZURE JUST HOURS BEFORE THE FINAL. HE PLAYS, BUT IS A SHELL OF THE PLAYER WHO'D LIT UP THE PREVIOUS MONTH. CONSPIRACY THEORIES ABOUND.

And we're sure no-one will notice that it's just Paul Warhurst in a rubber mask?

DESPITE BEING IN AN ALTERED STATE, LUCA VOWS TO NEVER AGAIN EAT CRAB PASTE BEFORE A BIG GAME.

What a turn-up for the books. If I'd known **this** was going to happen I'd have only had one dinner!

2002 RESURRECTION! TWO GOALS TO WIN THE FINAL FOR BRAZIL, THE GOLDEN BOOT AND A BOLD NEW LOOK TO START A TREND.

2006 SPEARHEADS BRAZIL'S ATTACK WITH ADRIANO, BUT EVEN THEIR INNOVATIVE HIGH-CARB DIET CANNOT PREVENT A QUARTER-FINAL EXIT.

AND HERE'S RONALDO IN THE SCI-FI WORLD OF 2017. HE'S NO DOUBT CONTEMPLATING THE PEACEFUL UTOPIA HUMANITY HAS CREATED, AS HE COMPETES ON THE PROFESSIONAL POKER CIRCUIT.

After this, **every**one's going to want to look like a twat!

A straight flush. Hand over that filthy lucre... lucre... lucre... lu

'uca... Luca... Luca... Luca. Wake up, man. The game's over.

Whu?...What happened?

We lost 3-0. We just couldn't cope with Ronaldo.

Ronaldo!

That hair cut! I must warn him!

Hey! Ronaldo! Wait!

Heh, did you guys see Marchegiani? I thought he was gonna poo himself.

Oh, hi, Luca. Um, what is it?

Nothing. Forget it.

JOHAN CRUYFF

2016 was a dangerous time to be a cultural icon. Whilst men and women of a certain age were still processing the loss of David Bowie, the news broke that Johan Cruyff had passed away too.

Cruyff was more than just a football player or a coach; he was a philosopher and a visionary. Always principled, often difficult, he thrived on conflict and argument. Sometimes he was deliberately vague. 'If I wanted you to understand it,' he once sniffed, 'I would have explained it better.' Presumably this famous quote was delivered during a press conference, rather than a team talk. A simple way of discovering whether you are as charismatic as Johan Cruyff is to try repeating this phrase to a loved one during your next disagreement about how to load the dishwasher correctly.* Chicken.

Cruyff cut a distinctive figure as a player. Limbs as long and skinny as the cigarettes he chain-smoked, his deep-set, intelligent eyes were bordered by shadows; even his hair was thin. Looking like a spare Ramone wouldn't have been enough for him to endure in the memory though. 'Without Cruyff,' said Rinus Michels, his manager at Ajax, Barcelona and Holland, 'I have no team.'

Few players are innovative enough to have a move named after them. There's Antonín Panenka's chipped penalty manoeuvre, of course; and in France, a powerful acrobatic volley is sometimes called *'Une Papinade'*, in honour of Jean-Pierre Papin, but it's the Cruyff Turn that most resonates (Andrei Kanchelskis may also have been able to patent the trick of running with the ball, then stopping and standing on it, if it hadn't been completely pointless). The turn was the result of a naturally inquisitive desire to experiment. In some ways he was football's answer to Bowie; both of them were willing to push boundaries and able to look sharp in a trench coat.

---

* Cutlery facing downwards.

JOHAN CRUYFF WAS THE GREATEST EUROPEAN FOOTBALLER OF ALL TIME AND FOLLOWED IN THE TRADITION OF PRODIGIOUS DUTCH ARTISTS.

BRUEGEL

REMBRANDT

VAN GOGH

WHEN THINKING OF CRUYFF, YOU INSTINCTIVELY RECALL HIS FAMOUS TURN AT THE 1974 WORLD CUP. IT WAS A MOVE THAT PRODUCED GASPS OF AWE AND LEFT SWEDEN'S JAN OLSSON AS BAFFLED AS A MAN WHO FINDS HIMSELF WAKING FROM A TRANCE, NEXT TO A SMIRKING HYPNOTIST.

Let's hear it for Jan! What a great sport. Jan!

WHILE THE TURN MAY SEEM STANDARD TO A GENERATION OF FANS RAISED ON A DIET OF YOUTUBE COMPILATIONS OF SICK SKILLZ...

kid fills out tax return by volleying football against keyboard

... IN 1974 IT WAS AS SURPRISING AS SEEING ONE OF YOUR PETS DIAGNOSE THE PROBLEM WITH YOUR IMMERSION HEATER.

Yeah, you just had a loose connection, mate.

Also, someone had blocked a pipe with a half-eaten sparrow, so that's a bit of a mystery.

CRUYFF EXEMPLIFIED THE NEW, CONFIDENT NETHERLANDS. HE WAS AWARE OF HIS VALUE AND FOUGHT HARD TO SECURE A WAGE TO MATCH THAT WORTH. HE ONCE SAID: 'WHEN MY CAREER ENDS, I CANNOT GO TO THE BAKER AND SAY, "I'M JOHAN CRUYFF, GIVE ME SOME BREAD"'. HE PROBABLY COULD HAVE, THOUGH.

I'm—

Oh, we know who you are, Mr Cruyff. I hope you don't mind, but we took the liberty of baking a bagel-eyed statue for you. On the house, naturally.

JOHAN CRUST

AN EXAMPLE OF HIS PRINCIPLED, SINGLE-MINDED ATTITUDE CAME WHEN HE REFUSED TO WEAR THE FAMOUS THREE STRIPES OF ADIDAS ON HOLLAND'S 1974 STRIP. A BESPOKE KIT, WITH JUST TWO STRIPES WAS MADE FOR CRUYFF. NO LOGO!

I refuse to be a walking billboard for a multi-national corporation. Especially when I already have a sponsorship deal with Puma.

That's Puma.

Puma.

HE'D JOINED AJAX'S YOUTH TEAM AT THE AGE OF 12. THEY'D BEEN PERSUADED TO SIGN HIM BY HIS MOTHER, WHO WAS A CLEANER AT THE CLUB'S OFFICES.

Nice little set up you've got here. It'd be a shame if it became incrementally dusty.

Christ, calm down.

It's the junior team. You only need to fill out a form.

THE ADOLESCENT JOHAN ACTUALLY PREFERRED BASEBALL, BUT WAS ENCOURAGED TO PURSUE A FOOTBALL CAREER BY HIS MOTHER. MARCO VAN BASTEN WOULD LATER THEORISE THAT CRUYFF WAS 'TECHNICALLY PERFECT' BY THE TIME HE WAS 20, ALLOWING HIM TO FOCUS ON LOFTIER, TACTICAL ISSUES.

What if one player on each team wore a big leather glove and the goalkeeper was given a long, hard stick to beat away shots with?

Let it go, son.

HE DEFIED CONVENTION THROUGHOUT HIS CAREER, FAMOUSLY OPTING TO WEAR THE NUMBER 14, RATHER THAN THE REGULAR 1-11. IN THE MODERN ERA, PLAYERS ARE FREE TO WEAR ANY COMBINATION OF NUMBERS, BUT BACK IN THE SEVENTIES THIS WAS AGAIN 'CAT FIXING CARBURETTOR' TERRITORY.

Yeah, it just needed the main mixture adjustment screw tightening, love.

Also, it was full of tiny bits of smelly gravel, so I think you might have a ghost.

AFTER WINNING A HAT-TRICK OF EUROPEAN CUPS WITH AJAX, HE MOVED TO BARCELONA. THEY WERE IN THE RELEGATION ZONE WHEN HE JOINED, BUT ENDED THE SEASON AS CHAMPIONS. CRUYFF FURTHER ENDEARED HIMSELF TO THE BARÇA FANS BY NAMING HIS SON 'JORDI' AFTER THE PATRON SAINT OF BOTH CATALONIA AND UNDERACHIEVING CHILDREN.

Hey, is that Ziggy Marley? Jordi Cruyff here. Fancy coming over to watch some Charlie Sheen films with Sean Lennon and me?

IN FAIRNESS, FEW COULD HAVE FOLLOWED IN THE FOOTSTEPS OF SUCH A GIFTED FATHER. ONCE JOHAN'S PLAYING DAYS WERE OVER, HE MOVED INTO COACHING AND BECAME THAT RAREST OF BEASTS: A GREAT PLAYER WHO WENT ON TO BE A GREAT MANAGER.

Hey, is that Hristo Stoichkov? Diego Maradona here. Fancy coming over to watch videos of Edgar Davids' Barnet with Lothar Matthäus and me?

CRUYFF WAS A FIRM BELIEVER IN INDIVIDUAL COACHING SESSIONS, WHICH HE USED THROUGHOUT HIS MANAGERIAL CAREER TO EXCELLENT EFFECT.

One...one...ONE...

HNNNG

ROMARIO

Bah! I'll just pay for the blasted liposuction.

Woo-hoo!

HE GUIDED AJAX TO VICTORY IN THE EUROPEAN CUP WINNERS' CUP IN 1987, BUT LEFT FOR BARCELONA A YEAR LATER AFTER A DISAGREEMENT ABOUT MONEY. A VEXED CRUYFF DESCRIBED AJAX PRESIDENT **TON HARMSEN** OF HAVING 'A GROCER'S MENTALITY'.

CONGRATULATION'S AJAX EUROPEAN CHAMPION'S

You see, this is exactly what I'm talking about.

WHILST AT AJAX, HE'D ALSO BROUGHT THROUGH A NEW GENERATION OF DUTCH STARS, SUCH AS DENNIS BERGKAMP, MARCO VAN BASTEN AND FRANK RIJKAARD. CRUYFF ALSO PUT INTO PLACE THE TACTICAL FRAMEWORK THAT WOULD BENEFIT FUTURE MANAGERS AND HELP AJAX TO WIN THE CHAMPIONS LEAGUE IN 1995.

Of course, this wouldn't have been possible without the vision of Johan Cruyff...

~ oh for...

Can we just have **one day** when we don't talk about that man?

AT BARCELONA, HIS EXALTED 'DREAM TEAM' WON FOUR CONSECUTIVE LA LIGA TITLES AND THE CLUB'S FIRST EUROPEAN CHAMPIONS CUP. HIS REAL LEGACY HAD BEEN SOWN BACK IN 1979, WHEN HE HAD HELPED TO SET UP **LA MASIA**, A YOUTH ACADEMY THAT WOULD DEVELOP PLAYERS OF THE ILK OF XAVI, INIESTA AND MESSI.

What are you using that old farmhouse for, President Núñez?

Good question. We thought we'd turn it into a boutique restaurant, specialising in cured meats, artisan cheeses and charging gullible tourists a fortune for tiny servings of food. Market it as 'tapas', sit back and get rich.

Well, you **could** do that...

Or, you could make it into a production line for players so talented that it would establish FC Barcelona as a genuine football powerhouse and global brand.

Change of plan, lads.

JAMÓN CRUYFF

IN LATER YEARS, AFTER HE'D STEPPED BACK FROM COACHING, HE CONTINUED TO PRESENT NEW IDEAS, CAPTIVATING FOOTBALL FANS AND CHALLENGING COMMON THINKING.

What if the football pitch was inside all of us the whole time?

Mind. Blown.

CRUYFF SUCCUMBED TO LUNG CANCER AT THE AGE OF 68, IN EARLY 2016. HIS DEATH RESULTED IN AN OUTPOURING OF HEARTFELT TRIBUTES, RECOGNISING THE INDELIBLE MARK HE HAD LEFT ON FOOTBALL AND WIDER SOCIETY. THE LOSS OF SUCH AN INTELLIGENT HUMAN BEING ALSO SEEMED TO BE THE THING THAT FINALLY PUSHED THE WORLD OVER THE EDGE.

Yeah, two litres of super-strength cider please. I'm not doing this sober any more.

PELÉ

It was while watching a particularly dull game in Australia's A-League that my friend's nine-year-old son suddenly announced to his father and me, 'Pelé was overrated'. Before allowing time for that statement to settle, he followed it up with, 'Neymar is better'. One of the drawbacks of living in a modern society, packed with fun things like Netflix, flat whites and zero-hour contracts, is that it's frowned upon to strike a child, especially if it's not your own, especially in public. Yes, even in Australia.

While my open palm quivered in the air, I paused to reflect upon his outrageous statement; perhaps my young friend wasn't talking utter fucking *bull*shit. After all, if you're nine, the only footage you'll have seen of Pelé will have been limited to clips on YouTube: a grainy yellow sprite drifting past pedestrian defenders and missing shots from the halfway line. Other than that, Pelé's just the old prune who turns up at FIFA events looking a bit like Grampa Simpson.

What my precocious companion was missing was the context of Pelé's achievements; the fact that when he broke onto the world football scene in 1958, Pelé was a skinny 17-year-old kid, ripping up the best defences in the world, doing things that no one had seen before. The first of his two goals in the final involved flicking the ball over the head of a Swedish defender and finishing with an unstoppable volley into the bottom corner. His second goal saw him score with a looping header from his impressively angular flat-top. This range of scoring goals would become a feature of his career: left foot, right foot, free-kick, dribble, short range, long range, flat-top; no wonder he scored 1,283 of them.

After that World Cup, the Brazilian government declared him a national treasure, in a bid to prevent him being snapped up by any European clubs. So he stayed at Santos, the club he'd joined as a 15-year-old. They made sure they got the most out of their newly famous starlet, embarking on a series of money-spinning world tours. On one such tour to Africa in 1969, legend has it that a ceasefire was declared in Nigeria's civil war, so that Federal and Rebel troops could watch Pelé play in Lagos. Whilst this story is difficult to verify, you don't see *Neymar* signing up to wow the warring factions in Syria, do you? Obviously not, it would be really dangerous and quite irresponsible.

Pelé was football's first truly global star. As well as physically travelling to all corners of the planet, his reputation grew at a time when televisions became commonplace, broadcasting his skills to the living rooms of people who couldn't make it to Lagos for a tour match. The players of previous generations had earned their fame through eyewitness accounts, newspaper reports or via the images created by the words of radio commentators. When your massive new wooden TV set only picked up three stations, and one of them is showing a lithe Brazilian lad motoring through visibly terrified defences, it's little wonder that Pelé became a household name.

Ah yes, the nickname. He was, of course, named Edson (after Thomas Edison), and nicknamed 'Dico' by his family. He remains unclear about the origins of the nickname Pelé, but he has said it may have been given to him by his classmates, as he used to mispronounce the name of the Vasco da Gama goalkeeper Bile as 'Pile'. However, his vagueness about the whole situation leads one to think that its origins are something far more embarrassing and probably disgusting. When he joined Santos, he was called 'Gasolina' (Gasoline). Given his fondness for a commercial opportunity, you'd imagine he'd have stuck with that one; it being far easier to shill for a petrol company than whatever filth a 'Pelé' is.

Amongst his countless achievements, Pelé would go on to win three World Cups, the only player to do so. Admittedly, fitness standards were lower and games were played at a slower pace, so maybe Neymar would score that many goals in such conditions, maybe my friend's son does have a point? Then again, he did also ask whether the stadium's food kiosk sold croissants, so it's hard to tell.

DESPITE HIS STATUS AS THE GREATEST FOOTBALLER OF ALL TIME, THERE IS OFTEN A LACK OF WARMTH TOWARDS PELÉ. THE PERCEPTION IS THAT HE'S A COMPANY MAN, WHOSE CLICHÉ-LADEN DICTION — COMBINING BLAND RELIGIOSITY WITH FOOTBALL JARGON — CONTRADICTS THE EYE-POPPING TALENTS HE DISPLAYED AS A PLAYER. FOR EXAMPLE, AFTER SCORING HIS THOUSANDTH PROFESSIONAL GOAL, HE DECLARED TO A MOB OF JOURNALISTS...

Let us protect the needy little children. For the love of God, the Brazilian people can't forget the children.

Children. Right. Gotcha.

God.

BUT BY THE TIME THE 1970 WORLD CUP ROLLED AROUND, HE WAS A GLOBAL ICON. A SURVEY HELD LATER THAT DECADE REVEALED THAT PELÉ WAS THE SECOND MOST RECOGNISABLE 'BRAND' IN EUROPE, AFTER COCA-COLA.

Pelé

I'LL PUT MY NAME TO LITERALLY ANYTHING

WHATEVER THAT MEANS. HE'D RETIRED FROM INTERNATIONAL FOOTBALL AFTER THE 1966 WORLD CUP, WHERE HE'D BEEN SUBJECTED TO MORE FOUL PLAY THAN HE WAS DURING 'ESCAPE TO VICTORY'.

That's for saying I can't hide out in Brazil after the war, idiot.

Pelé did not sign up for this.

HE ANNOUNCED WITH FURY THAT HE'D PLAYED HIS LAST EVER WORLD CUP MATCH, A PROCLAMATION THAT TURNED OUT TO BE AS BOLLOCKS AS MOST OF HIS OTHER PREDICTIONS.

Pelé foresees that this year's World Cup will be won by....

David Bowie's Tin Machine!

HIS RETURN TO THE NATIONAL TEAM SAW BRAZIL QUALIFY EASILY FOR THE WORLD CUP. THE SQUAD ARRIVED IN MEXICO THREE WEEKS EARLY, TO ACCLIMATISE. THE LOCAL PUBLIC ADORED THE BRAZILIANS, BUT SECURITY WAS TIGHTENED AMID RUMOURS THAT PELÉ WOULD BE THE VICTIM OF A KIDNAPPING ATTEMPT.

Who the hell is this?

You said get the second most recognised brand name in Europe.

TEAM MORALE WAS HIGH, AND PELÉ INSTIGATED GROUP PRAYER MEETINGS, WHICH TOOK PLACE EVERY DAY DURING DINNER. EVEN THOSE WHO WEREN'T RELIGIOUS WERE COMPELLED TO PARTICIPATE.

Gather round everyone! Hey, teammate, put down that plate of food and fetch my guitar, would you?

God.

That's the spirit!

THEY BEGAN WITH A 4-1 WIN AGAINST CZECHOSLOVAKIA. PELÉ WAS ON THE SCORESHEET, BUT THE HIGHLIGHT WAS HIS BOLD EFFORT FROM THE HALFWAY LINE, WHICH DRIFTED WIDE, AGONISINGLY. BEFORE THE GAME, THE CZECH COACH, JOZEF MARKO, CALLED PELÉ 'A SPENT FORCE'. THIS PERFORMANCE MAY HAVE CHANGED HIS OPINION.

Pfft. I suppose he'll add that one to his billion-goal tally, along with ones he's scored in his garden and whilst playing Subbuteo.

AFTERWARDS, A JOURNALIST ASKED HIM IF HE HAD ATTEMPTED THE SHOT TO PROVE HE WASN'T SHORT-SIGHTED, AS CLAIMED BY THE FORMER BRAZIL COACH, JOÃO SALDANHA.

No, my friend. The goalkeeper was off his line and God helped me to see the opportunity to bring joy to the people of Brazil, to the childr-

OK, forget it.

NEXT CAME A 1-0 WIN AGAINST ENGLAND, DURING WHICH PELÉ WAS DENIED A GOAL BY A FAMOUS FLYING SAVE FROM GORDON BANKS. THE RESULT SHOWED THAT BRAZIL WERE A GENUINE FORCE, AS ENGLAND WERE REIGNING WORLD CHAMPIONS AND STRONGLY FANCIED. YES, ENGLAND.

VICTORIES AGAINST ROMANIA AND PERU THEN SET UP A SEMI-FINAL AGAINST THE DREADED URUGUAY AND PAINFUL MEMORIES OF BRAZIL'S HUMILIATION AT THEIR HANDS IN 1950. THAT DAY, THE NINE-YEAR OLD PELÉ HAD TOLD HIS FATHER THAT BRAZIL WOULDN'T HAVE LOST IF HE'D BEEN PLAYING. AGAIN, THIS WAS PATENTLY BOLLOCKS.

Heh, the past is a foreign country, eh, Alf?

If by that you mean the food tastes funny and you can't trust no one, then yes, Gordon; it is.

Out of the way, kid.

A CLEARLY SPOOKED BRAZIL FELL BEHIND TO AN EARLY, CALAMITOUS, GOAL. PELÉ WAS AGAIN THE FOCUS FOR BRUTAL TREATMENT, BUT UNLIKE IN '66, HE RESPONDED IN KIND, AT ONE POINT BRAINING A URUGUAYAN, WITHOUT PUNISHMENT

Pelé predicts a mild concussion and a headache in the morning.

He got one right!

A CLODOALDO EQUALISER AND A HALF-TIME TALKING TO FROM MARIO ZAGALLO SET BRAZIL UP FOR A MORE CONTROLLED SECOND HALF AND A 3-1 WIN. AGAIN, IT WAS THE IMPROVISATION OF PELÉ THAT WOULD PROVIDE THE GAMES LASTING IMAGE, AS HE AUDACIOUSLY DUMMIED URUGUAY'S GOALKEEPER, MAZURKIEWICZ, BEFORE DRAGGING A SHOT JUST WIDE.

Another one for the scrapbook, eh, Edson. A billion and two goals now, is it?

Why are you still even here?

AND SO TO A FINAL AGAINST ITALY IN THE SHIMMERING AFTERNOON HEAT OF THE AZTECA STADIUM. IT WAS BRAZIL WHO STRUCK FIRST, PELÉ RISING ABOVE BURGNICH TO PLANT A HEADER PAST ALBERTOSI.

ITALY FOUGHT BACK AND DREW LEVEL WHEN BONINSEGNA TOOK ADVANTAGE OF A MISPLACED BACKHEEL FROM CLODOALDO, BUT THEY WILTED UNDER BRAZIL'S RELENTLESS PRESSURE. GOALS FROM GÉRSON AND JAIRZINHO PUT THEM OUT OF REACH BEFORE PELÉ LAID THE BALL OFF TO CARLOS ALBERTO TO FINISH THE MOST BEAUTIFUL TEAM GOAL EVER SCORED AT A WORLD CUP.

* COUGH Argentina v Serbia & Montenegro, 2006 COUGH *

ALTITUDE ALTIT

RIDICULOUS KICK-OFF TIME

CINZANO   CINZAN

IT WAS A GOAL THAT WOULD BE REPLAYED COUNTLESS TIMES AND WAS A FITTING WAY FOR PELÉ TO BOW OUT OF INTERNATIONAL FOOTBALL, AS A WORLD CHAMPION FOR THE THIRD TIME. IT WAS A HAPPY ENDING THAT EVERYONE COULD ENJOY.

That was amazing. We should let the hostage watch the trophy presentation.

Um...

Oh Jesus.

What did you do, Ernesto?

What did you do?

MIDDLE MEN

The modern midfielder is a perfect specimen; an inverted triangle of muscle and sinew. The data collected from those bras they all wear now reveals the incredible distances they cover each game. You'd be exhausted if you travelled that far by bus. It's amazing how they achieve such levels of stamina by consuming nothing but protein snacks and a copy of *Men's Health*.

The term 'midfielder' encompasses a variety of roles. There is the playmaker, who used to be recognisable by unrolled socks and an untucked shirt. Such was Glenn Hoddle's dedication to this look, it sometimes seemed that he was pulling the strings in the Tottenham midfield wearing a pristine white summer dress. When combined with leadership skills, these players are transformed into midfield generals: those who can pass and point.

Then there are the wide players. Once their job was simply to find some space and ping a cross towards the lummox of a centre-forward who'd charged upfield like a startled cow. Now they are expected to take on additional defensive responsibilities, putting in extra work for no extra pay; the ruinous effects of the erosion of the trade-union movement impacting upon a generation of downtrodden, impoverished wingers.

For those of a more defensive disposition, there is the holding role: the job of the person who likes to get in the way, to frustrate the opposition; like a slow-walker on a rush-hour pavement. And if that all sounds a bit too complicated, there's always the room for the bog-standard workhorse. Even the sophisticated modern game needs players who can barge people over and skulk off, re-adjusting the captain's armband.

GHEORGHE HAGI

By rights, Paul Bodin should have been congratulated. The Welsh left-back had thundered a penalty against the crossbar in the second half of a vital World Cup qualifier against Romania, with the scores level at 1–1. Had Bodin's effort been a few centimetres lower, it would probably have been Wales who'd have gone to USA '94, robbing the world of the spectacle of the most exciting team of the tournament. However, the Cardiff crowd groaned, Romania rallied and snatched the game with a late winner from Florin Răducioiu, and Wales fans never forgave Bodin. Not even the consolation of him drilling home a perfectly competent spot-kick for Swindon Town just three days later could lift their spirits.

Opening the scoring that night was Gheorghe Hagi, Romania's mercurial number 10. The captain had cut inside and hit a weak left-footed skidder that had squirmed under the considerable body of Wales' legendary Neville Southall. At this stage of his career, Hagi was playing his football for Brescia in Serie B, having been sold by Real Madrid after two indifferent seasons at the Bernabéu. Previously, he had impressed with Steaua Bucharest, where his flair as an advanced playmaker had helped them progress to the semi-finals of the European Cup in 1988, and the final a year later. There is as much chance of a Romanian club side reaching the Champions League Final now as there is of Paul Bodin playing in it.

Hagi's performances at the World Cup earned him a move to Barcelona, and then, in 1996, he switched to Galatasaray. It was in Turkey where he enjoyed the most successful spell of his career, winning four consecutive league titles and, in 2000, the UEFA Cup against Arsenal. Typically, the surly Hagi wasn't on the field when victory was secured in a penalty shoot-out, as he'd been sent off in extra-time for clouting Tony Adams. However, on this occasion he could feel hard done by, as Adams had taken three swings at him with his elbows before Hagi landed one gentle retaliatory blow on his back. But Hagi will be best remembered for his performances for Romania during a sweltering American summer; and particularly for a vintage encounter with Argentina. Thank you, Paul Bodin!

THERE WAS A TIME WHEN IT WAS COMPULSORY FOR EVERY TOWN, CITY, COUNTRY OR REGION TO HAVE ITS OWN 'MARADONA'. FOR EXAMPLE, THERE WAS...

THE MARADONA OF WEST ANTARCTICA

THE MARADONA OF THE ADELAIDE DISTRICT OVER-75s LAWN BOWLS SCENE.

THE MARADONA OF THE SHROPSHIRE CARPET AND FLOOR TILE RETAIL INDUSTRY.

AND, BEST OF ALL, THE MARADONA OF THE CARPATHIANS, GHEORGHE HAGI.

WITH ROMANIA SET TO FACE ARGENTINA ON A SUN-DRENCHED PASADENA AFTERNOON, HAGI WOULD CUP UP AGAINST THE ORIGINAL MARADONA: MARADONA! HOWEVER, EL DIEGO HAD RECENTLY REVEALED HIMSELF TO BE THE MARADONA OF FAILING DRUG TESTS, SO WAS FORCED TO WATCH THE GAME FROM THE COMMENTARY BOX.

That looked like a clean tackle to me, Diego...

Cleaner than my urine after a perfectly legal energising supplement, if that's possible, which it isn't. Gary.

ROMANIA HAD STARTED THE WORLD CUP STRONGLY, WITH HAGI AT THE HEART OF THEIR BEST WORK. HIS INSANE AND PROBABLY DELIBERATE 40-YARD LOB AGAINST COLOMBIA HAD SET THE TONE, HELPING ROMANIA TO A 3-1 WIN AGAINST ONE OF THE PRE-TOURNAMENT FAVOURITES.

The 1994 World Cup will be won by... COLOMBIA!

Oh for...

Pack light, lads; we won't be staying long.

HE THEN SCORED ROMANIA'S ONLY GOAL IN A SURPRISE 4-1 DEFEAT TO ROY HODGSON'S SWITZERLAND...

THE MARADONA OF FLUFFY-HAIRED BRITISH MANAGERS WHO ARE A CURIOSITY BECAUSE THEY WORK ABROAD, THE WEIRDOS.

...BEFORE ORCHESTRATING A NARROW 1-0 WIN AGAINST THE USA TO SET UP A SECOND-ROUND MATCH WITH ARGENTINA.

IT WAS A WORLD CUP CLASSIC, WITH A FLURRY OF EARLY GOALS. A HAGI-LIKE FREE KICK FROM ROMANIA'S ILIE DUMITRESCU WAS PEGGED BACK BY A BATISTUTA PENALTY, BUT THEN ROMANIA SWEPT FORWARD IN A MOVE THAT SAW HAGI PLAY TWO DEFENCE-SPLITTING PASSES, THE SECOND OF WHICH SET UP DUMITRESCU TO SIDE-FOOT HOME.

THEIR THIRD CAME FROM A LIGHTNING-QUICK BREAK. BASUALDO LOST POSSESSION AND DUMITRESCU RACED UP-FIELD, SQUARING TO HAGI, WHO WAS IN SO MUCH SPACE HE COULD HAVE SCOFFED A BAG OF MUSHROOMS AND FOUND HIMSELF.

Whoa...

INSTEAD, HE SLAMMED THE BALL INTO THE NET FOR 3-1.

ABEL BALBO PULLED ONE BACK, WHICH LED TO A NERVY LAST 15 MINUTES, BUT ROMANIA HELD ON FOR A FAMOUS WIN. THEY WOULD LATER BE NAMED TEAM OF THE TOURNAMENT AND HAGI ONE OF ITS BEST PLAYERS. NOTHING COULD STOP THEM NOW.

Weak Beer Wee

SWEDEN 2
ROMANIA 2
SWEDEN WINS 5-4 ON PENALTIES

Oh this is a bad trip.

ANDREA PIRLO

The Architect. That's what Andrea Pirlo's teammates in the Italian national team called him. Yes, he had a lustrous beard, an array of leather-bound books and a collection of artwork that didn't come from Ikea, but also he was the master craftsman whose creative vision was the foundation of success for Milan, Juventus and Italy.

Pirlo played the game at his own pace, as if he were strolling through the backstreet markets of a North African city, pausing occasionally to breathe in the visual delight of an arrangement of colourful spices, or to knock a through-ball to Hernán Crespo. Pirlo rarely wasted a delivery. For the first 15 years of the twenty-first century, he was the supreme artisan of Serie A, taking as much pride in his work as if he'd sanded and oiled each pass individually in the sepia light of a dusty, sun-drenched workshop.

It was Milan boss Carlo Ancelotti who first saw the benefit of moving Pirlo to a deeper position, raising an approving eyebrow when he saw the beauty Andrea could produce when removed from the hurly-burly of central midfield. From there, the classy playmaker could create wonder, like the roots of a grapevine that yields an exquisite wine, a good one that costs in excess of £15. It was a move that would help Pirlo become a world champion, starring in the Italian national team that won football's ultimate prize in Germany in 2006.

Naturally, Pirlo's long career was not without setbacks; he nearly quit football after Milan threw away a three-goal lead to relinquish the 2005 Champions League final to Liverpool. For Pirlo, it was an experience as traumatic as getting his soft , TRESemmé-infused hair butchered by a bus-station barber. However, Milan returned to avenge the defeat in the final two years later, and, once his contract expired, he joined Juventus. Inspired by their classic use of bold black and white lines, he would win four consecutive Scudettos. As much a victory for design as for *calcio*.

A move to New York City followed; a natural fit for a modern man like Pirlo, at home among other classy sophisticates, like Donald Trump and his Patrick Bateman sons. He settled happily into his new surroundings, as evidenced by the Thanksgiving portrait he released in November 2015 . . .

RUUD GULLIT

An indication of Ruud Gullit's vast knowledge of the game is shown by his publication of a book titled, *How to Watch Football*. The wealth of experience Gullit built over forty years as a player, coach and television pundit is compressed into the tome, which enables readers to better understand football. It is only fair that someone who has had the benefit of working alongside Jason McAteer shares his learnings.

Curiously, there are no chapters about 'Scrolling through your phone within two minutes of kick-off', 'Talking to your mate about work, or boxing, or the key elements that constitute the perfect fried breakfast', or 'Wondering idly whether everything that's rotten about the modern game can be boiled down to the prevalence of base layers'. Still, he's wise to keep some decent content back for the second book: Gullit again showing a clarity of vision, the likes of which some of us can only dream of possessing.

Gullit was a commanding presence in the all-conquering Milan team of the late-eighties, captaining them to back-to-back European Cup wins, and lifting the European Championship trophy for the Netherlands in 1988. He was famous for his ability to play anywhere throughout the centre of the park, from the advanced position of a second forward, to the depths of a sweeper; Gullit was a true son of Total Football.

At the outset of his career, Gullit played alongside Johan Cruyff at Feyenoord, a priceless learning experience in balance, the use of space and how to be argumentative. These were all skills that would become crucial facets to his game, and ones that he was able to pass on to the next generation when he turned his hand to coaching. Whilst his management career is yet to match the highs of his playing days, Gullit is currently the assistant to Dutch national coach, Dick Advocaat; the same manager whom he walked out on, on the eve of the 1994 World Cup, when a disagreement between the pair snowballed.

WHEN YOU WERE RAISED ON A DIET OF NEIL WEBB AND PETER REID, THE SIGHT OF RUUD GULLIT WAS AS MOMENTOUS AS SEEING PRINCE OR BOY GEORGE ON 'TOP OF THE POPS' FOR THE FIRST TIME. DREADLOCKED, STATUESQUE AND OPINIONATED, FOOTBALLERS JUST WEREN'T SUPPOSED TO BE LIKE THIS.

UNLIKE MANY FOOTBALLERS, GULLIT WAS ALSO RAISED IN A COMFORTABLE, MIDDLE-CLASS ENVIRONMENT. HIS FATHER WAS AN ECONOMICS TEACHER, WHO'D TRAVELLED TO HOLLAND FROM SURINAME WITH FRANK RIJKAARD'S FATHER. THE TWO SONS BECAME LIFELONG FRIENDS, GROWING UP TO FORM THE MIDFIELD AXIS OF THE IMMENSE MILAN SIDE OF THE LATE EIGHTIES.

Look how far we've come, Ruud.

Yes, it's a far cry from the days we'd be forced to play in well-equipped facilities in leafy suburbia, using a ball crafted from leather.

ALWAYS OUTSPOKEN, UPON SIGNING HE SAID TO THE PRESS:

They told me in Holland that there are three daily sports papers here and that they're generally full of rubbish. Is that true?

Well I wouldn't have put it like that...

ON ANOTHER OCCASION, HE WAS QUOTED AS SAYING:

What happens if Milan don't qualify for Europe? That's an absurd question, we'll see what happens at the end of the season. If my mother had a cock, she'd be my father.

Riiight...

INJURIES CURTAILED HIS CAREER AT MILAN, AND AFTER A SHORT SPELL AT SAMPDORIA (AND A BRIEF RETURN TO MILAN), HE JOINED CHELSEA IN 1995. A YEAR LATER HE WAS NAMED PLAYER-MANAGER AND WON THE FA CUP - CHELSEA'S FIRST TROPHY IN 26 YEARS. HOWEVER, HE WAS SOON SACKED BY CHAIRMAN KEN BATES, WHO THOUGHT GULLIT WAS ARROGANT.

Wait. I'm black?

GULLIT WAS ALSO THAT RAREST OF BEASTS: A POLITICISED FOOTBALLER. WHEN HE WON THE BALLON D'OR IN 1987, HE DEDICATED IT TO NELSON MANDELA, WHO WAS STILL IMPRISONED AT THE TIME. GULLIT ALSO HAD A HIT RECORD IN HOLLAND WITH AN ANTI-APARTHEID SONG, YET HAS STATED HE ONLY DISCOVERED HE WAS BLACK WHEN HE WAS TEN YEARS OLD.

You don't mind if I just follow you around this shopping centre until you feel intimidated enough to leave, right? Better to be safe than sorry...

SECURITY

Wait. Am I black?

HE WAS OFFERED THREE TIMES HIS SALARY AT PSV EINDHOVEN TO JOIN MILAN. HE AND MARCO VAN BASTEN WERE SIGNED TO REPLACE RAY WILKINS AND MARK HATELEY.

The pressure! I can't handle the pressure!

I feel it too, Marco; but we have to be strong. Just think, at least we aren't replacing Luther Blissett.

PERHAPS AN INDICATION OF HIS PROPENSITY FOR SPEAKING HIS MIND IS THE FACT THAT, AT THE TIME OF WRITING, HE HAS BEEN MARRIED AND DIVORCED THREE TIMES.

So, if your season is over, does that mean you're free to come to my cousin's barbecue on the 18th?

Hey, if my mother had a co

HE WAS UNABLE TO REPLICATE HIS PLAYING SUCCESS AS A COACH, BUT MEDIA WORK OFFERED A NEW CAREER DIRECTION. IT WAS WHILE WORKING FOR THE BBC DURING EURO'96 THAT GULLIT COINED THE TERM 'SEXY FOOTBALL', A PHRASE THAT WOULDN'T HAVE RESONATED WITH VIEWERS IF ONE OF HIS FELLOW PUNDITS HAD COME UP WITH IT.

You know, the sticky young bodies, going at it, lost in passion on a humid summer's night...

XAVI HERNÁNDEZ & ANDRÉS INIESTA

Pass. Pass. Pass. Pass. Pass. Pass. Pass. Pass. Pass. Pass. Pass. Pass. Pass. Pass. Pass. Pass. Pass. Pass. No, not how an appearance on *Mastermind* by Harry Redknapp would play out, but the unstoppable rhythmic combinations of Xavi Hernández and Andrés Iniesta.

For a period in the early 2010s, Barcelona and Spain seemed invincible. Both sides played a brand of possession-based football that no one else could live with. Key to that was Xavi and Iniesta's midfield partnership, which left opponents hopelessly entranced, like moths drifting into a bug zapper. 'They get you on that carousel and they make you dizzy with their passing,' Alex Ferguson once observed. 'The lights spinning, the honk of the generator, the smell of grease from the chip van. Before you know it, you're puking up your toffee apple behind the coconut shy whilst Mike Phelan strokes your hair,' he didn't say.

Both players were products of La Masia; the famous Barcelona youth academy founded by Johan Cruyff. The training centre was like a Hogwarts for children with magical talents for creating triangles and playing 'piggy in the middle' for eight hours a day. It was here that the principles of tiki-taka were instilled in them; along with fellow graduates Lionel Messi, Carles Puyol and Sergio Busquets. Under the management of Pep Guardiola they formed part of the Barcelona side that became the first to twice win the treble of winning a league title, domestic cup and Champions League. Their invulnerability was repeated at international level; Spain winning three consecutive major tournaments: A World Cup in 2010 sandwiched by European Championship triumphs in 2008 and 2012.

In their wake the pair left a trail of cross-eyed opponents; drained from chasing the shadows of these two tireless tiny pixies: one who looked like Robert Downey Jr, the other who looked like a ghost; an inseparable, unstoppable force (until the Iron Man one went off to Qatar).

Pass. Pass. Pass. Pass. Pass. Pass. Pass. Pass. Pass. Pass. Pass. Pass. Pass. Pass. Pass. Pass. Pass. Pass.

PAUL GASCOIGNE

I only saw Gascoigne play once in the flesh. It was April 1990, in an international friendly between England and Czechoslovakia at Wembley that was reported as being the impetuous midfielder's last chance to prove to manager Bobby Robson that he could be trusted. It turned out to be one of his most influential performances at national level, as he was involved in all of England's goals in a 4–2 win.

First, he scooped a brilliant right-footed pass into the path of Steve Bull to score; then he swung in a corner that resulted in a Stuart Pearce goal; after that he went on a driving run past two opponents on the flank and delivered a perfect cross onto the head of Bull for three; and finally he burst into the penalty area, chest out, socks rolled down, and lifted a left-footed shot into the top corner.

Before any of that, Gascoigne had also clattered into a Czech player within minutes of the kick-off (apologising to the referee by ruffling his hair). It was a foul not dissimilar to the lunge that would earn him a booking in the World Cup semi-final a few months later, although it was not quite as wild as the hack on Gary Charles that would derail his career in the FA Cup Final the following year.

Robson had no choice but to take Gascoigne to the upcoming World Cup after that showing; the manager sat beaming to his backroom staff, enjoying the youngster's performance as much as the rest of us. Not that I could see his warm reaction from the other side of the stadium; besides, I was already distracted by the massive scrap taking place near the exit between two rival factions of Wolves supporters. England games are weird.

By this stage, Gascoigne was already the most exciting prospect in the country. He'd first caught the public's imagination playing for his local club, Newcastle United. There, his outrageous individual displays were reported alongside stories about his colourful pranks and fondness for Mars bars. He left the north-east for Tottenham Hotspur in 1988, joining them in preference to Manchester United after the London club had agreed to buy his family a house and his sister a sunbed. A common theory has it that, under the watchful eye of Alex Ferguson, Gascoigne's self-destructive tendencies would have been kept in check. Whilst Ferguson had worked to eliminate the culture of heavy drinking at Old Trafford, the mental-health problems and torments of addiction that have plagued Gascoigne throughout his life were possibly too complex to be resolved by a Scottish man yelling at him.

The 1990 World Cup changed everything for Gascoigne. His performances in Italy catapulted him into the world of celebrity, this at a time when British football was still recovering from the traumas of the previous decade and was very much the preserve of the back pages. Suddenly, here was a footballer appearing on prime-time chat shows, releasing records and being discussed at dinner parties. England supporters who were more interested in his abilities as an attacking midfielder than his pop career had reason to feel excited about the future. Still only 23 years old, Gascoigne would surely mature into one of Europe's most dominant players; all he had to do was keep out of trouble and stay injury free.

The season that followed the World Cup, the best of his career, did little to dent the optimism. Gascoigne played a key role in getting Spurs to the FA Cup final, most memorably smashing a long-range free kick past David Seaman in the semi-final win against Arsenal. However, the self-inflicted cruciate ligament injury he suffered in the final, a result of that reckless foul on Charles, proved to be a pivotal moment in Gascoigne's life. In total, he was sidelined for 16 months and was never the same player again.

Gascoigne's love for playing never diminished, though. So desperate was he to keep going that at the age of 35 he went off to play in the Gobi Desert for Chinese team, Gansu Tianma. Post-retirement, the alcoholism that he had battled throughout his career submerged him; alarming photographs of his physical appearance accompanying tabloid stories of his latest downfall have become commonplace. The tragic figure of a broken middle-aged man, unrecognisable from the barrel-chested effervescence of his youth.

The last stable period of Gascoigne's life came in the mid-nineties. Having signed for Rangers after three stop-start-but-mostly-stop seasons in Italy with Lazio, Gascoigne enjoyed a solid campaign in the lead up to the 1996 European Championships. Questions again lingered about his temperament and fitness, but in a match against Scotland on a sunny afternoon at Wembley, Gascoigne would show that his unique talent had never diminished.

GASCOIGNE'S TIME AT RANGERS WAS PERHAPS THE MOST SETTLED OF HIS CAREER. HIS PERFORMANCES DREW WIDESPREAD ACCLAIM, HE WON TWO LEAGUE TITLES AND A COUPLE OF CUP WINNER'S MEDALS AND ONLY CAUSED ONE MAJOR SECTARIAN INCIDENT.

Is Gazza alright for this, boss?

Oh yes, I've reminded Paul of the delicate political context of the Old Firm Derby and he understands the need for sensitivity.

THE 1995-6 SEASON WAS ONE OF GASCOIGNE'S BEST. HE PROVIDED REGULAR REMINDERS OF THE PLAYER HE'D BEEN BEFORE INJURIES BLUNTED HIS POWER AND RESPONDED WELL TO THE MANAGEMENT OF WALTER SMITH, WHO LOOKED LIKE A GRUFF, OFF-DUTY DETECTIVE.

Aye...

'Looked like'...

THE ENGLAND MANAGER, TERRY VENABLES, WAS ANOTHER MAN WHO GOT THE BEST OUT OF GASCOIGNE. HE BELIEVED IN TREATING PLAYERS LIKE ADULTS, RATHER THAN THE EGOCENTRIC MAN-CHILDREN THEY BLATANTLY ARE.

We're off into town to try out that new nightclub. Maybe a curry after. We'll be back by dawn; big game tomorrow; we know.

Stop right there!

I'll just fetch me new leather jacket...

THREE WEEKS BEFORE THE START OF EURO '96, VENABLES TOOK THE ENGLAND SQUAD ON A TOUR OF CHINA AND HONG KONG TO RELAX AND BUILD TEAM SPIRIT. GIVEN A NIGHT OFF, THE PLAYERS RESPONDED WELL TO THE TRUST PLACED IN THEM BY THE MANAGER.

This is more fun than a hundred consecutive stag dos!

UNSURPRISINGLY, THERE WAS MORAL OUTRAGE FROM THE ENGLISH TABLOID PRESS, WHO WERE WELL-POSITIONED TO CRITICISE THE BEHAVIOUR OF OTHERS.

Pint?

No, quality journalism is the only drug I need, thank you. Also, I need to hack into this minor Royal's voice messages.

ENGLAND PLAYED AS IF THEY WERE RECOVERING FROM A MASSIVE LONG-HAUL BENDER IN THEIR OPENING GAME: AN INSIPID 1-1 DRAW WITH ROY HODGSON'S SWITZERLAND. THIS WOULD NOT BE THE LAST TIME THAT ENGLAND SUPPORTERS WOULD BE FRUSTRATED BY HODGSON

You're our best striker, so I want you to take all the corners, Harry.

Um... ok.

THERE WERE FEW SIGNS OF IMPROVEMENT IN THE FIRST HALF OF THEIR NEXT MATCH, AGAINST SCOTLAND. VENABLES DECIDED THAT AN EXTRA MAN IN MIDFIELD WAS REQUIRED, SO WITHDREW THE FULL-BACK, STUART PEARCE. THE PROBING INTELLIGENCE OF JAMIE REDKNAPP WOULD TURN THE GAME

ALAN SHEARER HEADED ENGLAND INTO THE LEAD SOON AFTER THE RE-START, BUT SCOTLAND RALLIED AND WERE AWARDED A PENALTY. AS GARY McALLISTER STEPPED UP TO TAKE IT, THE BALL MYSTERIOUSLY MOVED ON THE SPOT AND HIS SHOT WAS SAVED BY DAVID SEAMAN. MOMENTS LATER, THE BALL WAS WORKED UPFIELD TO GASCOIGNE, WHO'D BEEN LARGELY ANONYMOUS TO THIS POINT. AS DEFENDER COLIN HENDRY MOVES ACROSS TO MEET HIM, GASCOIGNE DINKS THE BOUNCING BALL OVER HIS HEAD WITH HIS LEFT FOOT...

... AND SMACKS A RIGHT-FOOTED VOLLEY PAST ANDY GORAM FOR 2-0.

NO OTHER ENGLAND PLAYER WOULD HAVE HAD THE IMAGINATION TO EVEN **THINK** OF SUCH A MOVE, LET ALONE BOAST THE SKILL TO PULL IT OFF.

TISSIER ...OK.

THE SCOTLAND TEAM HAD WATCHED BRAVEHEART THE NIGHT BEFORE. PERHAPS IT WAS WILLIAM WALLACE THAT HENDRY THOUGHT OF AS HE WAS EVISCERATED IN PUBLIC; THE SOLEMN ECHO OF A DISTANT CELTIC PIPE PLAYING IN HIS MIND, A KEEPSAKE FROM HIS WIFE FALLING FROM HIS HAND.

I said we should have watched Jumanji...

GASCOIGNE RACED AWAY, COLLAPSING IN A HEAP BESIDE THE GOAL. HIS GLEEFUL TEAMMATES JOINED HIM. TEDDY SHERINGHAM, FIRST ON THE SCENE, SPRAYED A BOTTLE OF WATER INTO THE SCORER'S MOUTH - A HOMAGE TO THE INFAMOUS DENTIST'S CHAIR INCIDENT. A SCORNFUL VENABLES LOOKED ON.

GIVEN THAT ALCOHOLISM WOULD COME TO CONSUME GASCOIGNE'S LIFE, THE IMAGE NOW JARS. PERHAPS A MORE GENTEEL CELEBRATION WOULD HAVE WEIGHED LESS HEAVILY IN TIME.

Wahey! Nice one, lads! Lager, lager, lager, lager lager. Shouting. Lager lag...

More tea, Teddy?

THE DAILY MIRROR'S EDITOR, PIERS MORGAN HAD BEEN CALLING FOR GASCOIGNE TO BE DROPPED, BUT NOW PRINTED AN APOLOGY TO HIM. ENGLAND WENT ON TO THRASH HOLLAND, 4-1, AND EDGE PAST SPAIN ON PENALTIES TO SET UP A SEMI-FINAL WITH GERMANY. MORGAN RAN WITH THE CULTURALLY SENSITIVE HEADLINE: 'ACHTUNG! SURRENDER'.

Pint?

No, being a relentless, thundering bellend is the only drug I need thank you.

ENGLAND PLAYED BRAVELY, BUT WOULD INEVITABLY LOSE ON PENALTIES. GASCOIGNE WAS SUPERB, AND IN GOLDEN GOAL EXTRA-TIME MISSED CONNECTING WITH A PASS ACROSS AN OPEN GOAL BY A FRACTION OF A SECOND. IT WAS A FAMILIAR STORY OF TRAGICALLY MISSED OPPORTUNITIES.

A GAP IN TIME SIMILAR TO THE SIZE IN WHICH 'COOL BRITANNIA' WAS CONSIDERED TO BE A VIABLE CONCEPT.

PIONEERS

The survival of the human race has always required people to blaze a trail. Without those innovative souls, the kind of people who saw something fall out of a chicken's arse and decided to call it breakfast, we'd all still be eating moss and using dial-up internet. Football, as a sport predominantly played by humans (despite what the makers of the *Soccer Dog* film franchise would have you believe) is no different. If it weren't for individuals with big, bold ideas, the game wouldn't have progressed past the 'wrestling an inflated pig bladder from one field to another' stage.

Some of the people included in this chapter had the vision to think about football in a different way; to use science, technology or Russian computers to explore new boundaries; or to consider the use of space with the ingenuity of an interior designer on one of those home-renovation shows where they put millions on the value of a house by plumping up some fucking cushions.

Others were different kinds of pioneers; the sort of people who refused to let the bigotry or prejudice of others prevent them from playing the sport they loved; those who made life marginally easier for the people who followed. Just look at the biggest leagues in the world now, they are a picture of ethnic and gender diversity; players from all over the planet competing in an environment of respect and harmony. Race or gender is no longer a barrier to employment unless you want to hold a position of management.

CHARLES REEP

When Wing Commander Charles Reep returned to Britain in 1947, he couldn't believe his eyes. He'd been posted to Germany after the war, but now he was back and was met with a confronting sight. Before the war, he'd been a fan of the way Herbert Chapman's Arsenal team got the ball forward with the minimum of faff, so it came as a horrible shock to see that Chapman's methods hadn't been widely adopted. Instead, teams were dithering about, building neat triangles in central midfield – such wastefulness in a time of post-war austerity. Reep sank to his knees and threw his hands in the air, like Charlton Heston at the end of *Planet of the Apes.*

Once he'd calmed down a bit, he began to collect data, scribbled in notepads. Soon he had enough evidence upon which to build a theory. The most effective way for a team to score, Reep concluded, was to lump the ball up the pitch as quickly as possible. He coined the term 'Reacher' to describe 'a single pass from the defensive third to the attacking third of the pitch'.

Reep's analytics and ideas were soon adopted by a number of like-minded coaches, and his regular newspaper columns allowed him to share his theories broadly. People at the most senior levels of the Football Association were sympathetic to his concepts, which, in time would come to influence the direction of coaching throughout the nation. Clubs that applied his methods with success included Watford and Wimbledon; and at international level the Republic of Ireland and Norway.

The Reepian influence on English football waned as the Premier League became more cosmopolitan, with the influx of foreign coaches and players; however, its DNA survives. One of the most fanatical champions of Reep's ideas was John Beck, whose Cambridge United team of the early-nineties nearly won promotion to the Premier League by catapulting the ball towards beanstalk centre-forward Dion Dublin. Beck is now part of the English coaching set-up, training people to get their UEFA coaching licenses, and Dublin is able to surreptitiously control the minds of the nation's daytime television viewers through his role as a presenter on *Homes Under the Hammer.* Wake up, sheeple!

Before heat maps and pass-completion percentages, there was CHARLES REEP; professional football's original performance analyst....

Of course!

IN THE MIXER

THE FORMER RAF WING COMMANDER BEGAN COLLECTING MATCH DATA IN 1950, HAVING GROWN FRUSTRATED BY WATCHING SWINDON TOWN UNCHARACTERISTICALLY LABOUR TO ACHIEVE A STATE OF FOOTBALLING NIRVANA.

I wish I'd kept some of those cyanide capsules.

It hasn't even started yet.

Christ.

REEP'S INTERPRETATION OF THE DATA LED HIM TO CONCLUDE THAT MOST GOALS WERE SCORED AFTER FEWER THAN FOUR PASSES. THEREFORE, HE ARGUED, IT WAS VITAL TO LAUNCH THE BALL FORWARD AS QUICKLY AS POSSIBLE AND TO AVOID ALL THAT POSSESSION NONSENSE.

HE ACHIEVED SUCCESS AS AN ADVISER FOR BRENTFORD AND WOLVES. IN THE EARLY EIGHTIES HE PROVIDED MATCH PERFORMANCE STATISTICS FOR GRAHAM TAYLOR AT WATFORD, EDUCATING THE YOUNG MANAGER IN THE REEP PHILOSOPHY.

First learn to stand, then learn to hoof. Nature rule, Graham son, not mine.

REEP'S METHODS WERE ALSO ADOPTED BY WIMBLEDON. THE FAMOUS 'CRAZY GANG' ROSE THROUGH THE DIVISIONS AND WON THE FA CUP IN 1988. FOR A FEW YEARS, THEIR ROUTE ONE AND MEGA LOLZ GAME UPSET FOOTBALL'S NATURAL ORDER.

Hmn, I don't recall saying anything about filling Clive Goodyear's bungalow with cat faeces.

Heh. Daft buggers.

THE FA'S DIRECTOR OF COACHING, CHARLES HUGHES, ALSO SUBSCRIBED TO REEP'S METHODOLOGY. HUGHES DEVELOPED THE CONCEPT OF 'POSITIONS OF MAXIMUM OPPORTUNITY'; AREAS FROM WHICH A PLAYER WOULD BE MOST LIKELY TO SCORE. GET THE BALL THERE QUICKLY AND YOU'D REAP THE REWARDS.

Those Continental lads who've been passing the ball through our midfield are going to feel **pretty** stupid when I punish them from the 'POMO', where I've been stood to no avail for the last hour.

THIS ARGUABLY LED TO A STATE OF AFFAIRS WHEREBY SUCCESSIVE GENERATIONS OF ENGLISH FOOTBALLERS WERE LEFT BEREFT OF TECHNICAL ABILITY AND WITH A LACK OF CONFIDENCE AROUND A FOOTBALL.

Careful, Jayden; it might hatch.

REEP'S IDEAS FELL OUT OF FASHION AS MORE FOREIGN PLAYERS AND MANAGERS JOINED PREMIER LEAGUE CLUBS. YET HE WAS STILL REVERED IN NORWAY, WHERE THE NATIONAL TEAM MANAGER, EGIL OLSEN, WAS A REEP DISCIPLE. WHEN NORWAY MET GRAHAM TAYLOR'S ENGLAND IN A WORLD CUP QUALIFIER IN 1993, REEP SAT IN THE STANDS AS A GUEST OF HONOUR.

Hit Les! Hit Les!

Hit Jan Åge! Hit Jan Åge!

Good, good...

ENGLAND LOST 2-0, BEATEN AT THEIR OWN LONG-BALL GAME.

IN RECENT YEARS, THE STATISTICAL ANALYSIS UPON WHICH REEP BASED HIS THEORIES HAS BEEN EXPOSED AS BEING FLAWED. SHOULD HUMANS EVER CRACK THE SECRETS OF TIME TRAVEL, PERHAPS WE SHOULD SEND SOMEONE BACK TO SET HIM STRAIGHT.

You're back! But England are still useless. What happened?

I got distracted.

HOWEVER, EVEN THE WORST IDEAS SOMETIMES EXPERIENCE A REVIVAL (E.G. DOUBLE DENIM, FASCISM ETC.), SO IT MAY NOT BE LONG UNTIL A MODERN MANAGER TRIES TO MAKE REEP'S SYSTEM COOL AGAIN.

Get a load of fertiliser on the corners. We need to make that grass like a jungle, so the ball will stick when our full-backs lump it forward.

RINUS MICHELS

Total Football was Rinus Michels' gift to the world; a tactical system that essentially boiled down to a team achieving a higher state of consciousness whereby each player in a team is fit enough and skilled enough to fill the space vacated by a teammate. In real-world workplace terms, it would be like if some Human Resources genius initiated a 'hot-desking' policy in which you not only have to get used to sitting in a different seat in the office every day, but also have to do the job of the last person to sit there. Oh great, now I have to learn how to do pivot tables in Excel, thanks a lot, *Rinus*.

Michels transformed Dutch football, and his coaching legacy lives on to this day. His appointment as Ajax coach in 1963 coincided with a period of investment from wealthy benefactors, but in demanding an increased level of fitness and professionalism from his players, he was able to bring the club a level of success previously unimaginable. They won the Dutch league four times between 1966 and 1970 and reached the European Cup final in 1969. They lost 4–1 to AC Milan, but with Ruud Krol added to the team as sweeper, they lifted the trophy in 1971, comfortably beating Panathinaikos 2–0 at Wembley. Michels then cleared off to Barcelona, signed Cruyff and Neeskens, and won the league there too.

It was Michels' achievements with the national team for which he's best remembered. The Dutch side that he coached to the 1974 World Cup final played some of the most exhilarating football ever seen; a buzzing, rotating swarm of brilliant orange, overwhelming all before them with their extrasensory passing and movement. If they hadn't scored so early in the final against West Germany, they might even have won it.

However, Michels would return to Munich's Olympiastadion 14 years later, with a new generation of gifted Dutch players, including the likes of Marco van Basten, Frank Rijkaard and Ruud Gullit. Holland lifted the European Championship trophy with a 2–0 win against the USSR, but his most satisfying win came with a cathartic semi-final defeat of West Germany; a success he celebrated with the self-restraint one would expect from a visionary football intellectual.

IN 1988, MICHELS MANAGED HOLLAND TO VICTORY IN THE EUROPEAN CHAMPIONSHIPS, LAYING TO REST THE GHOSTS OF DEFEAT IN THE 1974 WORLD CUP FINAL. HE ALSO CAME CLOSE TO RETAINING HIS COMPOSURE DURING THE SEMI-FINAL WIN AGAINST WEST GERMANY.

HE PLAYED 269 TIMES FOR AJAX, SCORING 121 GOALS. IN THE PROCESS, HE WON TWO LEAGUE TITLES AND MADE FIVE APPEARANCES FOR HOLLAND, WHO AT THIS TIME WERE RUBBISH. RINUS RETIRED IN 1958 TO BECOME A GYMNASTICS TEACHER.

PHYSICAL FITNESS WAS A KEY COMPONENT OF MICHELS' FOOTBALL PHILOSOPHY. AT AJAX, HIS PLAYERS WERE EXPECTED TO TRAIN UP TO FOUR TIMES A DAY, IN ORDER TO MAKE THEM FIT ENOUGH TO PRESS OPPONENTS AND COVER SPACE ON THE PITCH.

HE'S BEST REMEMBERED FOR HIS LAUDED DUTCH TEAM OF 1974, WHO PRODUCED SOME OF THE FINEST FOOTBALL EVER SEEN. THIS ACHIEVEMENT WAS ALL THE MORE REMARKABLE CONSIDERING THE TEAM BEGAN THEIR WORLD CUP CAMPAIGN IN TRADITIONAL STYLE.

MOST OF HIS SUCCESSFUL AJAX SIDE HAD GROWN UP TOGETHER, PROGRESSING THROUGH THE CLUB'S YOUTH RANKS. THERE EXISTED A KIND OF TELEPATHY BETWEEN THEM, SO FAMILIAR WERE THEY WITH MICHELS' SYSTEM.

THE NON-LINEAR SPATIALLY-INTERCHANGEABLE STORY OF RINUS MICHELS

AJAX APPOINTED MICHELS AS MANAGER IN 1964; WITHIN SIX YEARS THEY WOULD BE EUROPEAN CHAMPIONS. HIS SUCCESS WAS AIDED BY AJAX TURNING PROFESSIONAL, MEANING PLAYERS NO LONGER NEEDED SECONDARY INCOMES.

HE LED AJAX TO THE TITLE IN HIS FIRST SEASON AND SPANKED LIVERPOOL 5-1 DURING THE FOLLOWING YEAR'S EUROPEAN CUP. THE RESULT MADE LIVERPOOL'S BOSS BILL SHANKLY REVISE HIS TACTICAL APPROACH AND PROVOKED A FAMOUSLY WRY QUIP:

MICHELS' GREAT LEGACY WAS THE YOUTH ACADEMY HE ESTABLISHED AT AJAX. ITS MOST GIFTED PUPIL, JOHAN CRUYFF, WOULD LATER FOLLOW ITS TEMPLATE TO SET UP LA MASIA AT BARCELONA - THE PRODUCER OF SOME OF THE WORLD'S FINEST TALENT.

WALTER TULL

One of the first people of mixed heritage to play top-flight football in Britain was the talented midfielder – and war hero – Walter Tull.

Tull was orphaned by the age of nine, and was sent with his brother Edward to a children's home in Bethnal Green. Life then delivered another punch in the neck when Edward was adopted by a family in Glasgow. However, it was in the orphanage where Walter learned to play football, and once he'd grown into a man, he started playing with distinction at amateur level for Clapton, who reportedly never lost a game with Tull in the side. At the age of 21 he was signed by Tottenham Hotspur, where he played ten matches and scored two goals.

Perhaps his career at Spurs would have lasted longer if it weren't for the appalling racial abuse he was repeatedly subjected to, most notoriously during an FA Cup tie at Bristol City. A journalist for the *Football Star* newspaper wrote that 'a section of the spectators made a cowardly attack on him in language lower than Billingsgate'. It's unlikely that this was an isolated incident.

A transfer to Herbert Chapman's Northampton Town followed. Tull had appeared 111 times for the club before the outbreak of the First World War, and had built such a reputation that an agreement had been made for him to sign for Glasgow Rangers once the war was over, allowing him to be closer to his brother.

Tull was part of the Football Battalion of the Middlesex Regiment, which consisted of current and former players and was established to try and encourage fans to sign up. He fought at the Battle of the Somme and achieved the rank of second lieutenant, becoming the first black infantry officer in the British Army. He later fought on the Italian Front and was commended for his 'gallantry and coolness'. When Tull led an attack into no-man's-land during Germany's Spring Offensive in March 1918, he was shot and killed, his body never recovered, despite the desperate efforts of his platoon; especially Private Tom Billingham, Leicester's goalkeeper.

Tull's commanding officers told Edward that Walter had been recommended for the Military Cross for his actions in Italy, but it was never forthcoming. Nearly a century later, and despite a lengthy campaign, the Ministry of Defence still refuses to award Tull his posthumous medal. However, in 1999, Northampton Town unveiled a memorial in Tull's honour, which included the following words . . .

Through his actions...

W.D.J. Tull ridiculed the barriers of ignorance...

...that tried to deny people of colour equality with their contemporaries.

His life stands as a testament to determination...

...to confront those people and those obstacles that sought to diminish him...

...and the world in which he lived.

It reveals a man,

though rendered breathless in his prime...

...whose strong heart still beats loudly.

VALERIY LOBANOVSKYI

After clinching the Soviet Top League title with Dynamo Kyiv in 1961, talented winger, Valeriy Lobanovskyi mused to a celebrating teammate: 'A realised dream ceases to be a dream.' This was not a young man burdened by sentimentality. Instead, Lobanovskyi saw football as a scientific challenge, one that he came close to solving.

His first coaching appointment was at Dnipro Dnipropetrovsk, where he teamed up with the academic Anatoly Zelentsov. They developed a system of statistical analysis and used a computer program to measure the speed of the players, calculate how long they spent in specific areas of the pitch, observe how they supported one another if drawn out of position, and evaluate how they worked with and without the ball. Thus 'The Methodological Basis of the Development of Training Models' was born. They were too busy decrypting football to think of a punchier title.

The pair achieved limited success at Dnipro, but teamed up again at Dynamo Kyiv in 1973. It was here that they would crack the code. Under Lobanovskyi's judicious eye, Dynamo won eight Soviet championships, six Soviet cups and three Soviet super cups. They also became the first team from the Soviet Union to win a European trophy; beating Ferencváros 3–0 in the European Cup Winners' Cup final in 1975.

Lobanovskyi's achievements saw him appointed as national coach of the USSR. His first spell in the role ended acrimoniously, when the players went on strike, sick of the excessive demands of his training regime. He was reinstated in 1986 and built his team mostly on the Dynamo Kyiv players whom he had again led to victory in that year's European Cup Winners' Cup final, this time beating Atlético Madrid 3–0. The Kyiv players were familiar with Lobanovskyi's system and expectations. Together, they reached the final of the 1988 European Championships, where they faced a Holland team managed by Rinus Michels. The two coaches shared similar football principles: the high press, the intelligent use of space, and that players should have the ability to slot into each other's positions. The key difference was that Michels had Marco van Basten to smack in a volley that – infuriatingly for Lobanovskyi – defied the laws of logic.

COMPUTERS ARE THE FUTURE; ONE DAY THERE WILL BE ONE IN EVERY HOME. INNOVATIVE COACH, **VALERIY LOBANOVSKYI**, REALISED THIS AND USED THEM TO DEVELOP PROGRAMS TO TEST PLAYERS FOR THE KEY SKILLS THEY WOULD NEED ON THE PITCH. VERSATILE MIDFIELDER, VASYL RATS, IS INVITED TO PARTICIPATE IN SUCH A TEST...

Come on in to the lab, Rats.

Did you get me all the way down here just to do that joke?

Do I strike you as a man who wastes time on clownery?

No, sorry, I didn't mean—

Just sit down.

Lab rats

MATHS

COMPUTER

SCIENCE

This game has been designed to test your reflexes, spatial awareness, and ability to rescue princesses.

Did you draw the cover yourself?

I did, actually.

SUPER VALERIY

Why is he a plumber?

Because I trained to be a plumber. Look, there's a whole back story, but the main point is that you need to guide your little sprite to the space at the top of the screen and avoid all the baddies.

When you're ready to start, fast forward the tape to number 442 on the counter and press play. I'll be in the next room, studying a VHS tape of potential European opponents, acquired through the black market.

And remember, I'll be comparing your performance to your teammates' and there will be a small prize for the highest score. Maybe you will be the one to get the cheese, Rats.

Oh, come on.

This does not look like Dukla Prague.

π

LILY PARR

In today's society of blissful gender equality, women employees can earn up to a quarter of their male counterparts' salaries. Some believe this situation has gone too far, and that the bloody *feminazis* have made it impossible for a bro to even compliment a co-worker on her waist measurements as she attempts to simply earn a living without having to put up with this constant avalanche of bullshit.

Football does not exist in isolation from the rest of society, and it also provides an environment of respect and equal opportunity. A cursory scroll through the twitter replies of any woman footballer usually reveals a depressingly long diatribe of abuse from micro-cocked adult virgins experiencing their only interaction with a member of the opposite sex. Women are not excluded from the epic banter.

However, football hasn't always been so accepting. For over 50 years, women were banned from playing the game in England, as the Football Association mistook their role in administering the game for that of the fucking Taliban. The massive crowds that gathered to watch women's football during the First World War were perceived as a threat to the men's game, so it was shut down.

The most popular women's team of the time was formed from a group of factory workers, and was led by a towering winger whose goal-scoring exploits rattled the establishment and helped raise vast amounts of money for charity; the first woman to be inducted into the National Football Museum's Hall of Fame: Lily Parr.

Football is quite unsuitable for ladies.

THE LADS AT THE FA HAD A POINT. WITH THEIR DELICATE FRAMES AND PROPENSITY FOR DRAMA, WOMEN WERE ILL-EQUIPPED TO COPE WITH THE PHYSICAL AND EMOTIONAL RIGOURS OF SOCCER. TAKE, FOR EXAMPLE, ENGLAND'S FIRST FEMALE FOOTBALL STAR, THE SIX FOOT TALL, CHAIN-SMOKING, WINGER, LILY PARR...

Crush the Patriarchy...

INTEREST IN THE WOMEN'S GAME GREW DURING THE FIRST WORLD WAR. AT THE FOREFRONT WAS PARR'S TEAM, 'DICK KERR'S LADIES', FORMED FROM THE FEMALE WORKFORCE OF A LANCASHIRE MUNITIONS FACTORY.

PARR WAS PLAYING FOR ST HELENS WHEN SHE WAS SPOTTED BY DICK KERR'S. SHE WAS GIVEN A JOB AT THE FACTORY AND RECRUITED FOR THE TEAM, BEING PAID 10 SHILLINGS PER GAME. PARR WOULD SCORE 43 GOALS IN HER FIRST SEASON. SHE WAS 14 YEARS OLD.

CLANG! Ooooh! Unlucky.

Casualty of the horrific theatre of war?

Tried to stop a Lily Parr shot.

You only have yourself to blame.

PARR PLAYED IN THE FIRST EVER RECOGNISED WOMEN'S INTERNATIONAL. DICK KERR'S REPRESENTED ENGLAND IN FOUR MATCHES AGAINST FRANCE, WHO WERE CAPTAINED BY ALICE MILLIAT, WHOSE TIRELESS LOBBYING WOULD RESULT IN WOMEN BEING ALLOWED TO COMPETE IN THE OLYMPICS.

Waaaah! What next; girls taking the lead roles in children's sci-fi fantasy stories? They're ruining my childhood memories! WAAAH!

WOMEN'S FOOTBALL REMAINED HUGELY POPULAR AFTER THE WAR. ON BOXING DAY IN 1920, 56,000 PEOPLE TURNED OUT TO SEE DICK KERR'S PLAY AT GOODISON PARK. SUCH A LARGE CROWD NO DOUBT CAUSED A MASS OUTBREAK OF FAINTING AMONGST THOSE BIOLOGICALLY PRE-DISPOSED TO FRAGILITY.

Look at the size of the crowd! Perhaps one day soon, women's football will be more popular than men's!

Oh...

CLEARLY THIS WASN'T A SITUATION THAT COULD BE ALLOWED TO CONTINUE. FEELING THREATENED, THE FA BANNED WOMEN FROM PLAYING AT THE GROUNDS OF THEIR MEMBER CLUBS, EFFECTIVELY BANISHING THEM TO THE PARK LEVEL.

RANGER

NO BALL GAMES

NO CRUSHING THE PATRIARCHY

Yep, that seems about right.

PARR PLAYED ON UNTIL 1951, BY WHICH TIME SHE WAS 46. CONSERVATIVE ESTIMATES SUGGEST SHE SCORED OVER 900 CAREER GOALS. SADLY, SHE PASSED AWAY IN 1978, BUT SURVIVED TO SEE THE FA'S BAN ON WOMEN'S FOOTBALL LIFTED IN 1971.

I can't wait for you to see what they do to Ghostbusters.

I don't know what that is.

FORWARD THINKERS

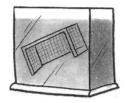

Centre-forward. The glamour role. Nobody grows up dreaming of being a full-back. In his more whimsical moments, even Gary Neville must have dreamt of being a striker; out-muscling a ponderous defender and blasting an unstoppable shot that leaves a smouldering, football-shaped hole in the goalkeeper's midriff. His brother Phil leans over from the top bunk, 'What are you doing under the duvet, Gary? Why are you making those noises? Are you hurt? Shall I get Mam?' NO! SHUT UP, PHILIP! Stupid Philip.

Gary wasn't to blame for harbouring these sinful thoughts; who hasn't fantasised about indulging their basest desires to surrender completely to greed? The good news is that there are no impediments to playing as a forward. No person is too tall, too small, too slow, too wide or too useless to take on the role. There are literally thousands of football clubs, professional and amateur, and they all need vainglorious poster boys with ice in their veins to bang in the goals and demand separate dressing rooms for their entourage.

When your club signs a new striker, it can instil within you a sense of hope. Beautiful, false hope. Perhaps *this* hired gun will be the final piece in the jigsaw; the chosen one that the weirdos who hang round the club shop every day prophesy will elevate the team to its rightful position as champions of the universe. *Fine*, so a cursory google reveals that he looks like a balloon sculpture filled with sausage meat, and *yes*, his track record suggests that his boots are made of Lego, but perhaps *yours* will be the club where everything clicks. You'd better go and loiter around the training ground car park to make sure.

Forward players come in a range of shapes and sizes, enabling them to fulfil a number of roles. There is your classic target man, whose genetics have equipped him with a natural advantage when it comes to nodding down long passes and towering above defenders at set-pieces. The target man will sometimes be employed in a partnership with a scuttling short-arse. An example of this Big Man/Little Man combination could be seen in the attacking union of Peter Crouch and Michael Owen, which must have left some Stoke City fans wondering if they were watching an am-dram adaptation of *The Hobbit*.

Advances in nutrition and sport science mean you are less likely these days to see what was euphemistically described as the barrel-chested centre-forward (BCCF). The Brazilian international Hulk never quite had the confidence to go 'The Full Jon Parkin' and truly explore the advantages that a vast heaving bosom can give you when a free-kick is arced into the penalty box. An opportunity wasted. A subset of the BCCF is 'The Beast'. This is a term exclusively reserved for heavy-set black players, a handy way of reminding us that football is still stuck in the 1950s. Hooray!

The role of the forward has evolved in recent years, with most players now given responsibilities beyond simply standing on the edge of the area with their hand raised and – *ugh* – scoring goals; many are now expected to 'link up play' and 'work for the team'. Sometimes, their efforts can be overlooked by tactically illiterate football fans who fail to see the subtlety at play when the number 9's first touch knocks the ball 20 metres away from its intended direction. Thankfully, pundits are on hand to remind us of our ignorance. We couldn't possibly understand the merits of dribbling the ball straight out of play for a goal kick; we haven't played the game.

However, there is still room in football for The Poacher; those dead-eyed souls who live only for goals. They circle the penalty area like sharks, electroreceptors enabling them to sense when a cross is going to be aimed to the near post. They would eat you in your sleep if they thought it would help them win a Golden Boot. Then they would just toss it into their basement, along with their other baubles and skeletons, already thinking about the next prize.

MARCO VAN BASTEN

Van Basten was the complete striker, capable of scoring with both feet, from near in or miles out. He could rise above opponents and power in headers, or motor through defences and stroke the ball into the net. If his career hadn't been curtailed by injury, he'd undoubtedly have added to his collection of medals and personal accolades. 'The Swan of Utrecht' blamed the surgeons who had operated on his troublesome ankle for the fact that he was forced to retire by the time he was 28, saying that they had done more damage than any opponent ever did.

It was at AC Milan where van Basten's reputation as the most lethal striker of his generation would be forged. His rampant performances on the pitch were matched only by his crazy antics off it. Whether playing backgammon with the youth team, or staying in and listening to George Michael CDs with his wife, Lisbeth, people knew they were in for a wild time when Marco was around.

Van Basten made his debut for Ajax in 1982, coming on as substitute for Johan Cruyff, in a symbolic passing of the baton. The introduction of batons in football was not one of the rule changes van Basten would later propose in his role as a member of FIFA's technical committee, but he did suggest scrapping the offside rule (once a striker . . .). His ideas were critiqued with the respect you'd expect for a man of van Basten's standing in the game, with the Rennes manager Christian Gourcuff describing them as 'immeasurable bullshit'.

However, the real legacy that van Basten will leave football will be the memory of his impossible goal for the Netherlands against the Soviet Union in the 1988 European Championships final . . .

THE NETHERLANDS WENT INTO THE SECOND HALF HOLDING A SLENDER 1-0 LEAD, COURTESY OF A RUUD GULLIT HEADER. TEN MINUTES AFTER THE RE-START, AN OFF-BALANCE ARNOLD MUHREN FLOATS A DIAGONAL PASS TOWARDS MARCO VAN BASTEN, WHO NOW HAS A DECISION TO MAKE...

Ruud's in the middle, a defender's closing in. Do I bring this ball down, cross it first-time, or try something else?

Something nuts...?

VAN BASTEN HAD STARTED THE TOURNAMENT ON THE BENCH, AFTER AN INJURY-PLAGUED SEASON WITH MILAN. SUCH INJURIES WOULD END HIS CAREER PREMATURELY, DESPITE THE OFFER OF ONE MILANISTA TO DONATE A PORTION OF HIS ANKLE CARTILAGE TO 'THE ICE MAN'.

Look, man, I just want part of me to be in you, you know, forever.

Right. And you cut that out yourself, you say?

Oh yeah.

HOWEVER, HIS RETURN TO THE TEAM PAID INSTANT DIVIDENDS WITH A HAT-TRICK AGAINST ENGLAND. THE PICK OF THE GOALS FEATURED A SHARP TURN THAT WOULD HAVE BEEN WORTHY OF VAN BASTEN'S EARLY MENTOR, JOHAN CRUYFF.

Maaaarco... make Tony Adams look like a tiiiiiiit.

I will. I will make Tony Adams look like a tit!

AFTER A LUCKY WIN AGAINST IRELAND, THE DUTCH OVER-CAME WEST GERMANY IN A HIGHLY CHARGED SEMI-FINAL. VAN BASTEN HIT AN 88TH-MINUTE WINNER, AND AFTER THE GAME, RONALD KOEMAN PRETENDED TO USE OLAF THON'S SHIRT TO WIPE HIS BUM.

NIEDERLANDE

Hey, Ronald, I was just wondering if you wanted me to sign that... oh.

BUT FOR NOW, VAN BASTEN HAD TO WORK OUT WHAT TO DO WITH THIS LOOPING PASS AND THE FULL-BACK MOVING TOWARDS HIM.

Ah, what the hell...

ONE OF THE MOST SPECTACULAR, RIDICULOUS GOALS OF ALL TIME HAD GIVEN HOLLAND AN – AS IT TURNED OUT – UNASSAILABLE LEAD. THEIR COACH, RINUS MICHELS, RAN HIS HANDS OVER HIS FACE IN AMAZEMENT; OTHERS REACTED DIFFERENTLY.

My accumulator!

Maaaarco... you probably learned that from meeeee...!

Hey, man, I was free, what the hell?

Right. Yeah. Sorry.

MARCO

ZLATAN IBRAHIMOVIĆ

Unrepentant bicycle thief, world-class swearer, scourge of defenders and teammates alike; players like Zlatan Ibrahimović are as rare as people who enjoy the company of José Mourinho.

For the last two decades, fans across the world have grown accustomed to Ibra's regular displays of outrageous skill and dexterity – an awe-inspiring fusion of centre-forward and local martial-arts instructor. There he is, executing a flying karate kick to back-heel a cross into the top corner; there he is round-housing a half-volley past a goalkeeper; there he is using the five-point palm exploding heart technique on a marker who dares touch his sleeve while awaiting a corner. Step from me, for I am Zlatan and I can make your kidneys explode with my thinks.

Ibrahimović was raised in the rough Rosengård Estate, east of Malmö, where he first began to play football. Throughout his career, his approach rarely changed. Never one to back down from a confrontation, nor to pass up the opportunity to humiliate an opponent, Zlatan was always the lanky windmill-legged lad all the other kids' parents tutted about. When he signed for Malmö, the older players found his fondness for doing cocky tricks at inopportune moments irritating. They were surprised when Ajax paid €8.7 million for him, an amount roughly the equivalent of a round of drinks in most Swedish cities.

At Ajax, Zlatan was mentored by one of the few coaches whose authority he respected: Marco van Basten. Suddenly, the impressively beaked showman was willing to listen and learn. He would go on to be one of the most successful forwards of his generation; becoming the only man to have won 13 league titles in four different countries, as of 2017. Yet it took a 30-yard bicycle kick in a friendly against England in 2012 to prove that he wasn't absolute garbage, outwitting Joe Hart being the ultimate test of a footballer's ability.

'I AM ZLATAN!'

Zlatan does not play by your rules, normals. Zlatan elbows the face of convention and authority. There's some authority, Zlatan smash!

'Zlatan is a martial arts warrior - a fact rarely mentioned. No mortal is spared the wrath of Zlatan, be they man, beast or junior teammate. Zlatan once put Gennaro Gattuso in a dustbin after the little fucker had thrown grapes at Zlatan.'

RIFIUTI

'Only a handful of humans have been able to tame Zlatan.'

'Guardiola was not one of them - him and his troupe of tiny conformist goodies can stick it'.

Sir, Ibrahimović called you a shit Jason Statham.

'Even as a teenager at Malmö, Zlatan's more experienced, decrepit colleagues could only stand and admire Zlatan's range of mad skills'.

Sakes.

'Zlatan's arrogant persona is really a mask for his insecurities, Zlatan is actually quite complex and vulnerable.

'The English media doubted Zlatan...'

It's all very well to win the league with Ajax, Juventus, Barcelona, Inter and PSG, but how many goals has he ever scored against Watford?

'... but once Zlatan had conquered their muddy island, they would kneel before him'.

Henceforth, we shall only refer to him by his first name.

'If the circumstances permitted, Zlatan would karate chop an orca.'

Zlatan is top of the food chain, seal fucker!

Somebody call security.

This is all **fascinating**, but did you want to buy any petrol?

Zlatan would also like a Twix.

JUST FONTAINE

No one will ever score more goals than Just Fontaine did at a single World Cup in 1958. Not unless FIFA does something completely insane like expanding the tournament to include an improbable number of participants in an obvious attempt to line their pockets with more filthy, filthy, money. Yes, your record is safe, Monsieur.

Going into the World Cup, Fontaine had little international pedigree. OK, he'd scored a hat-trick on his debut in 1953, but it was in a dead rubber against Luxembourg, as part of an 8–0 demolition. In 1953 there emphatically was such a thing as an easy game at that level. He'd only made four more appearances for France before the tournament, and his performances in the warm-up matches didn't exactly inspire confidence; he kept slipping over because the studs in his boots were worn out. He ended up borrowing a pair from teammate Stéphane Bruey.

It's not documented whether Bruey had found the boots in the dusty attic of a deceased relative who'd been a prolific goal-scorer in a bygone era; nor whether the boots contained magical properties that transformed those who wore them into unstoppable goal machines; but, frankly, it's unlikely.

Fontaine was employed as a lone striker for the World Cup, after his attacking partner René Bliard busted his ankle in a pre-tournament friendly. The duo had starred together in the Reims side that had just claimed a league and cup double, with Fontaine scoring 34 goals. Reims had signed Fontaine as a replacement for the great Raymond Kopa, who had departed for Real Madrid, but the pair would link up superbly for France. Kopa was named player of the tournament, having provided a succession of perfectly threaded passes for the grateful Fontaine to lash home with his borrowed boots that, as we have established, had no supernatural powers because they were just shoes.

JUST FONTAINE'S 13 GOALS AT THE 1958 WORLD CUP

AN OPENING GAME HAT-TRICK IN A 7-3 WIN AGAINST PARAGUAY. THE FIRST TWO CAME FROM IDENTICAL THROUGH BALLS, LOFTED OVER PARAGUAY'S DEFENCE.

FRANCE DEFENDED LIKE PARAGUAYANS IN THEIR 3-2 DEFEAT TO YUGOSLAVIA, BUT FONTAINE SCORED TWO MORE: A TAP-IN AND AN AUDACIOUS LOB.

THE SECOND GOAL IN A 2-1 VICTORY OVER SCOTLAND, TO SEND FRANCE THROUGH TO THE QUARTER-FINALS.

A GLANCING HEADER AND A NEAT FINISH IN A 4-0 WIN AGAINST NORTHERN IRELAND, WHO WERE FORCED TO PICK INJURED GOAL-KEEPER HARRY GREGG, EVEN THOUGH HE'D BEEN USING A WALKING STICK TO HOBBLE AROUND THE TEAM HOTEL.

EVENTUAL CHAMPIONS BRAZIL BEAT FRANCE 5-2, BUT FONTAINE BROUGHT LES BLEUS LEVEL AT ONE POINT, AFTER DRIBBLING AROUND THE GOALKEEPER, GYLMAR.

NEEDING THREE GOALS TO BEAT SÁNDOR KOCSIS' RECORD FOR THE MOST GOALS SCORED AT A WORLD CUP, FONTAINE SCORED FOUR IN THE THIRD-PLACE PLAY-OFF AGAINST WEST GERMANY (FINAL SCORE: 6-3). THERE WAS NO GOLDEN BOOT IN THOSE DAYS, BUT HE WAS PRESENTED WITH AN AIR RIFLE BY A LOCAL NEWSPAPER.

WILLIAM 'DIXIE' DEAN

Middlesbrough's striker George Camsell probably thought his haul of 59 goals in a single season would never be bettered. As it turned out, his record would stand for just one season. In the 1927–28 campaign, Everton's 21-year-old striker, William 'Dixie' Dean, surpassed Camsell with a 60-goal tally. *Sixty.* As the delirious Everton supporters ran onto the pitch to celebrate his achievement, a thin distant cry echoed across the land from a north-easterly direction. It was the sound of George Camsell shouting the word 'Bastard' at the sky.

Dean was a football obsessive. He left school at 14 and became an apprentice fitter, working in the sheds at Wirral Railways. He opted to work the night shift so he could play football during the day. He and his fellow night workers held competitions to obliterate yard rats by booting them against a wall. Whichever way you look at it, it was grim.

There are conflicting theories about the basis of his nickname 'Dixie'. The most common was that it was a reference to his dark hair and complexion, which apparently resembled the people of the southern states of the USA. He preferred to be called Bill, but given that this was the 1920s, his nickname could have been a *lot* worse.

There was a violence to Dean's language when he discussed scoring. He spoke of 'butting' goals, as if the stadium was a pub car park and the ball the nose of a patron who'd spilled his pint of mild. However, despite being a tough competitor, Dean was never booked or sent off, and the statue of him that stands outside Goodison Park is inscribed with the words: *'Footballer. Gentleman. Evertonian.'*

Looking back on his career, Dean noted that while Liverpool were always recognised for their great goalkeepers, Everton were renowned for their centre-forwards. This tradition would persist, with the likes of Stuart Barlow, Brett Angell and James Beattie all pulling on the famous blue shirt, but it was Dean who set the standard.

DIXIE DEAN'S DEDICATION TO FOOTBALL WAS ABSOLUTE. HIS RECORD-BREAKING CAREER BEGAN AT TRANMERE ROVERS AT THE AGE OF 16. HIS COMMITMENT WAS NEVER BETTER ILLUSTRATED THAN WHEN A ROUGH CHALLENGE IN A RESERVE GAME SAW HIM LOSE A BOLLOCK. HE RESPONDED WITH CHARACTERISTIC BREVITY.

Don't rub them, just count them!

Ahhh. Seriously though, this is going to have to come off.

DEAN'S HEART BELONGED TO EVERTON, THOUGH. HIS DREAM MOVE BECAME REALITY WHEN THEY SIGNED HIM FOR £3,000 IN 1925, AT THE AGE OF 18. HE WAS SO EXCITED THAT HE RAN 2.5 MILES FROM HIS HOUSE TO MEET THE EVERTON SECRETARY AT A LOCAL HOTEL. THIS SET THE BENCHMARK FOR DESIRE AND INDUSTRY FOR ALL FUTURE EVERTON PLAYERS.

Your ball, Andy!

VAN DER MEYDE 7

Screw that, man; it's the weekend.

HE SCORED 32 GOALS IN HIS FIRST SEASON. EVERTON FINISHED IN MID-TABLE, BUT SPIRITS IN THE CAMP WERE HIGH. ACCORDING TO DEAN, THE SIDE CONTAINED NINE COMEDIANS, WHICH MUST HAVE BEEN TIRING FOR THE OTHER TWO.

Salt in the sugar bowl. Again. Nice one, lads.

He drank it! He actually drank it!

OPPOSITION PLAYERS WEREN'T SPARED EITHER. BEFORE EACH MERSEYSIDE DERBY, DEAN WOULD SEND A NOTE AND A BOTTLE OF ASPIRIN TO LIVERPOOL'S GOALKEEPER, ELISHA SCOTT.

"Get some sleep tonight, because I'll be on you tomorrow."

It's him again, isn't it? You have to **tell** someone.

Damn it, Alice; let me handle this.

DEAN'S PROLIFIC GOAL-SCORING PROPELLED EVERTON UP THE TABLE TO BECOME CHAMPIONS IN 1928. ON THE LAST DAY OF THE SEASON, HE BAGGED A HAT-TRICK AGAINST ARSENAL TO SET A NEW RECORD FOR THE MOST GOALS SCORED IN A SEASON (60). THE VITAL STRIKE - A TRADE-MARK HEADER - SPARKED WILD CELEBRATIONS.

Congratulations, Dixie.

Settle down, John; it's not the Rio Carnival, you maniac.

AWARE THAT HE WOULD BE MOBBED BY THE FANS UPON THE FINAL WHISTLE, DEAN ASKED THE REFEREE IF HE COULD LEAVE THE PITCH EARLY, TELLING THE OTHER PLAYERS THAT HE NEEDED TO USE THE TOILET.

Hah, yeah, what the hell. I think we've established by now that football in this era is completely nuts. Someone has just scored 60 goals in a season, for example.

Ta, ref.

JUST LIKE HIS RECORD, DEAN'S LOVE FOR EVERTON ENDURED. HE PASSED AWAY ON 1 MARCH 1980, HAVING SUFFERED A HEART ATTACK WHILST WATCHING THE MERSEYSIDE DERBY AT GOODISON PARK. IT WAS PERHAPS FITTING THAT HIS FINAL ACT WAS TO WATCH THE CLUB HE'D RACED THROUGH THE STREETS TO SIGN FOR AS A YOUNG MAN.

DENNIS BERGKAMP

At least once a season, Dennis Bergkamp would do something so outrageous that you would think he was playing a different game to everyone else. In a way, Bergkamp's Arsenal teammate Jérémie Aliadière could create this illusion too.

At the outset of his career, Bergkamp played alongside Marco van Basten in Johan Cruyff's Ajax team. His exquisite touch, balance and finishing skills earned him a move to Inter, but he endured a difficult couple of seasons in the world's toughest league. Arsenal manager Bruce Rioch came to his rescue in the summer of 1995, with a £7.5 million transfer; a move Bergkamp found out about via Ceefax. Rioch, Ceefax, Serie A being good: it was a scenario that couldn't have been more typically 'nineties' if the transfer was negotiated with Pogs.

Bergkamp didn't score in his first seven games for Arsenal, but broke his duck with two against Southampton; from there on in, he was flying. Or rather, he wasn't. Bergkamp was famously aviophobic; and unlike the rest of us, was unable to deal with his anxieties about falling from the sky in a burning cylinder of screaming tourists with a large dose of Valium and six pints in the airport bar. This made those long European away trips a literal pain in the buttocks.

Despite his on-field persona as an ice-cool assassin, according to teammate Ray Parlour Bergkamp was a dressing-room prankster whose favourite stunt was to yank down the trousers and pants of his unsuspecting colleagues. A good way of seeing whether you have achieved the god-like status of Dennis Bergkamp is to try this manoeuvre in your own workplace.

Bergkamp was also adept at pulling down the pants of even the best defences. His most celebrated goal probably came when he was playing for the Netherlands against Argentina in the quarter-finals of the 1998 World Cup. You've seen it. The long flat pass from Frank de Boer. The touch to kill the ball dead. The second touch to take it past Roberto Ayala. The finish with the outside of the right boot, past the outstretched hand of Carlos Roa, his shorts metaphorically tangled round his ankles, smooth white bottom and genitals exposed to an astonished global audience. Dennis had struck again.

SCORE GOALS THE DENNIS BERGKAMP WAY

PREPARATION IS KEY. IDEALLY, YOU'LL HAVE ENJOYED A RELAXING TEN-HOUR BUS JOURNEY, WHILST YOUR TEAM-MATES SLUM IT ON A PRIVATE JET.

"...I'm lovin' angels inste—

YOUR STATUS AS ALPHA PRACTICAL JOKER IS INDISPUTABLE, BUT UPON MEETING UP WITH THE REST OF THE SQUAD, THROW PASCAL CYGAN'S SHOE OVER THE STADIUM AS A REMINDER.

Naw...!

RIGHT, TIME TO FOCUS. THINK OF ALL THE PEOPLE WHO HAVE HELPED YOU TO GET TO THIS POINT.

JOHAN CRUYFF
MICHELS
RINUS
BRUCE
RIOCH

A LONG BALL IS PUMPED TOWARDS YOU, A DEFENDER MOVES IN YOUR DIRECTION, BUT YOU'LL HAVE ALREADY SOFTENED HIM UP WITH AN UNPUNISHED LATE TACKLE.

Balletic!

KILL THE DROPPING BALL DEAD WITH YOUR FIRST TOUCH. WITH YOUR SECOND TOUCH, DO SOMETHING SO FANCY THAT IT SENDS YOUR MARKER SO FAR OUT OF THE GAME THAT HE'LL NEED A TRAVEL GUIDE TO GET BACK.

NOW STEER THE BALL INTO THE ROOF OF THE NET WITH THE OUTSIDE OF YOUR BOOT

SOAK UP THE ADULATION OF THE CROWD. ON THE TOUCHLINE, YOUR MANAGER PUMPS HIS FISTS IN DELIGHT.

That should see me sweet for another dozen years at least.

THREE POINTS IN THE BAG, TIME TO SECURE A LIFT HOME. BUT BEFORE YOU DEPART, GIFT YOUR COLLEAGUES WITH ANOTHER REMINDER OF YOUR POTENCY.

Naw...!

Ooh, shall we pick up that hitchhiker?

Are you mad?

CULT HEROES (PART TWO)

During the early 1970s, a curious breed of footballer stalked the British Isles. An errant rabble of extroverts, bringing colour and sass to the grey landscape, they left in their wake a scattered trail of broken hearts and after-dinner anecdotes. These were The Mavericks and they could be spotted by their long hair, non-conformist sideburns, and skills that were so silky they could line a knee-length camel hair trench coat.

Perhaps the ultimate maverick was Robin Friday, a wild hedonist whose professional career lasted only four years, but who would shine with a brightness that would eclipse even the glamorous locations where he performed: Reading and Cardiff.

In the summer of 1972, Friday was contracted to play football at amateur level with Hayes. Working to earn some extra money during the off-season, he was applying asphalt to a roof when he fell and was impaled on a spike. It passed through a buttock, pierced his stomach and narrowly missed a lung. Presumably, this is the kind of life-changing experience that leaves you with a laissez-faire attitude to wearing shin pads.

The many stories that surround his on- and off-field exploits may have been embellished over the years. While there are plenty of contemporary accounts that attest to his ability as a player, there is sadly no evidence to support the claim that, after being sent off in his last ever professional game, for Cardiff at Brighton, he did a poo in the kit bag of opposition central defender, Mark Lawrenson. However, it is worth pausing for a second to consider what Lawrenson's face would have looked like had this event occurred.

Friday quit football at the age of just 25 and would tragically succumb to his drinking and drug addictions, dying at the age of 38 from a heart attack that was thought to have been brought on by a heroin overdose. While Friday's career was limited exclusively to the relative obscurity of the lower leagues, most other mavericks were prancing about in the upper echelons of the First Division, where their displays could catch the eye of a succession of England managers, who would then immediately dismiss them as being silly.

There was Stan Bowles, the artful attacking midfielder whose performances with QPR took them to within 14 minutes of winning the league championship, before Liverpool scored three late goals in their game at Wolves to pip them to the post. When QPR played an away game in Bowles' native north-west, he'd sometimes stay up there and turn out for one of the local pub teams on a Sunday. The only activity he loved more than playing football was gambling; he was a semi-permanent fixture at the White City dog track and was once forced to sell his greenhouse to settle his gambling debts. The only drawback to this was that Stan was renting the house from QPR's chairman, John Gregory.

Bowles was only ever capped five times for England, but Arsenal's flair player, Charlie George, was only ever picked once. Having acquitted himself well in the first half of a friendly against the Republic of Ireland, the forward got into a heated argument with Don Revie at half-time, when the manager told him to play on the left wing. He was substituted after an hour, mouthed off at Revie on his way to the bench, and never played for England again.

Frank Worthington was awarded eight caps for the national team, but was also regarded with suspicion. When he was called up to play for the under-23 squad, he almost gave Alf Ramsey a coronary by turning up at Heathrow wearing high-heeled cowboy boots, a red silk shirt and a lime velvet jacket. In fairness to Ramsey, that does sound like a horrible outfit.

Worthington played for 24 clubs during his long career, but it could have been different had he signed for Liverpool in 1972. A medical revealed that Huddersfield's most prolific lothario was suffering from high blood pressure, so the Reds' manager Bill Shankly advised him to go on holiday and relax. Curiously, a week of intensive R'n'R with strangers in Majorca didn't help him to unwind and he failed the test again upon his return and signed for Leicester instead.

Chelsea's legendary playmaker, Peter Osgood, fared no better for England, only ever being given two starts. It was the same story for his teammate Alan

Hudson. The duo had helped transform Chelsea into one of the most exciting teams in the country, but weren't trusted at international level. Both would later grace the glitzy playground of the North American Soccer League; the natural habitat of men who wore their shirts unbuttoned to their navel. There, they were joined by the wisecracking Rodney Marsh and, briefly, Tony Currie.

Of all the 1970s showmen, Currie won the most England caps (17), but the overriding attitude towards these entertainers was one of wariness. To Alf Ramsey and Don Revie, these incorrigible rogues were a needless luxury. It was a clash of intergenerational attitudes that had all the ingredients of a classic British sitcom. No, really, it did.

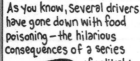

WEMBLEY BUS DEPOT

Don.

Alf.

As you know, several drivers have gone down with food poisoning — the hilarious consequences of a series of unlikely events that ended up with me having to cook in the staff canteen.

You haven't eaten your fish fingers, Gordon.

I don't feel too good...

As a result, we've had to draft in some replacements from the Wayward Showmen Recruitment Agency. I don't anticipate no problems.

We'll get these buses out and back in time for a nice round of carpet bowls, Alf.

Hmn.

FOUR HOURS LATER

Where the hell are they? I never had this trouble with Martin Peters. Or Martin Chivers. Not with any of the Martins.

GENERIC 1970s ROCK MUSIC..

This looks like someone now...

Hey, dudes. Frank Worthington.

From the agency, yeah.

Dolly birds? Cowboy boots? Dolly birds? Where's your uniform? This is a bus depot, not a vegetarian, Ban the Bomb, free-love orgy, you long-haired malcontent!

TSSSS-TS-TSSSSSSS-T

What's that sound?

Oi!

Watch it, Ossie; it's old man Revie!

TSSSS-TS-TSSS

OSGOOD IS GOOD

Osgood and Hudson, I might have known. Oh you'll swing for this, you mark my words.

MATTHIAS SINDELAR

The only footage that exists of Matthias Sindelar can be glimpsed in scratchy newsreels; brief images of a gaunt man with a bulbous head and slicked-back hair, bony legs protruding from sail-like shorts, working ten to the dozen. It's a mildly comedic image to modern eyes, but he must even have looked different to other footballers in the 1920s; his elegant appearance earning him the nickname 'The Paperman' from his fanboys on the Viennese coffee house scene.

It was in one such joint – 'The Ring Café' – that the patrons convinced Austria's coach Hugo Meisl, to recall their delicate hero to the national team. Despite scoring four goals in his first three games at international level, Meisl had dropped Sindelar in favour of Josef Uridil, whose contrasting style and appearance was evidenced by his nickname: 'The Tank'.

In perhaps the only recorded instance of gobshites in a greasy spoon being right, once Sindelar was restored to the starting line-up, Austria experienced a fantastic run of form. This began with a 5–0 thrashing of Scotland in 1931, and extended through to the 1934 World Cup. 'Das Wunderteam' got as far as the semi-finals before succumbing to Italy on a boggy San Siro pitch that made their neat passing game impossible. The game's decisive goal came when Giuseppe Meazza barged Austria's goalkeeper, Peter Platzer, over the line.

Sadly, it would be Sindelar's last World Cup appearance. By the time the next tournament rolled around, Europe was on the brink of war, Austria had been annexed and Sindelar's story would have a tragic end.

WHEN NAZI GERMANY ANNEXED AUSTRIA, THE FAMOUS WUNDERTEAM WAS ALSO SWALLOWED UP. A 'RECONCILIATION MATCH' WAS ORGANISED IN VIENNA IN APRIL 1938, TO CELEBRATE.

It's coming home, it's coming home, it's coming, the Thousand Year Reich of death and fire is coming home.

IN TRUTH, HITLER CARED LITTLE FOR FOOTBALL, BUT KNEW OF ITS POWER. HE ONLY EVER ATTENDED ONE MATCH, AT THE BERLIN OLYMPICS IN 1936. GERMANY LOST 2-0 TO NORWAY AND THE FÜHRER HUFFED OFF EARLY.

Ten minutes left? Game delicately poised? Let's leave now to beat the traffic. Come on, kids...

AS BAD AS ADOLF HITLER.

SINDELAR, IT APPEARS, DID NOT NEED THAT FASCIST GROOVE THANG. HE SPENT THE FIRST HALF TOYING WITH HIS GERMAN OPPONENTS, BUT MISSED NUMEROUS SIMPLE CHANCES. ONE THEORY HAS IT THAT THIS WAS A DELIBERATE, SARCASTIC WAY OF RIDICULING ORDERS TO NOT SCORE AGAINST THE FATHERLAND.

HAH!

But Matthias, you've blasted the ball into Berlin again.

Precisely.

THE BITTER LIBTARD SNOWFLAKES HAVE GONE TOO FAR THIS TIME. NO MORE MISTER NICE TOTALITARIAN FROM NOW ON.

AUSTRIA COULDN'T RESIST THE TEMPTATION, THOUGH. SINDELAR GAVE THEM A SECOND-HALF LEAD AND WHEN SCHASTI SESTA MADE IT 2-0, THE PAPERMAN DANCED IN FRONT OF THE SEETHING SENIOR NAZI OFFICIALS.

WITHIN A YEAR HE WAS DEAD. AFTER DECLINING TO PLAY FOR THE UNIFIED GERMANY TEAM, HE BOUGHT A CAFÉ FROM A JEWISH MAN WHO'D BEEN FORCED TO SELL UNDER NAZI LAW. SINDELAR WAS LATER CENSURED FOR REFUSING TO PUT UP NAZI PROPAGANDA POSTERS.

What is this outrage?

I believe it's called twerking, sir.

Add him to the list.

Yeah, your whole genocidal race hate theme is really at odds with the chilled out jazz café vibe I'm going for.

HE WAS FOUND DEAD IN HIS APARTMENT IN 1939, LYING IN BED WITH HIS GIRLFRIEND, CAMILLA CASTAGNOLA, WHO LATER DIED IN HOSPITAL. THE OFFICIAL VERDICT STATED THAT THEY HAD SUFFERED CARBON MONOXIDE POISONING.

HOWEVER, THE PUBLIC PROSECUTOR WAS STILL TO REACH A CONCLUSION WHEN THE NAZIS ORDERED THE CASE TO BE CLOSED. SUSPICIONS ABOUND, BUT HIS NEIGHBOURS HAD COMPLAINED ABOUT A DEFECTIVE CHIMNEY STACK JUST DAYS BEFORE. VIENNA MOURNED, WITH 20,000 PEOPLE ATTENDING HIS FUNERAL.

DER PAPIERENE   1903~1939

SCOURGE OF THE NAZIS ~ GREAT COFFEE

ANTONIO CASSANO

While undoubtedly blessed with outstanding natural talent, Antonio Cassano – 'The Jewel of Old Bari' – is widely regarded to be flakier than the *Singing Detective*, eating a bowl of Bran Flakes, whilst brushing dandruff out of his hair. With a Flake.

Within eight days of signing for Verona in July 2017, he shocked the club by announcing his immediate retirement from football. Then, later that day, he told a press conference that he'd reconsidered and was looking forward to the season starting. Another U-turn followed a week later, with a declaration that he was in fact calling it quits. If it were anyone else, you'd be shocked, but this was fairly standard behaviour for Cassano. His former coach, Fabio Capello, even had a term for it: *Cassanata*, or 'Cassano-ism'

However, when he was on form, his eccentricities were a small price to pay. Within a week of making his professional debut, Italy knew he was special. Making just his second appearance for his local club Bari, against Inter, he controlled a 40-yard pass with his heel, accelerated into space, skipped between Laurent Blanc and Christian Panucci, and finished calmly. He then hurdled the advertising board and was mobbed by a pack of photographers and officials on the athletics track. The only person in the Stadio San Nicola who was unimpressed was the referee, who booked him.

Two seasons later, at the age of 19, he signed for Roma for 60 billion lire, making him the most expensive teenager in the world. Although he played well, he clashed with coach Capello and teammate Francesco Totti; two battles he was never going to win. He was transferred to Real Madrid in 2006 and made a solid start, but the club soon grew concerned by his poor diet and alarming weight gain. In his autobiography *Dico tutto* ('I'll tell you everything'), Cassano claimed to have slept with '600 to 700' women and that he used to sneak them into his room on the night before Real Madrid matches. He also said he'd celebrate each conquest with three or four croissants', delivered by a waiter friend. This must have been a bleak duty for the waiter. Phone chirps up at 2 a.m. Oh God, it's Antonio, has he had an accident? Ah, no, he just wants more sex pastries. This is really stretching the definition of friendship. Yes, I'll get the custard ones.

However, his fun was to come to an end when Real Madrid appointed his old boss Fabio Capello as coach.

ANTONIO CASSANO AND FABIO CAPELLO HAD ALWAYS ENDURED A ROCKY RELATIONSHIP AT ROMA, BUT WHEN THEY WERE REUNITED AT REAL MADRID, CASSANO REALISED THAT HE HAD TO MAKE AMENDS. IN AN ATTEMPT TO CONVINCE HIS NEW BOSS THAT HE HAS CHANGED HIS WAYS, ANTONIO INVITES FABIO ROUND FOR DINNER...

Ah, Capo; come in, come in!

Hello, Antonio.

Hope you brought your appetite, we're having grilled chicken and steamed asparagus. No more junk food for me – a complete lifestyle overhaul; the destructive habits and behaviour are behind me.

Hmm. And my coat goes in here, I take it.

Oh, yes, but let me—

I'm quite capable, thank you.

What is that you've painted on the walls; neutral white? Bit racy for my tastes, but it is 2006 I suppose.

Unfortunately.

....

Sit down, sit down; have some crisp bread and mulched carrot dip. Heh.

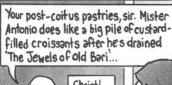

LATER... Well, that was adequate. Now, what's this I read about you being prepared to 'walk back to Italy to re-sign for Roma'?

Ah.

I've changed my mind about that.

How far have I walked now?

Four hundred metres, sir.

Screw it, I'll just cook the old bastard dinner.

I'm pleased to hear it. I believe we can do great work here, Antonio.

Really? Great, I—

KNOCK KNOCK KNOCK

What's this; more guests?

Your post-coitus pastries, sir. Mister Antonio does like a big pile of custard-filled croissants after he's drained 'The Jewels of old Bari...

Christ! Not now, Parsons!

OH DOES HE?

I'll see you at five a.m. for death by shuttle run!

NAW!

Ooh, croissants!

LEN SHACKLETON

When the new World Champions, West Germany, arrived in London in 1954 to play a friendly at Wembley, England's selection committee was faced with a headache. Most of their first-team regulars were ruled out through injury, leaving them with no choice other than to pick a wayward misfit like Len Shackleton. He was definitely going to do something embarrassing, like knocking a one-two off a corner flag to humiliate a full-back, or – *worse* – sullying the famous shirt by looking like he was *enjoying* himself. It was a total bloody nightmare.

Shackleton was one of English football's first true mavericks. 'The Clown Prince of Soccer' they called him. His jet-age jocularity was mixed with an outspoken honesty and a healthy streak of cynicism towards authority, which some found confronting. Famously, his autobiography included a chapter titled 'The Average Director's Knowledge of Football', which sat above a blank page.

Sometimes, Shackleton's ire would be directed towards his own teammates. He didn't get on well with Sunderland midfielder Trevor Ford, so would deliver him passes that looked perfect, but were in fact hit with enough backspin to make them almost impossible to control. That he even had the ability to do that set him apart from most of his peers. Oh God, what if he did that to Stanley Matthews?

As it turned out, the selectors needn't have worried; Shackleton put in his best performance in an England shirt as the team recorded a comfortable 3–1 win; the highlight of which was his flitting dribble into the box and composed chip over the goalkeeper, Fritz Herkenrath. By this stage, Shackleton was already 32 years old, and this would be the last of his five caps for England. *Phew!*

LEN SHACKLETON WAS ONE OF THE FIRST FLAIR PLAYERS TO FALL FOUL OF THE ENGLISH FOOTBALL ESTABLISHMENT'S ENDURING SUSPICION OF INDIVIDUALITY. HE WAS CAPPED ONLY FIVE TIMES AND THE ATTITUDE TOWARDS HIM WAS SUMMED UP NEATLY BY ONE SELECTOR, WHO SNIFFED:

We play at Wembley Stadium, not the London Palladium.

WHILST 'SHACK' WAS ONE OF THE MOST EXCITING PROSPECTS OF HIS GENERATION, THE STUFFY OLD BLAZERS HAD A POINT: WEMBLEY STADIUM ISN'T A PLACE FOR ENTERTAINMENT.

ED SHEERAN!

'THE DEFINITIVE PROOF THAT, AS A SPECIES, WE ARE DONE' TOUR

HE WAS ACCUSTOMED TO OVERCOMING REJECTION, THOUGH. AT THE OUTSET OF HIS CAREER HE WAS LET GO BY ARSENAL. THEIR MANAGER, GEORGE ALLISON, ALLOWED HIM TO SEE HIS NEW TV SET AS A CONSOLATION.

State of the art, full black and white colour, one channel. You won't have seen anything like this back home in Yorkshire. Do you have electricity up there yet?

SHACKLETON RETURNED TO HIS HOMETOWN IN 1939, SIGNING FOR BRADFORD PARK AVENUE AND WORKING IN THE COAL MINES DURING THE WAR. HE LATER CAUSED PUBLIC ANNOYANCE BY CONFESSING THAT HE 'HADN'T OVER-WORKED HIMSELF' DURING THIS ASSIGNMENT.

Can you lot stop moving around? I think it's interfering with the reception.

HE SIGNED FOR NEWCASTLE AFTER THE WAR, SCORING SIX GOALS ON HIS DEBUT, IN A 13-0 ROUT AGAINST NEWPORT COUNTY. ACCORDING TO JACKIE MILBURN, HE SCORED HIS SIXTH GOAL WITH HIS ARSE. OTHER REPORTS STATED IT WENT IN OFF A NEWPORT PLAYER'S ARSE. THANKFULLY, PUBLIC SERVICES WERE WELL-STAFFED BACK THEN, SO THE DISPUTE WAS SETTLED QUICKLY.

DUBIOUS ARSE COMMITTEE

It's ringing!

HE DIDN'T STAY THERE LONG – WITHIN 18 MONTHS HE'D SIGNED FOR SUNDERLAND FOR £20,500. THIS WAS A HUGE SUM FOR THE TIME, BUT SUNDERLAND WERE KNOWN AS 'THE BANK OF ENGLAND CLUB' DUE TO THEIR LAVISH SPENDING. LUCKILY, GOOD SENSE HAS SINCE PREVAILED.

We've signed Didier Ndong for £13.8 million!

That must mean he's twice as good as Jozy Altidore! How is that even possible?

HIS PROLIFIC GOAL RECORD AND EXHIBITIONISM MADE HIM A HIT WITH THE CROWDS. ON ONE OCCASION, WHEN 2-1 UP AGAINST ARSENAL, HE DRIBBLED INTO THE PENALTY AREA BEFORE STANDING ON THE BALL AND PRETENDING TO CHECK HIS WATCH AND COMB HIS HAIR, TO WIDESPREAD DELIGHT.

OFTEN OUTSPOKEN, SHACKLETON BECAME A SPORTS JOURNALIST AFTER HANGING UP HIS BOOTS IN 1957. HE LIVED HIS LIFE AS HE PLAYED – NEVER AFRAID TO TRY NEW THINGS. FOR EXAMPLE, WHILE AT SUNDERLAND HE OPENED A BARBER SHOP.

THE AVERAGE MAVERICK INSIDE FORWARD'S KNOWLEDGE OF THE HIGH QUIFF-POMPADOUR

FAUSTINO ASPRILLA

Only a small group of footballers can claim to have been photographed wearing a Tyrannosaurus Rex costume while riding a pony that is playing football with a huge inflatable ball. Whilst Faustino Asprilla may now be better known for his appearances on Colombian reality television shows, his own brand of flavoured condoms, or the Tyrannosaurus Rex thing, for a spell in the early nineties, he was one of the hottest prospects in world football.

In 1992, he left Atlético Nacional for a Parma side that was in the process of upsetting the Serie A elite.* It was his long-distance free kick that beat an AC Milan side that had previously enjoyed a 58-match unbeaten run, and it was his goals that helped the club reach their first European final; a feat previously unimaginable for the small club. The Parma side of this era are recalled with fondness by misty-eyed fans of a certain age. With their compact stadium, distinctive playing strip and open, attacking football, they became a staple of Sunday afternoon TV viewing.

Tino was tearing it up at international level too. He scored twice for Colombia in a historic 5–0 thumping of Argentina in Buenos Aires in 1993. The result made them one of the favourites for the following year's World Cup, but they cracked under the weight of expectation and the steady stream of helpful death threats from the drug cartels back home.

A move to the Premier League with Newcastle followed in 1996. He'd studied the league table and seen they were 12 points clear, and he'd looked at a map and observed Newcastle was by the coast. He therefore arrived gleefully expecting to parade the Premier League trophy in an open-top bus along the palm-tree lined streets of the tropical north-east. Instead, his arrival completely unbalanced the team, they slumped to second place and he froze his tits off.

However, Asprilla is still remembered affectionately on Tyneside, thanks to his unpredictable play, flashes of brilliance and half-arsed cartwheeling goal celebrations. He may have been pushed out of the team by the arrival of Alan Shearer, who at the time was one of the best strikers in the world, but there was one thing Shearer lacked: the entrepreneurial spirit to launch his own range of flavoured johnnies; something for which we should all be grateful.

---

* 'Elite' in the old sense of the word, rather than just people who admit to having read a book once.

FAUSTINO ASPRILLA

WAS NOT YOUR AVERAGE FOOTBALLER. NOT FOR HIM THE PLAYSTATION MARATHON OR SELFIE WITH A BLAND POP STAR. HERE ARE FEW OF HIS MORE MEMORABLE ANTICS.

SIGNS FOR NEWCASTLE IN **THIS**.

TINO'S BEST YEARS CAME AT PARMA; HIS GOALS HELPING THEM TO THE 1993 EUROPEAN CUP WINNERS' CUP FINAL. SADLY, HE MISSED THE GAME AFTER SMASHING HIS FOOT THROUGH THE GLASS DOORS OF A BUS DURING A CONFRONTATION WITH THE DRIVER.

Human male foot to scale

HIS ROAD SAFETY RECORD WASN'T THE BEST, THOUGH. HE HAD FIVE CAR ACCIDENTS DURING THE SUMMER OF 1992 ALONE.

Hey, man; jump in, I'll give you a lift.

Tino! Christ. Heh, no, I'm good thanks. Need the exercise, yeah.

AN EXCELLENT HOUSE GUEST, TINO WAS ARRESTED IN 1994 FOR FIRING UNLICENSED GUNS AT A NEW YEAR'S EVE PARTY.

1995, BITCHES!

HE MADE HIS NEWCASTLE DEBUT AT MIDDLESBROUGH. HE'D ONLY JUST MET THE TEAM OVER LUNCH, DURING WHICH HE HAD A GLASS OF WINE. HE WAS SURPRISED TO THEN BE NAMED AS A SUBSTITUTE, BUT CAME OFF THE BENCH TO HELP NEWCASTLE WIN, 2-1.

Warm up, Tino lad.

What does it **look** like I'm doing?

WHILST AT NEWCASTLE, HE WAS RENOWNED FOR INVITING RANDOM PEOPLE BACK TO HIS HOUSE FOR WILD PARTIES.

Back to mine, stranger! And bring your monkey friend!

Eh?

I'm Rob Lee. Your teammate, Rob Lee.

HIS FINEST MOMENT FOR NEWCASTLE CAME WITH A HAT-TRICK AGAINST BARCELONA. HOWEVER, HE'D NEARLY MISSED THE GAME THROUGH SHAGGING REASONS (THIS MAY HAVE BEEN A COVER-UP TO PROTECT HIS LOTHARIO REPUTATION).

RING BINDER WORLD!

See, I told you it was cool.

Oh God, Tomas; look at the **time**!

TINO ONCE APPEARED NAKED ON THE COVER OF A MAGAZINE. THIS, MERCIFULLY, DID NOT SET A TREND FOR HIS FORMER NEWCASTLE COLLEAGUES.

STUD FARM
PROUD PEACOCK
DARREN REVEALS ALL

BLIMEY. IN RETIREMENT, TINO HAS TAKEN TO KEEPING DANCING PONIES. HE ONCE LENT A £44,000 SHOW HORSE TO A FRIEND, WHO PROMPTLY GOT DRUNK AT A FAIR AND GAVE IT AWAY.

Go on, give me a free go and I'll let you keep my unicorn.

Go on then.

OH YEAH, DEFENDERS

The value of the defensive side of football is seldom recognised. Take for example this book, which has shoved them right to the back and can only muster four players for inclusion, all at the behest of the publisher. A damning indictment on the slack-mouthed consumerist football fan, who attributes more merit to a filthy *rabona* than a volleyed clearance into the camera gantry. Nobody ever put Chris Smalling on the cover of their video game franchise, for shame.

Fabio Cannavaro was the last defender to win the Ballon d'Or, in 2006, a decade after Matthias Sammer won it. Before that, you have to go back as far as Franz Beckenbauer. However, being a top-class defender is not about individuality (nobody wants a maverick back there), it's about being part of a cohesive unit; you're only as good as the right-back you scream at to step up.

The very existence of defenders adds value to goals. Without them there to block and harry, head and tackle, matches would become a farcical procession of high-fiving trots back to the halfway line. If you want to know what a sport looks like with no real barrier to goal-scoring, watch a game of Australian rules football. There you can experience the visceral thrill of seeing people in vests scrapping over an oval ball, like it's the last flat-screen in the January sales, in order to win the right to kick it between a set of unguarded posts. Teams usually rack up triple-figure scores, and although it's good when they do throw-ins (with the lineman flinging the ball backwards over their heads), the sheer number of goals reduces the dramatic tension. There's rarely such a thing as a game-changing goal in Aussie rules.*

It's no coincidence that half of the defenders in this, admittedly insultingly short, chapter are Italian. It was in Italy where Helenio Herrera honed the tactical system of *catenaccio*, bringing domestic and Continental success to Inter. This basically involved placing a sweeper behind the defence, to tidy up any loose balls, provide an extra layer of cover, launch counter-attacks and generally look dashing. Herrera claimed that *catenaccio* was, in principle, an attacking formation, and that it was those who later imitated the system that led to it being considered as ultra-defensive.

Despite *catenaccio* falling out of fashion, Italy still boasts an unequalled reputation for producing world-class defenders, whether they be graceful, intelligent ball-players like Maldini, Facchetti, Nesta or Scirea; wizened leaders like Baresi, Bergomi, or the other Baresi; or simply hard bastards like Claudio Gentile. They are also renowned for their mastering of 'the dark arts': the more underhand methods of players like Marco Materazzi would regularly infuriate opposition fans and players. Most spectacularly, Zinedine Zidane became so sick of Materazzi's chatter that he drove his own career off the edge of a cliff during the 2006 World Cup final.

This sort of behaviour was anathema to many people in the British Isles, who were more accustomed to the kind of old-fashioned centre-half who would wear his violence like a rosette. None of that sneaky shirt-pulling, pinching and name-calling; just honest, hard-working, shin-snapping tackles, followed by handshakes in the players' lounge afterwards. We preferred our defenders to be the kinds of people who would leap onto the ball like war heroes smothering a grenade in an orphanage. Until relatively recently, many British fans felt that a defender wasn't worthy of the name unless he left the field with a mist of arterial spray fizzing from his temple.

However, the more cosmopolitan nature of the Premier League has altered this perception, with many supporters now expecting that defenders be equipped with the skill to do something more productive than smashing the ball straight back to the opposition. It's the kind of craven intellectualism

---

* FACT CHECK: It turns out they *do* have defenders in Aussie rules, but it's still rubbish and long and stupid.

that will hopefully be outlawed after Brexit, when the country's thriving marmalade-based economy will give people the confidence to be as fucking stupid as they like. In your *face*, Lily Allen.

Anyway, defenders...

FRANCO BARESI

Franco Baresi's brother, Giuseppe, seemed the better prospect. Inter signed him in favour of the 14-year-old Franco, whom they considered a bit too weedy for the physical and mental rigours of Serie A. In fairness, it also took AC Milan three trials to see that the younger Baresi, although small and quiet, was as hard as a block of old Parmesan.

Franco had to be tough. At the age of 17, his father died in a car accident, just four years after the death of his mother, making an orphan of him, his two brothers and two sisters. It was around this time that he made his full debut for Milan; he would go on to enjoy a 20-year playing career at the club, coinciding with the most gilded period in their history.

This being Italy, the road to success was littered with potholes. He missed four months of the 1981–2 season with a blood disease and Milan were relegated to Serie B. However, despite offers from other clubs, he decided to stick around and was named as captain, at the age of 22. The arrival of Silvio Berlusconi, and the appointment of Arrigo Sacchi as coach proved pivotal. Along with Paulo Maldini, Billy Costacurta, Mauro Tassotti and Christian Panucci, Baresi formed part of the most formidable defence in world football, as Milan won back-to-back European Cups. In the 1987–8 Scudetto-winning campaign, they conceded just 14 goals all season.

In addition to his dominance as a defender, Baresi regularly contributed with goals during this period and was an adept penalty-taker, apart from that one time, which we won't dwell on. But it was the sight of the scruffy-haired sweeper frustrating a procession of strikers in the world's toughest league for which he will be best remembered.

FRANCO BARESI

BOBBY MOORE

West Ham's World Cup-winning captain exuded the qualities that many people like to believe reflect England's national characteristics: a calmness under pressure, a quiet dignity, a brave stoicism. All you need to do is stand outside Morrisons for five minutes and watch people come to blows over parking spots to see that these self-perpetuating stereotypes are plainly bollocks. However, like many of his countrymen, Moore did vote Tory and had a mid-level drink problem, so maybe there is something in it.

Alf Ramsey believed Moore to be his most important player ('my captain, my leader, my right-hand man . . . Without him England would never have won the World Cup'). Franz Beckenbauer said he was the best defender in the history of the game. His obvious defensive capabilities aside, Moore was also a player of exceptional vision, as evidenced by the two goals he set up in the 1966 World Cup final. Firstly he directed a quickly-taken free-kick onto the head of Geoff Hurst, and then, in the dying moments of extra-time, with Jack Charlton howling at him to punt the ball over the Wembley roof, his long pass played in Hurst to lash in England's fourth and put the game decisively beyond West Germany's reach.

Moore trained for hours to iron out the few defects in his game; this kind of studiousness was almost unheard of in British football at the time. Why would you want to do *extra* work? Maybe it was for this reason that the public never completely took Moore to their hearts. Nobody likes a try-hard, making the rest of us look bad by comparison. Certainly, his composed nature was frequently interpreted as aloofness and few people ever really got to know him.

Still, as someone who played 108 times for his country, and captained them to their only major success, you would think he would have been deserving of a little more affection. Oh, hang on, he played for West Ham. Yep, that's probably it. Carry on.

IF THERE WAS ONE PERFORMANCE THAT TYPIFIED THE CHARACTER OF BOBBY MOORE, IT WAS HIS IMPERIOUS DISPLAY AGAINST BRAZIL AT THE 1970 WORLD CUP. HE PRODUCED A STRING OF COOL-HEADED INTERVENTIONS IN SEARING CONDITIONS THAT WOULD HAVE MELTED THE RESOLVE OF MOST ENGLISHMEN.

MOORE WAS AS FASTIDIOUS ON THE PITCH AS HE WAS IN HIS PRIVATE LIFE; A PERFECTIONIST WHO DEMANDED NEATNESS AND ORDER.

THROUGHOUT HIS CAREER, HE PLAYED WITH THE SAME STRAIGHT-BACKED CONFIDENCE THAT HE SHOWED WHEN STARRING IN A TV COMMERCIAL ENCOURAGING PEOPLE TO VISIT THEIR LOCAL PUB.

HE WASN'T ESPECIALLY FAST OR STRONG, AND HEADERS WERE A RARITY, BUT HIS SENSE OF ANTICIPATION COUNTERED ANY DEFICIENCIES. JOCK STEIN ONCE SAID THAT MOORE COULD SEE TWENTY MINUTES INTO THE FUTURE.

MOORE'S SHOWING AGAINST BRAZIL WAS ALL THE MORE REMARKABLE CONSIDERING HE'D RECENTLY SUFFERED THE TRAUMA OF BEING WRONGLY-ACCUSED OF STEALING A BRACELET DURING A PRE-TOURNAMENT TRIP TO COLOMBIA. IT MUST HAVE BEEN A RELIEF TO RETURN HOME ONCE ENGLAND'S WORLD CUP WAS OVER.

BACK IN GUADALAJARA, IT WAS HIS PERFECTLY-TIMED PENALTY BOX TACKLE ON JAIRZINHO THAT WOULD GO DOWN AS THE FINEST PIECE OF DEFENDING IN ENGLISH FOOTBALL HISTORY.

THIS REMAINED THE CASE UNTIL 2010, WHEN JOHN TERRY TRIED TO STOP A SHOT BY A SLOVENIAN PLAYER BY DIVING AT IT HEADFIRST, MISSING BY A MATTER OF FEET.

EVEN MOORE COULDN'T KEEP BRAZIL AT BAY, THOUGH AND ENGLAND NARROWLY LOST, 1-0. UPON THE FINAL WHISTLE, PELÉ AND MOORE EMBRACED AND SWAPPED SHIRTS. TWO GIANTS OF THE GAME COMING TOGETHER TO CREATE ONE OF ITS MOST ICONIC IMAGES.

PAUL BREITNER

Former Wigan Athletic manager Paul Jewell has a tortoise called Trotsky. On the whole, though, footballers whose sympathies lie on the left side of politics are pretty rare. Unless Kyle Walker has a Little Red Book tucked away in his boot bag, there can't be many Maoist full-backs at top-level European clubs. Therefore, West Germany's left-back and commie pinko, Paul Breitner, was virtually unique (especially if you discount Inter legend Javier Zanetti, whose links with the Zapatistas in Mexico extended to actually helping to fund sports, water and health projects; rather than just having a poster of Che Guevara on his bedroom wall and a St. Pauli logo stencilled on his tortoise).

Breitner was more than just a bigmouth, banging on in the student union bar about the mobilisation of the peasantry. He was also one of the driving forces behind the success of Bayern Munich and West Germany in the 1970s. His Bayern debut came in 1971, after an injury crisis left them bereft of defenders. Coach Udo Lattek drafted the young midfielder Breitner as a full-back, perhaps reasoning that it's the easiest position on the pitch, so even the weird-looking wolf-child with Leo Sayer hair could play there. Breitner made it his own, and by the end of the season, he was making his international debut. Little more than a year later, he was playing a decisive role in the national team becoming European Champions.

Breitner's most successful year came in 1974, when he won the European Cup with Bayern and the World Cup with West Germany. He scored three goals in the tournament: a 25-yard winner against Chile, a 30-yard belter against Yugoslavia, and a textbook penalty that pulled Germany level in the final against Holland – a responsibility that had come his way by merit of being the person standing nearest to the ball. Later in his career, he made the great leap forward into midfield and linked up superbly with Karl-Heinz Rummenigge. Primarily though, he is recalled as a defender whose revolutionary attitude and handlebar moustache helped to overthrow the feudal oppression of opposition right-backs. *Smash the system!*

10 GREAT THINGS ABOUT PAUL BREITNER (THAT HAVE NOTHING TO DO WITH HIS HAIR)

HE SMOKED A PIPE.

HE ADOPTED A VIETNAMESE ORPHAN.

Oh. So it's not one of those things where you just pay a direct debit and get a letter once a year?

Nope.

HE APPEARED IN A SPAGHETTI WESTERN CALLED 'POTATO FRITZ', ABOUT A GROUP OF GERMANS WHO ENCOUNTER SOME GOLD THIEVES.

Right on, lads. All property is theft, yeah!

HE TRIED TO AVOID DOING HIS NATIONAL SERVICE BY HIDING IN A COAL SHED.

This is duller than one of Berti Vogts' board game evenings.

Quiet, child, or it's back to the orphanage with you.

HE TOOK A COPY OF MAO'S 'LITTLE RED BOOK' INTO TRAINING, PERHAPS GIVING PAT NEVIN THE MISPLACED CONFIDENCE TO TAKE A COPY OF THE NME INTO TRAINING AT CHELSEA.

HE WAS AN EXPERT AT CONTRITE APOLOGIES. AFTER BAYERN WON THE LEAGUE IN 1973, HE WAS PHOTOGRAPHED DANCING NAKED IN A SWIMMING POOL. WHEN REPRIMANDED, HE COMPLAINED:

At this shitty club, they can't even celebrate!

HE WAS A RIDDLE OF CONTRADICTION; ON ONE HAND DECRYING THE ABSENCE OF SOCIALISM IN THE BUNDESLIGA, ON THE OTHER LAMENTING THE FACT THAT HE COULDN'T TAKE HIS SPORTS CARS WITH HIM WHEN HE JOINED REAL MADRID.

To paraphrase Mao: 'I am a lone man, walking the world with a leaky umbrella. Which is why I need a kick-ass ride. Preferably in red.'

HE GREW TO REGRET THE STATEMENTS HE'D MADE IN HIS YOUTH, WAY BEFORE FACEBOOK MADE IT POPULAR.

Hey, remember when you spent a month posting nothing but Morrissey lyrics because that girl you liked wouldn't go out with you?

No sleep for you tonight, Romeo.

HE HAD A GOOD LINE IN INSULTS; ONCE LIKENING EINTRACHT BRAUNSCHWEIG - WHERE HE PLAYED FOR ONE SEASON - TO 'A VILLAGE SHOP WHERE EVERYONE GIBBERS ON ABOUT HORSE APPLES'.

Do you have any horse apple balm left from the horse apple festival?

Of course, it's in the horse apple by-products aisle.

Come on come on come on

IN 1998, HE WAS ANNOUNCED AS GERMANY MANAGER, ONLY FOR THE DFB TO CHANGE THEIR MINDS SEVENTEEN HOURS LATER, MAKING HIS STINT AS AN INTERNATIONAL COACH EVEN SHORTER THAN THAT OF ANOTHER COLOSSUS OF THE GAME.

Two more sambucas and a family pack of Scampi Fries, yeah.

GIACINTO FACCHETTI

There's a great photo of Giancinto Facchetti in his prime at Inter. Shoulders back, chin out, square jaw clenched, blond hair neatly parted. He's framed to the right of the portrait, with what appears to be a municipal golf course over his shoulder. The thick black and blue stripes of the famous shirt lead the eye up to his face, which holds the expression of a disappointed father-in-law silently judging your new decking.

As the picture suggests, Facchetti was an elegant defender; groundbreaking in becoming one of the first full-backs to venture beyond the halfway line. Technically adept with both feet, those long legs would motor him upfield to arc in crosses or drill in shots.

Born in Treviglio, near Bergamo, Facchetti had been on the verge of signing for Atalanta before something attracted him to the cash-rich Inter. He made his debut for them at the age of 18, having been recommended by Inter's youth coach, Giuseppe Meazza, and went on to play 476 Serie A games for the club. Little wonder that, upon his death in 2006, his famous number 3 shirt was retired. He represented Inter at all levels, becoming a member of the technical staff once his playing days were over and even enjoyed a spell as club President, a position in which that municipal golf course experience must have come in handy.

COUNTER-ATTACK WAS A VITAL COMPONENT OF HELENIO HERRERA'S CATENACCIO SYSTEM AT INTER, AND THIS CAME IN THE FORM OF GIACINTO FACCHETTI- A SPRING-HEELED ADONIS WHOSE OVERLAPPING RUNS FROM DEEP LEFT A TRAIL OF BEWILDERED OPPONENTS.

How?

HIS STYLE OF PLAY CAPTIVATED MILLIONS, INCLUDING FRANZ BECKENBAUER, WHO DECIDED THAT HE TOO SHOULD BE ALLOWED TO MARAUD FORWARD, FROM A MORE CENTRAL DEFENSIVE POSITION.

When I grow up, I'm going to be like Facchetti and there's not a thing you can do about it.

You're 23.

FACCHETTI WAS ALSO FAMED FOR HIS GENTLEMANLY CONDUCT. HE WAS SENT OFF ONLY ONCE IN HIS CAREER, ALBEIT FOR THAT MOST HEINOUS OF OFFENCES: SARCASM.

Good one.

Gia-cinto!

HIS REGULAR FORAYS UPFIELD WERE REWARDED IN GOALS-TEN OF THEM IN 1965-66. THIS WAS A RECORD TALLY FOR A SERIE A DEFENDER, AND REMAINED SO FOR TWENTY YEARS, UNTIL IT WAS SURPASSED BY DANIEL PASSARELLA OF FIORENTINA.

Good one.

FACCHETTI FORMED PART OF INTER'S INDOMITABLE BACK-LINE ALONGSIDE SUCH LUMINARIES AS ARMANDO PICCHI (THE WHITE FEATHER) TARCISIO BURGNICH (THE ROCK) AND ARISTIDE GUARNERI (NO NICKNAME).

I want you to start calling me 'T-Bone'.

We should call Tarcisio 'T-Bone.

I like that.

But your name begins with an A, Aristide.

T-Bone! T-Bone!

HERRERA'S TEAM BECAME A MAJOR EUROPEAN FORCE, BACKED BY THE WEALTH OF OIL TYCOON ANGELO MORATTI. HOWEVER, ALLEGATIONS PERSIST THAT SOME OF THAT FORTUNE WAS USED TO CURRY FAVOUR WITH UNSCRUPULOUS REFEREES.

Play on.

INDEED, 'GRANDE INTER' WERE UNPOPULAR CHAMPIONS. THEY WON THE EUROPEAN CUP WITH A 3-1 WIN AGAINST REAL MADRID IN 1964, THEN RETAINED IT THE NEXT YEAR. HOWEVER, THEY WERE DEEPLY NEGATIVE IN THEIR 1-0 WIN AGAINST BENFICA, DESPITE ENJOYING HOME ADVANTAGE AND WITH THE PORTUGUESE SIDE REDUCED TO TEN MEN AFTER AN INJURY TO THEIR GOALKEEPER, COSTA PEREIRA.

I am strong. I am calm. I will sit back and protect the lead, even though Benfica have a pile of bibs in goal.

NOT THAT FACCHETTI CAME IN FOR CRITICISM, HIS POPULARITY RARELY WAVERED. HE WAS ONE OF THE FEW PLAYERS WHOSE REPUTATION SURVIVED ITALY'S DEFEAT TO NORTH KOREA IN 1966, CAPTAINING THE AZZURRI TO A EUROPEAN NATIONS CUP WIN TWO YEARS LATER. HE EVEN WON THE COIN TOSS THAT DECIDED THE SEMI-FINAL AGAINST THE USSR.

Damn. I guess when it comes to high-pressure, match-deciding situations, you just can't beat the Italian national team.

CCCP

BIBLIOGRAPHY

BOOKS

Agnew, Paddy, *Forza Italia: A Journey in Search of Italy and its Football* (Ebury Press, 2006)

Ball, Phil, *Morbo: The Story of Spanish Football* (WSC Books, 2001)

Bellos, Alex, *Futebol: The Brazilian Way of Life* (Bloomsbury, 2002)

Brown, Paul, *The Victorian Football Miscellany* (Goal-Post, 2013)

Burns, Jimmy, *Maradona: The Hand of God* (Bloomsbury, 2010)

Castro, Ruy, *Garrincha: The Triumph and Tragedy of Brazil's Forgotten Hero* (Yellow Jersey Press, 2005)

Charlton, Sir Bobby, *The Autobiography: My Manchester United Years* (Headline, 2008)

Connolly, Kevin and MacWilliam, Rob, *Fields of Glory, Paths of Gold: The History of European Football* (Mainstream, 2006)

Dawson, Jeff, *Back Home: England and the 1970 World Cup* (Orion, 2001)

Downie, Andrew, *Doctor Socrates: Footballer, Philosopher, Legend* (Simon & Schuster, 2017)

Ferguson, Alex, *My Autobiography* (Hodder & Stoughton, 2013)

Foot, John, *Calcio: A History of Italian Football* (Fourth Estate, 2007)

Freddi, Cris, *Complete Book of the World Cup 2006* (HarperSport, 2006)

Glanville, Brian, *For Club and Country* (Guardian Books, 2008)

Glanville, Brian, *The Story of the World Cup* (Faber and Faber, 2005)

Goldblatt, Davd, *The Ball is Round: A Global History of Football* (Penguin 2007)

Hamilton, Duncan, *George Best: Immortal. The Approved Biography* (Windmill, 2013)

Hawkey, Ian, *Feet of the Chameleon: The Story of African Football* (Portico, 2009)

Henderson, Jon, *The Wizard: The Life of Stanley Matthews* (Yellow Jersey, 2013)

Hesse-Lichtenberger, Ulrich, *Tor! The Story of German Football* (WSC Books, 2002)

Hughes, Simon, *Red Machine: Liverpool FC in the 1980s* (Mainstream, 2013)

Keane, Roy, *Keane* (Penguin, 2002)

Kelly, Stephen, *Dalglish: The Biography* (Highdown, 2004)

Kuper, Simon, *Football Against the Enemy* (Orion, 1994)

Lawrence, Amy, *Invincible: Inside Arsenal's Unbeaten 2003-2004 Season* (Viking, 2014)

Lowe, Sid, *Fear and Loathing in La Liga: Barcelona vs Real Madrid* (Yellow Jersey Press, 2013)

Maradona, Diego, *El Diego* (Yellow Jersey Press, 2004)

Mattick, Dick, *100 Greats: Swindon Town Football Club* (Tempus, 2002)

McGuigan, Paul and Hewitt, Paolo, *The Greatest Footballer You Never Saw: The Robin Friday Story* (Mainstream Sport, 1997)

Pelé, *Pelé: The Autobiography* (Simon & Schuster, 2006)

Pirlo, Andrea, *I Think Therefore I Play* (BackPage Press, 2014)

Plenderleith, Ian, *Rock'n'Roll Soccer: The Short Life and Fast Times of the North American Soccer League* (Icon, 2014)

Spurling, Jon, *Death or Glory: The Dark History of the World Cup* (Vision Sports, 2010)

Steen, Rob, *The Mavericks: English Football When Flair Wore Flares* (Mainstream, 1994)

Wangerin, David, *Soccer in a Football World: The Story of America's Forgotten Game* (WSC Books, 2006)

When Saturday Comes, *The Half Decent Football Book* (Penguin, 2005)

Wilson, Jonathan, *Angels with Dirty Faces: The Footballing History of Argentina* (Orion, 2016)

Wilson, Jonathan, *Inverting the Pyramid: The History of Football Tactics* (Orion, 2008)

Wilson, Jonathan, *The Anatomy of England: A History in Ten Matches* (Orion, 2010)

Wilson, Jonathan, *The Outsider: A History of the Goalkeeper* (Orion 2012)

Wilson, Jonathan with Murray, Scott: *The Anatomy of Liverpool: A History in Ten Matches* (Orion, 2013)

Winner, David, *Brilliant Orange: The Neurotic Genius of Dutch Football* (Bloomsbury, 2000)

Winner, David, *Those Feet: An Intimate History of English Football* (Bloomsbury, 2005)

ARTICLES

Adams, Tom, 'Ronaldo's record-breaking season', *ESPN*

Austin, Jack, 'Top managers respond to Marco van Basten's "immeasurable bulls***"', *Independent*

Ayegbayo, Olaojo, 'When Pelé played in Nigeria during its civil war (did he really bring a ceasefire?)', *Africa is a Country*

Ball, Phil, 'Greatest Managers, No. 5: Herrera', *ESPN*

Bandini, Paolo, 'Paolo Maldini bows out at Milan with jeers in his ears', *Guardian*

Barker, Matt, 'Milan '88: The Inside Story of Sacchi's all-conquering kings, as told by them', *Four Four Two*

BBC, 'Len Shackleton: Clown Prince'

Bellos, Alex, 'He's won more World Cups than anyone, now Zagallo returns to plot another Brazil triumph', *Guardian*

Bird, Sheridan, 'An Appreciation of . . . Franco Baresi', *The Blizzard*, Issue 8

Campanile, Vittorio, '"Look at me. I am Giorgio Chinaglia. I beat you!" – Farewell to the footballing legend who made Pelé cry', *Goal.com*

Carter, Jon, 'Maradona brings success to Napoli', *ESPN*

Chaudhary, Vivek, 'Sir Alex cleared after motorway dash', *Guardian*

Christenson, Marcus, 'Tomas Brolin at Leeds: the worst signing ever? He
    doesn't think so', *Guardian*

Corbett, James, 'Bill Shankly: Life, death and football', *Guardian*

Davies, Tom, 'Golden Goal: Ilie Dumitrescu for Romania v Argentina (1994)',
    Guardian

de Menezes, Jack, 'Paul Gascoigne reveals he snubbed Manchester United
    for Tottenham because Spurs gave him a house and his sister a sunbed',
    Guardian

Doyle, Paul, 'The Joy of Six: blessings in disguise', *Guardian*

Doyle, Paul and Lutz, Tom, 'Joy of Six: Footballers who have overcome humble
    beginnings', *Guardian*

Early, Ken, 'Doctor Sócrates review: the thinking, drinking, footballing genius',
    Irish Times

Early, Ken, 'Johan Cruyff the great idealist who proved beauty is best',
    Irish Times

FIFA.com, 'Der Bomber and his record for eternity'

FIFA.com, 'Herrera: More than just catenaccio'

FIFA.com, 'Michel Platini - Elegance and intelligence personified in blue'

FIFA.com, 'The inimitable Giuseppe Meazza'

Flint, Andrew, 'The methodical, scientific wisdom of Valeriy Lobanovskyi',
    These Football Times

FourFourTwo, 'Faustino Asprilla: One-on-one'
    https://www.fourfourtwo.com/features/faustino-asprilla-one-one

FourFourTwo, 'Matt Le Tissier: One-on-one'

Goal.com, '70 Facts about Brazil legend Pele'

Gordon, Phil, 'Jimmy Johnstone: Celtic winger considered his club's greatest
    ever player', *Independent*

The *Guardian*, 'Football Weekly presents: The Ballad of Robin Friday'

The *Guardian*, 'From the Vault: Remembering the life and football of
    Bobby Moore'

Hackett, Robin, 'Faustino Asprilla: All guns blazing', *ESPN*

Hackett, Robin, 'Frank Worthington: All Shook Up', *ESPN*

Hackett, Robin, 'Paul Breitner: Playing on the left', *ESPN*

Haugstad, Thore, 'The incomparable legacy of Helenio Herrera',
    These Football Times

Heffernan, Conor, 'When Pelé literally became a national treasure in Brazil', *These Football Times*

Hills, David, 'The ten most entertaining transfers', *Guardian*

Horncastle, James, 'Gianluigi Buffon: a goalkeeper must be a masochist and egocentric', *Guardian*

Hurrey, Adam, ''90s Heroes: Dennis Bergkamp', *The Set Pieces*

Jacobs, Sean and Ross, Elliot, 'How Eusebio's soccer exploits challenged European and African identities', *Aljazeera*

Jenson, Pete, 'How to stop the Barcelona carousel leaving you dizzy', *Independent*

Jones, Simon, 'George Best was dubbed El Beatle 50 years ago as Manchester United thrashed Benfica 5-1 . . . it was the night he came of age on the European stage', *Daily Mail*

Keating, Frank, 'From the archive, 24 November 1977: The incomparable Dixie Dean', *Guardian*

Keating, Frank, Lacey, David, and McIlvanney, Hugh 'From the Vault: Remembering the life and football of Bobby Moore', *Guardian*

Kuper. Simon, 'Rijkaard finally gets frank', *Guardian*

Kuper, Simon, 'The Hamburg Factor', *The Blizzard*, Issue 10

Levin, Angela, 'Hero who won his Spurs in No Man's Land: The amazing life of football star Walter Tull - the first black army officer of WWI', *Daily Mail*

Lowe, Sid, 'Barcelona were transformed by Johan Cruyff not once but twice, and for ever', *Guardian*

McKinstry, Leo, 'Hero cast aside – Sir Alf Ramsey, 1970s', *Guardian*

McOwan, Gavin, 'Eusébio obituary', *Guardian*

McRae, Donald, 'Johan Cruyff: 'Maybe we were the real winners in 1974. The world remembers our team more', *Guardian*

Miller, Nick, 'The Joy of Six: Diego Maradona', *Guardian*

Molyneux-Carter, Jonathan, 'Gheorghe Hagi: The Maradona of the Carpathians', *ESPN*

Morgan, Steve, 'George Best's Greatest Night', *Manchester United.com*

Murray, Andrew (additional reporting by Alves, Marcus; Jonson, Alex; Renard, Arthur; and Santi Alberto) 'ZLATAN'. Australian *Four Four Two*

Murray, Scott, 'The Joy of Six: Route-one goals', *Guardian*

Murray, Trevor, 'How Dennis Bergkamp became a symbol of elegance at Arsenal'', *These Football Times*

Nakrani, Sachin, 'Golden goal: Paul Gascoigne for England v Scotland (1996)', *Guardian*

Newman, Blair, 'Valeriy Lobanovskyi and Dynamo Kyiv's scientific enlightenment', *These Football Times*

O'Brien, Colin, 'Napoli Still Diego Maradona's City Almost 3 Decades After the First Scudetto', *Bleacher Report*

O'Dea, Arthur James, 'Why Sir Alf Ramsey was English football's great man of the people', *These Football Times*

Paxton, Jonathan 'Stoke City 1946-47', *When Saturday Comes*, Issue 267, May 2009

Pearson, Harry, 'Brother world', *When Saturday Comes*, Issue 188, October 2002

Phillip, Robert, 'Salute to a true Cup final legend', *Telegraph*

Powley, Adam, 'Pride and Prejudice', *When Saturday Comes*, Issue 279, May 2010

Prior, Neil, 'Giorgio Chinaglia: Swansea to Italian and American stardom', *BBC*

Rainbow, Jamie, 'Garrincha, the never forgotten genius of Brazilian football', *World Soccer*

Roberts, John, 'Dixie Dean went off early to avoid being mobbed after his 60th goal. The ref conspired by saying he'd gone for a wee', *Sporting Intelligence*

Ronay, Barney, 'Grim Reep' *When Saturday Comes*, Issue 196, June 2003

Ronay, Barney, 'The Great Orator', *When Saturday Comes*, Issue 205, March 2004

Sharp, Will, 'Andoni Goikoetxea: The Butcher of Bilbao', *These Football Times*

Smith. Alan, 'Golden Goal: Eric Cantona for Manchester United v Liverpool (1996)'

Smyth, Rob, 'Golden Goal: Roberto Baggio for Juventus against Internazionale (1992)', *Guardian*

Smyth, Rob, 'The forgotten story of ... Just Fontaine's 13-goal World Cup', *Guardian*

Smyth, Rob, 'World Cup: 25 stunning moments ... No10: Dennis Bergkamp's wonder goal', *Guardian*

Spurling, Jon, 'Exit Strategy' *When Saturday Comes*, Issue 338, April 2015

Staunton, Peter, 'The Captain and The Foot Soldier: Ferenc Puskas was a hero on two fronts', *Goal.com*

Steinberg, Jacob, 'Golden goal: Matt Le Tissier for Southampton v Newcastle (1993)', *Guardian*

Steinberg, Jacob, 'Golden Goal: Paolo Di Canio for West Ham v Wimbledon (2000)', *Guardian*

Stevenson, Jonathan, 'Remembering the genius of Garrincha', *BBC*

Storey, Daniel, 'Portrait of an Icon: Eric Cantona', *Football 365*

Storey, Daniel, 'Portrait of an icon: Ferenc Puskas', *Football 365*

Storey, Daniel, 'The Big Interview: Jan Åge Fjørtoft on impersonating journos & the aeroplane', *Planet-Football.com*

Talbot, Simon, 'Alfredo Di Stefano: Icon', *Four Four Two*

Taylor, Louise, 'Bert Trautmann: from Nazi paratrooper to hero of Manchester City', *Guardian*

Taylor, Louise, 'Gianluigi Buffon's 1,000th career game is testament to a beacon of stability', *Guardian*

The Telegraph, 'Eusébio da Silva Ferreira – obituary', *Telegraph*

The Telegraph, 'Johan Cruyff, footballer - Obituary', *Telegraph*

Townsend, Jon, 'Bill Shankly: it's not how you arrive, it's how you leave', *These Football Times*

Townsend, Jon, 'Marco van Basten: an undisputed legend despite a premature end', *These Football Times*

Turnbull, Simon, 'Football: From prisoner of war to folklore', *Independent*

UEFA.com, 'Van Basten remembers 'fantastic' EURO '88'

Vickery, Tim, 'Mario Zagallo and Tostão', *The Blizzard*, Issue 3, December 2011

Wagner, Frank, 'Helenio Herrera: 10 Things You Didn't Know About the Coaching Legend', *Bleacher Report*

When Saturday Comes, 'The media-created Brian Clough was a pain' Issue 25, March 1989

Williams, Richard, 'Michel Platini's playing brilliance can be seen through the murk', *Guardian*

Wilson, Jonathan, 'Best, Beckenbauer, Platini, Zidane: Puskas topped them all', *Guardian*

Wilson, Jonathan, 'How Valeriy Lobanovskyi's appliance of science won hearts and trophies', *Guardian*

Wilson, Jonathan, 'Sindelar: the ballad of the tragic hero', *Guardian*

Winner, David, 'Johan Cruyff: father of modern game who also shaped Dutch culture', *Guardian*

Winter, Henry, 'The day Ronaldo received a standing ovation from all Old Trafford after his star turn against Manchester United', *Telegraph*

ACKNOWLEDGEMENTS

As soon as I finished writing my last book, I started working on this one. Therefore, everyone who I mentioned in the acknowledgements of *The Illustrated History of Football* was also vital in getting me over the line with this one.

First and foremost, I'd like to thank my partner, Sarah; without whose support, these books simply would not have happened. It's been a tough couple of years, but hopefully I can have a weekend off now. Thanks also to Sarah's parents, Laurelle and Bruce, and of course to my own mum and dad. Between them, they were probably responsible for about 70 per cent of the sales for the first book.

Huge thanks also to my agent Iain Macintosh and for the team at Penguin Random House; notably Ben Brusey and Huw Armstrong. Their constant encouragement and advice was invaluable, especially at times of distracting global news events such as Brexit, Trump and Swindon Town being relegated to League Two (that last one not really a surprise). Their hard work on my behalf was astonishing and humbling.

I'd also like to thank my colleagues at the *Guardian*, especially James Dart, Owen Gibson, and Ian Prior, who, to my weekly surprise, continue to provide a platform through which I can share my silly drawings. Their enthusiasm for my cartoons gives me the confidence to keep making them. Mike Hytner at *Guardian Australia* also continues to exceed his duties as a sports editor by providing me with weekly counselling sessions, as well as debriefs on the latest episodes of the Athletico Mince podcast.

Another of my *Guardian* colleagues, Dan Lucas, sadly passed away in March 2017. I'll do here what I never got a chance to do in person and thank Dan for his regular generous words, which helped me more than he could ever have realised.

Finally, I'd like to express my gratitude to my family and friends, who have remained patient as I became a hermit over the last couple of years. So massive thanks to Alastair Wilson, Paul Whitehead, Justin Smith, Kieran Holden, Mark Woolford, Elizabeth Aubrey, Simon Hodgon, Casper Hodgon (you might have had a point about Neymar), Paul Connolly, Ian Plenderleith, David Stubbs, Sachin Nakrani, John Mitchell, Pete McDougall, The Curry Club, and anyone who got in touch to say they'd enjoyed the first book; it encouraged me to keep going.

I might not ever get a chance to do another book, so despite what I said in the introduction about being too old to have a favourite footballer, here is a cartoon about mine . . .

JAN ÅGE FJØRTOFT

My friend Kieran phoned me from the payphone outside the County Ground. 'We've signed a player called George Spanker. From Bochum. He looks handy.' This was 1993; a time before the internet or widespread mobile phone ownership, I had no way of knowing that there was no such player, nor that Kieran was calling from his mum's hallway. However, Swindon Town *had* signed someone: a tall, blond Norwegian centre-forward called Jan Åge Fjørtoft.

Fjortoft would lead the line in Swindon Town's first ever season in the top flight. It's unlikely they'll ever get back there, unless this book sells a billion copies, and if you've read this far, you'll know that ain't happening (no Ronaldinho? No Gerrard? A cursory mention of Spanker? Ridiculous). Fjørtoft had been instrumental in Norway's historic 2–0 defeat of England a couple of months before, and his pre-season form gave Swindon fans cause for misplaced optimism.

Of course, Swindon were relegated. They didn't record a win until their sixteenth game, let in a hundred goals and finished bottom of the ladder. However, they scored a lot too, and once Fjørtoft found his feet, he was unstoppable. Not only was he deadly in front of goal, he also seemed to be enjoying himself. Not something that is always easy to do in Swindon. His enthusiasm and quirky Scandinavian humour made him a popular figure with the fans, not only at Swindon, but also with the other English clubs he later played for: Middlesbrough, Barnsley and Sheffield United.

My favourite goal of his came in a frenetic 2–2 draw with Manchester United at the County Ground, as he turned in a late equaliser that had the rusty old ground rocking. Just for a moment, he'd given Swindon fans the belief (again misplaced) that they were the equal of the best team in the country.

WHILST OTHER PLACES HAVE UNIVERSITIES AND CULTURE AND 'LIBRARIES', MY HOME TOWN OF SWINDON HAS **THE MAGIC ROUNDABOUT**. IMAGINE ARRIVING IN A STRANGE TOWN, IN A FOREIGN COUNTRY, AND BEING CONFRONTED WITH **THIS:**

THE MAGIC ROUNDABOUT
- STRANGERS TURN BACK

Ring Road
Cirencester
A4289

(M4)

Town
centre

Marlborough
Burford
Oxford
A4312

JAN ÅGE FJØRTOFT WASN'T LIKE OTHER FOOTBALLERS, THOUGH. HE DIDN'T HAVE AN AGENT, FOR STARTERS (WHICH COULD EXPLAIN HOW HE ENDED UP IN SWINDON). HE SIGNED FOR £500,000, A CLUB RECORD UNTIL THEY BLEW £850,000 ON JOEY BEAUCHAMP, WHO WAS AS EFFECTIVE AS A SOILED MATTRESS WITH A URINE STAIN FOR A FACE.

Your ball, Joey!

NOT THAT FJØRTOFT GOT OFF TO THE BEST OF STARTS EITHER. IN FACT, UP UNTIL THE NEW YEAR IT APPEARED HE WOULD BE INCAPABLE OF FINDING A CATTLE STATION WITH A SAT-NAV-ENABLED LORRY FULL OF BANJOS.

ARRANGEMENTS WERE MADE FOR HIM TO BE SENT OUT ON LOAN TO LILLESTRØM, IN NORWAY.

BUT THEN AN INJURY TO KEITH SCOTT GAVE HIM ANOTHER CHANCE IN AN FA CUP TIE AT IPSWICH, AND SURPRISINGLY **A GOAL!** AFTER THAT, HE COULDN'T STOP SCORING. A GOAL IN A 2-1 WIN AGAINST SPURS WAS FOLLOWED BY A HAT-TRICK AGAINST COVENTRY AND THE FIRST SIGHTING OF HIS FAMOUS AEROPLANE CELEBRATION.

He's still coming, right?

LILLESTRØM SK

LILLESTR

HE SCORED 13 GOALS IN HIS LAST 17 GAMES THAT SEASON AND THE SWINDON FANS FELL IN LOVE WITH HIM.

Wow.

SWINDON
COUNCIL
TIP

SWINDON WERE RELEGATED, BUT HIS PROLIFIC FORM CONTINUED THE NEXT SEASON. HE SCORED 25 IN ALL COMPETITIONS, INCLUDING A MEMORABLE CURLING STRIKE AGAINST MILLWALL IN A LEAGUE CUP QUARTER-FINAL. MILLWALL'S MANAGER, MICK McCARTHY SAID HE WOULD STAND NAKED IN A SHOP WINDOW IF FJØRTOFT HAD MEANT IT.

Jesus.

INEVITABLY, OTHER CLUBS BEGAN TO CIRCLE AROUND FJØRTOFT. EAGER TO FIND OUT MORE, HE PHONED THE SWINDON CHAIRMAN, PRETENDING TO BE A NORWEGIAN JOURNALIST, WHILE THE PAIR OF THEM WERE SITTING ON **THE SAME BUS.**

Ok, this is off the record and I'll have to whisper; he's only sat a few seats behind me.

Sure, sure.

SWINDON'S MANAGER, STEVE McMAHON RESENTED FJØRTOFT'S POPULARITY AND SOLD HIM TO MIDDLESBROUGH FOR A CUT-PRICE £1.3 MILLION. McMAHON REPLACED HIM WITH JASON DRYSDALE - A FULL-BACK FROM NEWCASTLE'S RESERVES. SWINDON FAILED TO SCORE IN SIX OF THEIR NEXT EIGHT MATCHES AND WERE RELEGATED AGAIN.